Victorian Fetishism

SUNY series, Studies in the Long Nineteenth Century
Pamela K. Gilbert, editor

Victorian Fetishism

INTELLECTUALS AND PRIMITIVES

Peter Melville Logan

STATE UNIVERSITY OF NEW YORK PRESS

Published by
State University of New York Press, Albany

For information, contact State University of New York Press, Albany, NY
www.sunypress.edu

Production by Marilyn P. Semerad
Marketing by Michael Campochiaro

Library of Congress Cataloging in Publication Data

Logan, Peter Melville, 1951-
  Victorian fetishism : intellectuals and primitives / Peter Melville Logan.
    p. cm. — (Suny series, studies in the long nineteenth century)
  This book examines Victorian discourse on culture.
  Includes bibliographical references (p.   ) and index.
  ISBN 978-0-7914-7661-1 (alk. paper)
  ISBN 978-0-7914-7662-8 (pbk. alk. paper)
  1. English prose literature—19th century—History and criticism. 2.
Culture—Philosophy—History—19th century. 3. Arnold, Matthew,
1822-1888—Criticism and interpretation. 4. Eliot, George,
1819-1880—Criticism and interpretation. 5. Tylor, Edward Burnett, Sir,
1832-1917—Criticism and interpretation. 6. Great Britain—Intellectual
life—19th century. 7. Criticism—Great Britain—History—19th century.
8. Culture in literature. 9. Fetishism in literature. 10. Primitivism
in literature. I. Title.
  PR788.C96L64 2008
  820.9'3552—dc22
                                                              2008003454

In loving memory of Mary Theresa Logan, 1949–1997.

Contents

The term "fetishism" almost has a life of its own. Instead of functioning as a metalanguage for the magical thinking of others, it turns against those who use it, and surreptitiously exposes their own magical thinking.

—Jean Baudrillard,
For a Critique of the Political Economy of the Sign (1981)

Preface

Where does *culture* come from? This study looks at the formulation of the culture concept in the nineteenth century. It argues that culture could only be imagined in relation to something that was not culture, a fantasy of a human existence without culture that I locate in a writing on "primitive" societies. The trope of fetishism has a lengthy history in this discourse, but it reached its apex in the middle of the nineteenth century, when British intellectuals were formulating the cultural theories that shaped subsequent Anglo-American writing on the topic. These writers used the fantasy of a primitive mind as the grounding assumption for their new theories—whether of "high" culture or culture as an entire way of life—and this study examines the consequences of that connection between fetishism and culture.

Comments on this manuscript and encouragement by colleagues at many institutions have improved my pedestrian ideas and influenced the shape of the argument at different points. I would particularly like to thank the two brilliant readers for the State University of New York Press, Nancy Armstrong and John Kucich, whose suggestions, while small in number, were large in consequence. Many other colleagues have been generous in their willingness to respond critically to different parts of the project: Alicia Carroll, Catherine Gallagher, Robbie B. H. Goh, Susan Hegeman, Anne Humpherys, Gerhard Joseph, Henrika Kuklick, Christopher Lane, Sally Shuttleworth, Kathy Psomiades, Rachel Teukolsky. I am grateful to Temple University for a Study Leave in Spring 2006 to work on this project. My colleagues there have been particularly helpful in fleshing out elements of this book: Deirdre David, Oliver Gaycken, Katherine Henry, Sally Mitchell, James Salazar, Larry Venuti, Sydney White; at the University of Alabama, I wish to thank Phillip Beidler, Celia Daileader, Gary Taylor, William Ulmer, and Fred Whiting. Talented graduate student Research Assistants were indispensable from start to finish: Andrea Cabus, Nick Moudry, Margaret

O'Brien, Collin Tracy. Finally, I need to thank my partner, Cathleen McCoy, who endured years of dinner conversation about fetishism and the sentence I wrote that day.

Portions of chapter 2 previously appeared in "Fetishism and Freedom in Matthew Arnold's Cultural Theory," *Victorian Literature and Culture* 31.2 (2003): 555–574; sections of chapter 3 were first published in "George Eliot's Fetish," in "Inauthentic Pleasures: Victorian Fakery and the Limitations of Form," ed. Shelton Waldrep, special issue of *Studies in the Literary Imagination* 35.2 (Fall 2002): 27–51. Illustration in chapter 3 is by Attilio Mussino © Giunti Editore Spa Firenze-Milano. Used with permission.

Abbreviations

CP   Arnold, Matthew. *The Complete Prose Works of Matthew Arnold*. Edited by R. H. Super. 11 vols. Ann Arbor: University of Michigan Press, 1960.

Essays   Eliot, George. *Essays of George Eliot*. Edited by Thomas Pinney. New York: Columbia University Press, 1963.

Journals Eliot, George. *The Journals of George Eliot*. Edited by Margaret Harris and Judith Johnston. Cambridge: Cambridge University Press, 1998.

Letters Eliot, George. *The George Eliot Letters*. Edited by Gordon S. Haight. 9 vols. New Haven: Yale University Press, 1954–78.

PC   Tylor, Edward B. *Primitive Culture: Researches into the Development of Mythology, Philosophy, Religion, Language, Art, and Custom*. 2nd ed. 2 vols. London: John Murray, 1873.

PP   Auguste Comte. *The Positive Philosophy of Auguste Comte*. Translated by Harriet Martineau. New York: Calvin Blanchard, 1855. Reprint, New York: AMS Press, 1974.

PS   Krafft-Ebing, Richard von. *Psychopathia Sexualis, with Especial Reference to the Antipathetic Sexual Instinct: A Medico-Forensic Study*. Translated by F. J. Rebman. 12th ed. New York: Physicians and Surgeons, 1922. Reprint, 1935.

SE   Freud, Sigmund. *The Standard Edition of the Complete Psychological Works of Sigmund Freud*. Translated by James Strachey. 24 vols. London: Hogarth, 1953–.

Introduction

During the 1860s and 1870s, two competing theories of culture were widely debated in England: Matthew Arnold's humanist ideal and Edward B. Tylor's anthropology. At present, scholars continue to debate the merits of a different but related theory of culture. This contemporary version began in the mid-1950s with the publication of Raymond Williams's *Culture and Society,* Richard Hoggart's *Uses of Literacy,* and, slightly later, E. P. Thompson's *Making of the English Working Class,* and out of this nexus of critical and historical works emerged the group of critical practices called "cultural studies."[1] Parallels exist between the newer and older debates, but their central questions are worlds apart. In literary criticism, recent discussion has focused on the vagueness of the culture concept. Scholars agree on the existence of a "definitional failure" in cultural theory, but they disagree on even the basic questions of whether this malleability is desirable or undesirable.[2] The Victorian debate had a completely different agenda. In response to Arnold's writing on culture, questions were raised about the utility of the concept and its political ramifications. The anthropological proposal led to questions about the proper method of studying it scientifically and, above all, to the development of culture over time. In the Victorian culture debate, we might say that problems of definition took a back seat to those of implementation: how it was to be evaluated, examined, and refined.[3]

What accounts for this difference from the present focus on definition? Clearly, it cannot be attributed to a superior Victorian precision in defining *culture.* Tylor produced a memorable definition that continued to serve anthropology after the rest of his ideas were retired. But Arnold? *Culture and Anarchy* famously lacked the kind of quotable definition found in Tylor, and most of the extracts commonly selected as shorthand for his culture idea do violence to it as a concept that was rooted in the justification of a broad, all-encompassing social utility. In one respect, however, the Victorian culture concept was considerably clearer in its outline than that of the present moment. Writing in 1980, E. P. Thompson insisted, "Any theory of culture must include the concept of the dialectical interaction between culture and something that is *not* culture."[4] In 1991, discussing writing on cultural theory, Catherine Gallagher similarly noted that "the puzzling thing about these writings is their almost programmatic refusal to tell us what *isn't* culture."[5] These comments suggest the extent to which the all-encompassing capaciousness of present-day cultural theory has been identified as the source of its definitional failure.

While Victorians were unable to explain precisely what culture was, they had far more success in identifying what it was not. Abstract claims about culture derive from contrasts with something that is not culture. Tylor defined it as learned behaviors, to differentiate culture from race. That distinction later proved too broad, and culture became some types of learned behaviors, distinct from other types that were not culture, such as economics and medicine. After Foucault's analysis of the discursive nature of social institutions, that distinction became considerably less tenable, and we entered the period of definitional failure. The case was different in the nineteenth century, when *culture* was frequently synonymous with *civilization*.[6] It existed in time as part of a developmental continuum from less culture to more, or undeveloped to advanced. As a result, *culture* had a historical register it has since lost. It was possible to imagine a beginning of culture, for example, as Tylor did, and thus even a time before culture. Both concepts became nonsensical after the early twentieth century, when evolutionary anthropology lost its purchase and anti-evolutionary paradigms took its place.[7] Culture is everywhere, but for Victorians this was not the case, and their stereotypes of primitives demonstrated a definite sense of something that was *not* culture.

This book examines the thread of culture's opposite in the Victorian discourse on culture. It should be clear at the outset that nowhere in this examination can we assume that culture is anything other than a verbal construct. This analysis is concerned with cultural rhetoric, rather than culture as an ontological category, because only in this way can we begin to understand the upper-middle-class episteme within which culture was imagined in the mid-Victorian decades.

Whether conceived as an absolute antithesis between culture and unculture, or as a shaded continuum from less to more, the condition of culturelessness permeated Victorian arguments about culture. It appeared, of course, in statements about the total lack of whatever constituted culture, but more often the condition showed up in a subtler form in descriptions of insufficiency: life with too little culture, life in an "undeveloped" culture.[8] Such statements emerged inevitably in descriptions of colonial life, but they were common also in images of uneducated Victorians. Examples litter the two nineteenth-century British foundational texts on culture, Arnold's *Culture and Anarchy* and Tylor's *Primitive Culture*. These two were born like twins in quick succession. Arnold's version—initially the circulation of the best ideas, but since then repackaged as the breadth of knowledge described by E. D. Hirsch in *Cultural Literacy*—appeared in 1869, while Tylor presented his anthropological definition two years later, in 1871.[9] Timing matters because despite the gulf between Arnold's idealist and Tylor's descriptive cultural theories, both imagined populations lacking culture in distinctly similar terms.[10] Given the closeness in age and social position of the two writers, the resemblance is not surprising, and it suggests the possibility that these rival theories of culture were in some sense different solutions to one and the same problem. Culture was the answer, but what, exactly, was the question?

Arnold and Tylor located culture's absence in completely different time periods. Arnold saw it in the Victorian present, where everyone "doing as one likes" produced the anarchy in *Culture and Anarchy*. Tylor located it in the furthest reaches of human prehistory, describing a more distant condition of insufficiency. Nonetheless, the characteristics both writers assigned to the condition of life without culture were generically similar problems of anthropomorphism. Without culture, both claimed, people lacked a factual understanding of the world around them. For Tylor, this took a Viconian turn: how did one explain thunder? For Arnold it was more often the incomprehensibility of the social world. Whether material or social, that unknown had to be explained, and in both cases explanations followed from acts of self-projection. Tylor's primitives imagined supernatural beings resembling themselves behind the thunder, much as Vico's primitive poets had done. For Arnold, people imagined the social body as a reflection of their own self-interests. In both cases, we see uncultured people explaining the unintelligible "outside" in terms of themselves. As a general rule, each writer's terminology was completely different—Arnold's idealist rhetoric ("sweetness and light," "the study of perfection") had little in common with Tylor's serviceable prose ("survivals," "complex whole")—but they both used the same label for this uncultured condition: *fetishism*. Tylor used it because he was immersed in the literature of ethnography, where *fetishism* had become the standard term for an anthropomorphic, "primitive" psychology. Arnold's usage is figurative, as when he complains about the Liberals "worshipping their fetish of the production of wealth" to differentiate "culture's" version of truth from the falsifications of self-serving, insufficiently cultured Victorian politicians.[11] The Victorian fetishist projects feeling, desire, and belief onto the world, but does so unawares. Then those projections are reflected back in alienated form, as though originating in the external world. This was not a new idea, of course, but its currency in the 1870s is suggested by a quote from Nietzsche, who wrote in 1873, "truths are illusions of which we have forgotten that they are illusions . . . . [And] precisely because of this forgetting, they arrive at the feeling of truth."[12] Victorian fetishism functioned in the same way.

As I explain in chapter 1, the immediate historical reason for Arnold's and Tylor's similar uses of *fetishism* lay in Auguste Comte's *Cours de philosophie positive*, which began circulating in earnest in Britain in 1853.[13] Comte defined the starting point for the evolution of human society as the state of *primitive fetishism*, meaning a fully anthropomorphic understanding of the world. The story of how this psychological process itself became associated with culture's opposite is far older than the term *fetishism;* it forms part of European philosophy since Greek antiquity. But its linkage to the signifier *fetishism* reached the acme of its currency in Britain during the half-century following *Cours*, roughly 1850–1900. The last years of this period saw the legitimacy of *fetishism* as a term decline in anthropology, when it was gradually replaced by the correlate terms, *animism* and (to a lesser extent) *totemism*. Thus the decades from 1850–1900 marked a unique era in the history of assumptions about primitive existence, one characterized by the dominance of evolutionary anthropology, wherein the concept of fetishism was knotted up with the idea of unculture. During these years, fetishism defined ideas about culture through difference, not by describing what it was but by defining what it was not, and what culture was not was fetishism.

The most familiar nineteenth-century expression of culture's relationship with the state of cultural insufficiency that I call "unculture" took the form of a difference in time; it relied on the commonplace assumption of an evolutionary continuum from uncultured primitive to highly-cultured modern. The Crystal Palace Exhibition in 1851 reflected this relationship, reinforcing a conviction among the English that they were the single most advanced culture the world had ever witnessed.[14] The Great Exhibition of the Works of Industry of All Nations was visited by one out of every five people in Britain during its six-month run in Hyde Park. Visitors arrived by train, forming crowds as large as one hundred thousand per day, passing through the entrance to the Exhibition and walking through an evolutionary narrative that concretely embodied their sense of place among the world's nations. From the main entrance one faced the center of the exhibition space, a high glass transept arching over the intact elms of Hyde Park. The transept bisected the Crystal Palace's two wings. On the left was the British section, including the British colonies. The Foreign Nave, on the right, represented the rest of Europe, as well as Asia, Africa, and the Americas. For the purposes of arrangement, the transept was treated like the equator. The countries and British colonies nearest it were clustered more or less according to latitude.[15] Within their individual spaces, each nation arranged its products in a given order: raw materials, followed by machinery, manufactures, and fine arts.[16] This arrangement made it possible to compare the products of different nations, while highlighting the differences between them in the range of products they displayed. As visitors proceeded through the Foreign Nave, they passed through the world's cultures in an order that progressed from the raw materials and handmade products of the less cultured equatorial countries to the machinery and arts of the more cultured France and Austria. The exhibit was not limited to machines. Next to stuffed animals, mannequins of primitives were arranged in didactic tableaux. The South African display went one step further, including two live children, Flora and Martinas, who had been taken from the San tribe along the Orange River.[17] The climax of this spatial narrative was the British display, in the Western Nave, which included sixty motive power machines, many driven by steam engines. There were steam printing presses, a steam hammer, mechanical looms, a riveting machine, new agricultural machinery, and even a gas cooking range. British pride of place was further reinforced by the Crystal Palace itself; built of glass panes on an iron frame, it arched over all other cultures as the ultimate symbol of British superiority. The exhibition not only taught Victorians about other societies, it also emphasized the place of Britain's culture in the overall range of advancement. That place was at one end of a continuum, as far removed as possible from their opposite number, Flora and Martinas, on display as living examples of culture's absence.

While distant on the evolutionary continuum, unculture was nonetheless close to home in practice because of its domestic use as metaphor. Victorian writers could and did employ the rhetoric of primitivism to label contemporary groups as lower down the line of cultural development, and so cultural insufficiency operated "to fulfil a social function of legitimating social differences," as Bourdieu points out.[18] Socially subordinate groups—rural villagers, women, the lower class, children—had traditionally been considered constitutionally inferior to the dominant male class, either in mind or body. From there it was a small step to account for this supposed inferiority by placing them further back in the evolutionary narrative. Such an approach appeared scientific and led to an increased interest in ethnology's accounts of cultural development. According to Kuklick, Victorians "wanted to know what relationships properly obtained between superior beings such as themselves—educated men—and the persons they somehow equated with inferior 'primitive' peoples—children, women, the mentally disordered, and the 'dangerous classes.'"[19]

We see the use of domestic primitivism—the adaptation of primitive themes to account for relations in modern life—in the writing of social commentators, like Arnold, and also in novels. In *The Mill on the Floss*, George Eliot's provincial child-heroine, Maggie Tulliver, imagines her "fetish" doll to be alive and to have feelings; indeed, the entire world of the Tulliver family has been rightly called an example of primitive fetishism.[20] Eliot read Max Müller's *Lectures on the Science of*

Language (1861) while writing *Romola*, John Lubbock's *Pre-Historic Times* (1865) while finishing *The Spanish Gypsy*, and Tylor's *Researches into the Early History of Mankind* (1865) while writing *Middlemarch*.[21] Her notebooks included quotations from all of these texts, and she appended a telling comment to one extract she copied from Tylor: "for savage customs and ideas."[22] None of Eliot's novels concerned "savages" as such, but they overflowed with detailed representations of earlier ways of life still practiced in provincial England, and these took on primitive characteristics in her hands. Eliot's example illustrates for us how readily the unculture of the past persisted in Victorian perceptions of the present as uncultured, so that the tension between the two evolutionary states was an immediate concern. It was locally present in England, rather than safely removed in the distant colonies of Africa, Asia, and the Caribbean.

For reasons besides its place in anthropological thought, the European second half of the nineteenth century can be called the "Era of the Fetish." Inheriting one form of fetishism, it produced two more. Sitting in the Reading Room of the British Library, Karl Marx produced the theory of commodity fetishism, first published in 1867 in volume one of *Das Kapital*; the first English translation appeared in 1886, making the text accessible to fin-de-siècle English readers. In the following year, the idea of fetishism as an element of human sexuality began to appear in the literature of sexology, when the French psychologist Alfred Binet published "Le fétichisme dans l'amour."[23] Despite these new uses and the shift in terminology within British anthropology, the older concept of the fetish was slow to disappear. When issued in 1911, the 11th edition of the *Encyclopedia Britannica* defined *fetishism* solely as a feature of primitive culture and was silent on the sexual and economic senses.[24] However, in the decades that followed, the two newer variants waxed in significance while the ethnographic usage waned as the fortunes of evolutionary anthropology slowly declined.[25] Even after Tylor's assumptions were laid to rest—some date this as early as the 1890s—references to fetishism persisted in one field of anthropology, the study of West African societies.[26] In 1883, A. B. Ellis titled his book on the region *The Land of Fetish*, and it was to West Africa that Mary Kingsley traveled in order "to study fetish," in 1893 and 1895.[27] In 1925, the Oxford School anthropologist Charles Kingsley Meek could still define African religion in terms of fetishism, in *The Northern Tribes of Nigeria*. However, his colleague R. S. Rattray was publishing an innovative series of books on the Ashanti simultaneously, and in *Ashanti* (1925), Stocking notes, he "was sharply critical of the prevailing tendency to reduce West African religion to 'fetishism'—which he believed to be the result of misinformation . . . ."[28] Rattray was the wave of the future, but the older usage was tenacious. Twenty years later, anthropologist Geoffrey Parrinder still felt it necessary to caution his peers, "It is best to drop this confusing and unfair word 'fetish' altogether, along with 'juju' and 'gree-gree'. They need to be relegated to the museums of the writings of early explorers."[29]

Primitive fetishism remains in that museum today as an embarrassment from a racist past.[30] Ultimately, it was always a European artifact, rather than an African condition; it was a projection of European assumptions onto African social practices, and so the concept of religious fetishism ultimately had little to do with African spiritualism as such. In this respect, it is useful to notice how the original sense of the word—as a reference to something artfully made—speaks more to the assumptions of westerners than the practices of Africans. The idea of African object worship was itself a skillfully made cultural construction, and in this artifice lies an ironic reversal, for the European idea of the fetish was itself a fetish and thus an example of the thing it claimed to describe. Ultimately, *fetishism* describes the cultural project of Europeans engaged in imagining Western Africa as the Land of Fetish, but the term applies more aptly to Europe in the second half of the nineteenth century than to any historical reality in Africa or other parts of the world.

For cultural theory, the question of culture's absence is unavoidable. Signs are meaningful through difference, so in a categorical sense the sign of unculture has to be specified for any sign of culture to emerge. Thus Arnold proved considerably more specific in analyzing the backward nature of Victorian unculture than in defining the culture he advocated. He worked through antithesis, painting pictures of what culture was not and using them to convey his famously vague idea of what it should be.[31] Victorian Britain assumed a connection between unculture and fetishism, and this created problems in writing about culture's opposite that were not only unavoidable but, more importantly, were irresolvable. The fetish is a peculiar concept, and the need to treat it with kid gloves affected the way that intelligent, self-conscious writers like Arnold, Eliot, and Tylor approached the topic. We can see their dilemma by considering how fetishism was imaginatively organized.

The story of fetishism's historical origins contains all of the key ingredients that make up its conceptual structure. Pietz points out that fetishism "originated in the cross-cultural spaces of the coast of West Africa during the sixteenth and seventeenth centuries" as an interpretation by Portuguese traders of religious practices on the Guinea Coast of Africa.[32] These expeditions, which began in 1436, brought together two radically different cultures, and fetishism emerged in the exchange. During their stays, the Portuguese observed behaviors that they took to be the worship of objects as if they possessed supernatural powers; they called these objects *feitiço*, meaning "magical."[33]

While this brief narrative is given as history, stripped of its historical specifics it becomes a parable that illustrates the major components of fetishism. First, it tells us that fetishism begins with the interpretation of someone else's acts or beliefs. It may seem counterintuitive to assert that, prior to this cultural intercourse, fetishism as such did not exist in Africa, and yet the West Africans could not possibly see their own practice as fetishism because the term refers not just to object worship but also to its falsity. The Africans in the historical narratives are sincere in their worship, and so there can be no sense of falsity for them. That sense first appears in the eyes of the trader, who interprets the worship as false. Thus we can say that fetishism originates in the outsider's interpretation and not in the practice being observed, and that "the notion of fetishism is strictly correlative to the gaze of the observer."[34] At bottom, the term is a label one party stamps on another's perceived assessment of something as having more value than it merits. Pietz is quite right when he points out, "The discourse of the fetish has always been a critical discourse about the false objective values of a culture from which the speaker is personally distanced."[35] Fetishism begins with a commentary on someone else's attribution of excess cultural value; to echo a later term from Freud, it depends on the "overvaluation" of an object.

The second lesson of this parable is that, while fetishism originates in one party, it is the product of a relationship between two parties. In the historical narrative, that relationship is between distinct cultures within a contact zone, and out of that relationship the concept of the fetish arises.[36] This means that *fetish* is a relative term, rather than a positive thing in itself, and it has no existence apart from the relationships that bring it into being. The fetish "must be viewed as proper to . . . no discrete society or culture, but to a cross-cultural situation formed by the ongoing encounter of the value codes of radically different social orders."[37] An expression of the difference between two parties, it designates a relationship rather than a thing. How is that relationship constituted? In schematic form, it contains three points, rather than two: (1) an object of some kind, real or imagined, (2) an "insider" who attributes supernatural qualities to the object, and, (3) an "outsider" who contradicts the insider and reasserts the simple materiality of the object. The three positions can be labeled as follows: the *fetish*, which can be either a thing or an idea; the *fetishist* who "worships" the fetish; and the *critic* who identifies the fetish as such. This last position is occupied by a skeptical spectator who interprets the fetishist's relationship to the fetish as a form of false evaluation.[38] This means that the critic, rather than the fetishist, occupies the philosophical position of the subject in this triangle, since fetishism is produced in the critic's interpretation. The fetishist is the one being subjected to interpretation.

This is a reasonably straightforward triangular structure, in which one person evaluates another's evaluation of something. However, it also produces a dialectical complication. In asserting the falsity of the fetishist's values, the critic simultaneously asserts the truth or accuracy of his or her own system of values. The claim that the object is a fetish, and thus overvalued as possessing qualities it lacks, is of course not a neutral or objective observation. The critic sees the fetish as lacking value, and that assessment is necessarily part of a larger structure of cultural values, within which the critic's perspective makes sense. The evaluation of a behavior as fetishistic can be understood as the interpretation of an (inexplicable) attitude toward an object whose symbolic or material value does not translate into the critical subject's culture. Thus the fetish is defined by what it lacks: while fetishism is the expression of cultural value, it is more precisely an assessment of negative value within the value system of the critic. Unavoidably, that same value system also contains positive values. The two—negative and positive values—are parts of the same differential structure, and so the assessment of an object as in fact lacking value also implies that "real," nonsubjective value exists elsewhere, in other objects. The critic thus asserts the naive grounds of truth within his or her own system of values, and that is where the difficulty begins.

In doing so, the critic becomes vulnerable to the claim of fetishism by another outsider. The West Africans who were first identified with fetishism viewed the attitude of Western traders towards African gold as itself a type of fetishism.[39] In this example, the second assessment of fetishism comes from the other culture in the fetishistic triangle, but it could also come from the critic in another culture observing the Portuguese trader's assessments of value. This relativism shows how the critic of the first triangle inevitably comes to occupy the position of the fetishist in a second fetish triangle the instant that the critic articulates a given set of values. In other words, the critic becomes the fetishist in the act of evaluating the fetish as such, and in this manner, the critique of fetishism produces a secondary fetishization of the critic's values. Because of this relativism, the discourse of fetishism is never about the fetish itself; instead, its business lies in constructing the sequence of relationships that produce the notion of the fetish. Within this discourse, representations of fetishism occur within a dialogue that entails competing claims of fetishism, in which the critic and fetishist become structurally interchangeable, locked in a match of dueling fetishisms defined by conflicting sets of values.[40]

When nineteenth-century cultural theory identified the absence of culture as a type of fetishism, it entered this never-never land of claim and counterclaim. Insofar as the definition of culture becomes liable to claims of fetishism, then culture begins to resemble its opposite, unculture. Like those antiquated ethnographers, whose assumptions about primitive fetishism proved to be themselves fetishes, Arnold, Eliot, and Tylor tended to reenact the same fetishism they identify with primitive culture, a point I take up in the chapters that follow. Their predicament was the product of the fetish dialectic, but instead of relegating them to the museums of the writings of early cultural theorists, we need to examine how these writers confronted what was ultimately an unsolvable problem without being reduced to silence.

We might hope that the only problem in writing about fetishism is this fetish dialectic—however, further complicating these writings is the antagonistic relationship that exists between fetishism and writing itself. Comte gestured toward this problem when he speculated:

> If Man had been no more capable than monkeys and carnivorous animals of comparing, abstracting, and generalizing, he would have remained for ever in the rude fetichism which their imperfect organization forbids their surmounting.[41]

Why should this be the case? To compare, abstract, and generalize requires a synthetic capacity for representing objects, mentally or physically. Each object in nature is unique, but in the abstract we combine the similarities of many particulars into a single representation of a general type, one that exists nowhere in nature. Thus the ability to generalize depends on differentiating the object in nature from its representation, so that a general ideal can stand in for many particular objects. In linguistic terms, the capacity for abstraction depends upon the ability to differentiate between a signifier and a signified. But in Comte's primitive fetishism, signifier and signified are indivisible; each object in nature is meaningful in and of itself, and it does not stand for anything. Representation signals a later stage of cultural development, one that makes possible the more advanced symbolic meanings found in the second phase of Comte's social progression, idol worship. While a fetish is a god, an idol represents a god; it is the signifier for a god that is not present. In fetishism, object and god, signifier and signified, are one and the same, fused in an unmediated anti-symbolic relationship. Fetishes are "perfectly aniconic . . . in the sense that they do not represent divinities, but are divinities."[42] Pietz elaborates: "The fetish is precisely *not* a material signifier referring beyond itself, but acts as a material space gathering an otherwise unconnected multiplicity into the unity of its enduring singularity."[43] Both writers are pointing out that, rather than a representation of meaning, the fetish is meaning itself.

This very communion of object with spirit, signifier with signified, makes the fetish antithetical to representation. As that which is not representation, it exists "outside" all representational systems, including the system of language. A represented "fetish" is in fact an icon or a symbol, precisely what the fetish as such is defined against, and so to represent it is to collapse the difference that makes the fetish a fetish. While we have a variety of words for fetishes, through the act of signifying they all assert that the fetish can be represented; the sign *fetish*, after all, does exactly that. But the anti-representational essence of fetishism makes such representation a contradiction in terms, for the fetish is defined against representation as precisely that which is not a representation of meaning but rather meaning itself. Its immediacy—or its animation, to use Comte's figure—is what makes the object a fetish rather than something else. He recognizes that "comparing, abstracting, and generalizing" are all forms of representation; once the primitive acquires the ability to abstract, primitive fetishism is dead because at that moment society passes from fetishism into the new era of representation. The antithesis between language and fetishism leads to the conclusion that when the subject matter of writing is fetishism, that is to say when fetishism is represented, then it is necessarily represented as overvaluation. The represented "fetish" is something which is said to be meaningful in itself but which has a meaning separable from the object, as the writer demonstrates through the act of writing. In other words, the represented "fetish" is, by definition, false.

Because of this predicament, writers concerned with conveying the immediacy of the fetish routinely relied on figurative language; they gestured toward its ineffability by describing it as something else. The most common of these is the figure of metamorphosis in which inert and imaginary objects spring to life. Marx famously explained that fetishism occurs when "the products of the human brain appear as autonomous figures endowed with a life of their own."[44] In commodity fetishism, products appear transformed by their entry into exchange relations. A wooden table is just a table, "[b]ut as soon as it emerges as a commodity, it changes into a thing which transcends sensuousness. It not only stands with its feet on the ground, but, in relation to all other commodities, it stands on its head, and evolves out of its wooden brain grotesque ideas, far more wonderful than if it were to begin dancing of its own free will" (163–64). Using a similar metaphor, Tylor retold the story (originally from Charles Darwin) of "two Malay women in Keeling Island who held a wooden spoon dressed in clothes like a doll; this spoon had been carried to the grave of a dead man, and becoming inspired at full moon, in fact lunatic, it danced about convulsively like a table or a hat at a modern spirit-séance."[45] Such rhetoric illustrates the mutability that characterizes representations of fetishism as a protean quality that involves crossing the line between notions of life and death.[46]

Thus, in terms of its content or stated subject matter, texts about fetishism are anti-fetishistic, because their act of representing tends to undermine the unrepresentative quality that makes the fetish a fetish. However, when turning away from questions of content to questions of form, the situation looks dramatically different. This second theoretical problem in the relationship between fetishism and representation is exactly the inverse of the first. The problem can be simply formulated as follows: fetishes cannot be represented, but representations can be fetishes. In the first instance, we are speaking about content, but in the second, we turn to questions of literary form: the organizing principles of a text, the rhetorical tropes it employs, the unstated logic that informs its explicit statements, the social ideologies that constitute its subtext.[47] The most familiar example of a fetishized textual representation is that of scripture, a form of writing that, because it has a metonymic proximity to the supernatural, acquires some of the value attributed to it, as though a god or spirit inhabits the writing. There are other forms of demi-scripture in which similar hauntings take place. Speaking of mid-twentieth century literary criticism, for example, Eagleton argues that it transformed poems into things, as though they existed in space, with tangible borders enclosing a mystical interior: "What New Criticism did, in fact, was to convert the poem into a fetish."[48] He points to a problem in the consumption of literature, but the problem extends as well to questions of literary production. A major goal of the realist novel in the nineteenth century was to make the represented world appear real to its readership, as if fictional characters were in fact alive. In that goal, representation actively seeks to fetishize itself, so that these nonexistent people and events can be taken as real. While I explore this further in chapter 3, similar logic applies to nonfiction as well. Tylor's *Primitive Culture* makes a greater claim to referentiality than does a work of make-believe, like *Pinocchio*.[49] It seeks to persuade the reader that Tylor's primitive man refers to an object that presumably exists (or existed) outside of his text, in the world of historical reality. He has thus taken a murky concept, given it flesh, and breathed life into it, convincing his readers that this primitive being once walked the very earth on which they tread. In this success, Tylor's primitive sheds the ethereality of abstraction and takes on the reality of the concrete in the mind of the reader, who reifies the representation into a living being. Such vicissitudes depend on a reader's willingness to invest representation with life, to forget its status as language, and to project a living spirit into words. Among other factors, that willingness depends on the rhetoric a text wields and its effectiveness in marshalling the social ideologies that constitute its subtext. In other words, convincing a reader to believe is more a function of literary form than content, and in this way, representation can invite its own fetishization.[50]

Thus two contradictory problems define the relationship between fetishism and representation. On the one hand, we have the incommensurability of the fetish with representation. This is a problem at the level of content. The very fact of representation strips the fetish of its essence as that which cannot be represented, and in this regard, representations of the fetish as such are implicit critiques; they fulfill the critic's role in the fetishistic triangle, so that anything identified as a fetish in writing is necessarily identified as false worship. At the level of content, representation is by definition anti-fetishistic. On the other hand, we have the various ways in which a representation can itself becomes fetishized. This is a problem at the level of form. An image might seem to "come to life," and thus transit from representation to fetish. This can happen in the process of reading, or it can be part of the goals and methods employed in writing.[51]

Given these two contradictory problems, nineteenth-century writers on culture were entering the land of paradox rather than that of logic and rationality. Whether producing nonfiction or fiction, their texts took on a paradoxical relationship to the fetishism they described. The basic parameters of that paradox are the following: Victorian writing on fetishism stood on an unstable ground of dueling fetishisms, in which the (anti-fetishistic) content of the representation contradicted its (fetishistic) form, and the form undermined the anti-fetishistic assertions of the content. Within the terms of Victorian writing on culture and unculture, this was not a solvable problem, barring writerly silence. Rather than diminishing their importance, recognizing the presence of this dilemma in the texts under consideration gives us a point of departure in analyzing their complexities and identifying the skill with which these writers navigated this paradox. Comte's solution was to call for a return to fetishism. Having argued, in *Cours*, that all of human development was an escape from the illusions of primitive fetishism, he decided that modern people need fetishism, and if they will not do without it, then Positivists must supply an object to channel their fetishism. He called this his new Religion of Humanity, in which people would worship the new god of humanity in proto-Catholic ceremonies replete with mystical regalia, statues, and religious iconology, so that their need for fetishistic beliefs would be directed at the human race as a whole, which he considered a far preferable fetish to supernatural gods. In different ways, each of the three writers under primary consideration—Matthew Arnold, George Eliot, and Edward B. Tylor—repeated Comte's move. They exposed fetishism as the absence of culture while employing it in defining their own versions of culture.

This paradox gives these texts a complexity with a distinctly contemporary tinge. Each text says two opposite things simultaneously—"no" in one aspect, "yes" in another. They are, in a word, ambivalent, and in this doubleness they reproduce the principle later defined as fetishistic disavowal. In 1927, Freud first argued that the erotic fetish always serves as a denial or a disavowal of the reality that the subject fears—in his oedipal narrative, this is the little boy's fear of castration.[52] The fetish is a substitute for the absent phallus, and it serves to reassure the subject. However, he points out that, simply in the fact of its existence and in the fact of the fetishist's very need for reassurance, the fetish also serves as an affirmation of the threat; at some level the fetishist recognizes the reality of the danger, and this unwanted recognition produces the need to disavow it with the object. The fetish is thus both a disavowal of the danger and an affirmation of its reality. It says two opposite things simultaneously. Freud's idea of fetishism derived from its ethnographic usage, and so the similarity between the structure of the two entities is more than coincidental, as I discuss in chapter 5. But by considering the structure of fetishism in Victorian writing, we can see that this ambivalence was present long before fetishism was transposed into the language of human sexuality.

Defining culture in terms of unculture obviously depends on how one formulates that opposite term. In *Culture and Anomie*, Christopher Herbert's insights into the instability at the root of the nineteenth-century culture concept have become a necessary starting point for thinking about culture in the twenty-first century. By defining the culture concept today as "the residue of an adversarial project native to the nineteenth century," he returns the problem to its historical articulation.[53] Herbert identifies that adversary as the Victorian middle-class fear of unbounded desire, a condition that occurs when social norms "cease to act effectively in their role of restraining influences" (69). Using Durkheim's term for this condition, *anomie*, he identifies it with the Christian theology of original sin and locates it in the evangelical Methodism of John Wesley, where the counter to anomie is figured as puritanical self-restraint—a Victorian cultural value if ever there was one. His study demonstrates the explanatory power of considering the emergence of the culture concept as a response to the problem of anomic desire, and in this sense it fulfills the only claim to finality possible in this kind of research, "to explore the world as best we can with the most productive and compelling paradigms we can discover, knowing all along that we can hope to attain only a relative mode of truth devoid of positive terms" (304).

My decision to consider culture as a response to fetishism, rather than anomie, does not indicate disagreement with Herbert: there were doubtless many lines of thought, many social biases, many contributing factors that figured into the assumptions of anthropological and elite theories about culture, and so there are different intellectual threads that need to be pursued before the study of culture as a historical artifact can attain provisional claims to comprehensiveness. Certainly, anomie and fetishism have much in common. Both are psychological states, both entail self-centered perspectives, both can be seen as means to attain a wanted sense of comfort or, at least, security. The differences, however, are significant, particularly in the different social resonances each carried in the nineteenth century. Anomie is a mode of turning one's attention inward, toward desires and their satisfaction. While fetishism is also ultimately subjective, it describes attention directed outward, toward the external world of natural events. Fetishism is an anthropomorphic means of explaining the unpredictability of nature, so we can see it as belonging in the same historical category as other understandings of the external world, such as empiricism and science. Anomie belongs to the category of moral systems for thinking about inner life, and so it has associations with religion, as Herbert shows in his many references to Wesleyanism. Where anomie is a moral condition related to religion, fetishism is an epistemological problem related to science. Thus the two terms, *anomie* and *fetishism*, resonate with the two sides of the Victorian contest between religion and science.

Considering the culture idea in relation to fetishism leads us in a direction different from that of anomie. Instead of the religious mythology of original sin, we need to look at the secular mythology of primitive society; instead of John Wesley, we need to look at Auguste Comte. The chapters that follow are designed to document the prominence of fetishism as a synonym for the absence of culture and to identify the effect it had in shaping the Victorian discourse of culture. The historical aspect of this argument depends on establishing the connection between primitive fetishism and unculture in the second half of the nineteenth century. Chapter 1 lays out the evidence for that claim, taking us from classical antiquity through Comte's *Cours*.

Chapters 2–4 look at the treatment of unculture in three writers who made major contributions to twentieth- and twenty-first-century ideas about culture. Each illustrates a different approach to the problem. Matthew Arnold, in chapter 2, and George Eliot, in chapter 3, are both proponents of the humanities theory of culture. Arnold's cultural theory matters to literary study in particular because historically it formed the basis for the establishment of criticism as a profession, and his ghost still inhabits English, foreign language, and comparative literature departments. His idealist notion of culture as a world apart has always been fraught with difficulty, and in looking at how he engaged the paradox of fetishism, we can see why his legacy has been both stifling and liberating for literary critics. His particular strategy, I argue, was to mask the problem by obscuring it within his rhetoric of intellectual freedom. In the main, George Eliot's views on culture were consistent with Arnold's, but where Arnold was a theorist, Eliot was engaged in cultural practice as the preeminent author of the Victorian realist novel. Underlying her practice were theoretical assumptions about realism that, although never programmatically explained, were spelled out in different journalistic reviews and essays. In her treatment of the paradox of fetishism, Eliot was more aggressive than Arnold, and her response to it was more in line with

Comte's late, enthusiastic embrace than with Arnold's sleight of hand. As chapter 4 shows, Edward B. Tylor's engagement with unculture was the most deliberate of the three. His project was to define a universal pattern for cultural evolution, and this he did with a meticulous examination of primitive psychology and its underlying fetishism. His principle goal was to establish the "science of culture," or socio-cultural anthropology. This project meant that he had to develop a justifiable scientific methodology for the study of culture. I show that, within that methodology, the paradox of fetishism resurfaced as an integral part of the study of primitive fetishism. Tylor's response to the problem was more straightforward in acknowledging its self-contradiction than Arnold's, but Tylor was also less enthusiastic than Eliot about the paradox his use of fetishism presented.

Much of my overall argument hinges on the concept of fetishistic ambivalence, and so it seemed necessary to account for the connection between ethnographic fetishism and the later concept of fetishistic disavowal in psychoanalytic theory, which I discuss in chapter 5. For reasons of space, I do not attempt to carry this discussion beyond Freud, though there are good reasons for doing so. Fortunately, revisionist uses of Freud in the twentieth century are a well-researched field, particularly in the case of Lacan and in psychoanalytic feminism, the two areas where fetishism has been most thoroughly revisited. Nor do I pursue Marx's concept of commodity fetishism beyond describing it, though this is also a topic that has been carefully documented elsewhere.[54] This last chapter also marks the end of the era during which primitive fetishism was an integral part of writing on culture, and so it forms a natural terminus for this study. In this regard, Freud stands as Comte's counterpart, who marks its beginning. My conclusion briefly summarizes my findings and discusses the relationship between fetishism and culture today.

1

Primitive Fetishism
from Antiquity to 1860

Fetishism exists today in multiple senses. In psychiatry, it is one of the Paraphilias, a group of sexual conditions that also includes exhibitionism, voyeurism, frotteurism (touching nonconsenting people), pedophilia, masochism, sadism, and transvestic fetishism (cross-dressing). The principle diagnostic criteria for sexual fetishism is that the subject has "recurrent, intense sexually arousing fantasies, sexual urges, or behaviors involving the use of nonliving objects (e.g., female undergarments)."[1] It circulates in a more abstract sense in current psychoanalytic theory and criticism derived from Freud, who saw it as an eroticization of objects that served to protect the subject against an unacceptable psychological reality.[2] In analyses of culture and economics, the term continues to signify the way that capitalism fosters the illusion of an independent value in commodities, as Marx theorized in his analysis of commodity fetishism.[3] From this same base, it also appears in postmodern theory and criticism, as the fetishization of commodity objects: a "car fetish," for example.[4] The term has become general enough to refer to any unreasonable fixation on an object or idea, as when a student editorial complains, "It's as if the entire male population at the University has a cap fetish," or the president of a prominent academic organization editorializes against "the elitism of the Best-Student Fetish" in college admissions.[5] These closely related usages all developed from the earlier ethnographic accounts of religious fetishism. In this older form, the primitive mind was considered limited in its ability to think abstractly; instead, it projected its own fears and hopes unaware onto the objects and events of the material world, so that they appeared to possess supernatural qualities. Broadly speaking, while fetishism today refers to commodification, sexual attraction, or mental fixation, in the nineteenth century it more familiarly conjured up images of primitives worshipping material deities, and in this sense it was used metaphorically to describe Victorian beliefs as irrational.

The central writer in considering Victorian beliefs about fetishism is Auguste Comte, the French philosopher of positivism. When Comte wrote about primitive fetishism in *Cours de philosophie positive,* he was entering into an existing debate within philosophy, history, and theology over the condition of the first humans, a discussion that stretched back at least to classical antiquity. By viewing Comte's ideas in their historical context, we can begin examining the commonplace associations that defined Victorian fetishism and can thereby establish the cultural terms which Victorian writers on the topic took for granted. While this earlier fetishism had a different meaning than today's erotic, economic, and popular versions, it operated in a related fashion, and so the specificity of Victorian fetishism does not leave us on entirely unfamiliar ground.

——◊◊◊——

The Portuguese traders to West Africa applied the term *feitiço* to objects they thought the Africans treated as magical.[6] This usage was subsequently adopted by the French, where it became *fétiche,* and the English, who spelled it either *fetich* or *fetish.* The term derived from the Latin *factitius,* "made by artifice," and it already existed in both languages, with slightly different senses. Old French had *faitis,* "well made, beautiful." Middle English had *fetis,* which Chaucer used regularly for people ("well made, graceful, pretty, handsome"), things ("well made, elegant"), and actions (*fetisly*: "skillfully, handsomely, elegantly").[7] Thus, in *The Romaunt of the Rose,* Chaucer writes of "[f]ul fetys damyseles two," and calls a solid door "fetys and so lite."[8] Chaucer's usage derived from the Anglo-Norman *fetiz,* but even in these few examples from his writing it is clear that the term was associated in England from a very early date with an exceptionally positive qualitative assessment of something or someone. This sense was subsequently extended from passive states—an object's beauty, for example—to a sense of active power in the object, such as its ability to attract one's notice or captivate. As philosophers of aesthetics know, it can be a maddeningly fluid line between these two states, one that hinges on the question of whether beauty is imminent in the object or is a product of perception. And in its history, the term *fetishism* straddled both sides of the line, referring to an assessment of the (passive) object as "fetis," or the (active) effect produced by the object in the perceiver.[9] It is this second form that dominates post-Renaissance usage, in which fetishes are thought of as objects with supernatural powers.

The assumed fetishism of the West Africans was only one episode in the long history of western ideas about how humans first arrived at the idea of supernaturalism. In particular, it illustrated one of the most enduring elements of this debate: the argument that primitive humans anthropomorphized the world around them by engaging in a fetish-like act of self-projection. Speculation on the topic began as early as classical antiquity, in the materialist school of Epicurus. This philosophy flatly denied the existence of an afterlife and thus was uniquely interested in explaining how such a false belief could become virtually universal. The same aspect of Epicureanism later led Christian theologians to hold it in particularly low esteem, if they deigned to mention it at all. This orthodoxy explains why Dante included Epicurus in *The Inferno* only to consign the pagan materialist to the sixth circle of hell.[10]

The dominant account of primitive life during the Middle Ages was supplied by the narrative of Genesis, which held that the true nature of God was revealed to the first humans, and this revealed truth was passed down to each subsequent generation, even as they populated new lands. This view was still espoused in major anthropological texts of the early nineteenth century, when it found its ultimate expression in James Cowles Prichard's *Researches into the Physical History of Man,* first published in 1813 and revised until his death in 1847. A renewed interest in Epicureanism began early in the Renaissance, when the philosophy was promoted by Erasmus and Michel de Montaigne, among others.[11] The late-Renaissance French philosopher Pierre Gassendi (1592–1655) played a prominent role in completing the philosopher's resurrection. His *Eight Books on the Life and Manners of Epicurus* (1647) influenced Thomas Hobbes and John Locke, after which the materialist strand of thought on the ancient past took on a new and vital role in Enlightenment thinking. As Nichols has explained, the emerging rationalism "understood itself to be a new departure in philosophy and very consciously defined itself in opposition to the orthodox school that descended from Aristotle and Plato. In antiquity, Epicureanism had been the most powerful and radical opponent of Platonism and Aristotelianism, in most of its fundamental teachings. For this reason, Epicurus and Lucretius were widely read in the seventeenth and eighteenth centuries and were a source of inspiration in many ways for the new philosophic-scientific enterprise."[12] Thus the philosophy of Epicureanism found a new home in the seventeenth-century reaction against established modes of knowledge. At this point, the materialist view of primitive life resurfaced within the mainstream of western philosophical and scientific writing.

The reemergence of Greek and Roman mythology itself further challenged the dominant status of primitive monotheism in orthodox teaching. Here was testimony from the earliest of all known societies that showed a flourishing polytheism. According to orthodox dogma, they clearly should have been either monotheistic or in a state of primitive degeneration, yet they were neither. Combined with the record of Egyptian antiquities, the historical evidence told strongly against the orthodox thesis, and by the later seventeenth century, there was a vigorous debate over the nature of primitive religion and the historical validity of scripture's account of it.

—*∿*—

Epicureanism was based on the materialist philosophy of the pre-Socratic thinker Democritus (460–370 BCE). He argued that the universe and everything within it was composed of physical atoms moving in a vacuum. As Epicurus (341–270 BCE) recognized, if everything consisted of material atoms, then where did that leave the soul? He claimed that the soul did in fact exist, though not in immaterial form. Instead, it had to be a material entity that consisted of atoms in a vacuum, like every other object in the universe. While more ethereal than the body, it was also part of the body and when the body died, so too did this corporeal soul. Since the soul was mortal, there could be no possibility of an afterlife. Nonetheless, Epicureanism was not a philosophy of atheism. "Gods exist," Epicurus said, but they reside in a remote and tranquil state of "blessedness," and such a state precluded any involvement in the stress and unpredictability (*ataraxia*) of human affairs.[13] In other words, the human world was on its own. No one watched over or kept track of men's deeds, nor were there any rewards and punishments in the hereafter. Epicurus questioned the reasons for the prevalent and apparently universal belief in the soul's existence after death. It was without question an illusion, but what psychological process could account for the widespread belief in the shade's descent into the underworld? In this attempt to imagine a primitive psychology, the Epicureans formulated the earliest known link between a primitive mind and fetishistic thinking. The first element of that connection was the assumption that primitives had to be immersed in the concrete facts of their own material existence. Their intimacy with nature gave them a heightened comprehension of the physical world, in all of its particularity. At the same time, the primitive mind lacked any capacity for abstraction. It was locked into the world of sensual experience and unable to comprehend objects in any manner except through their immediacy as distinct, present singularities.

In book 5 of *De Rerum Natura,* the Epicurean poet Lucretius (99–55 BCE)—the source for much of our understanding of Epicureanism—narrates the story of the first humans.[14] The primal earth was turbulent and extraordinarily fertile; from this womb emerged all of the different forms of life, including humans. They were larger and stronger than their modern descendents, and each lived a solitary existence scavenging in the woods and feeding on whatever came to hand. Sporadically, male and female giants encountered one another, and through force or consent mated before returning to their separate existences. Because they were intimately familiar with nature, these isolated giants had no need of superstitions to explain natural phenomena. At the sun's daily disappearance, "They did not try to trail him across the fields / With loud lament and panic," because they had seen this "from their earliest childhood," and so took for granted the sun's return, "with no wondering, no dread."[15]

Later, isolated giants began to form lasting relationships with one another, perhaps traveling in small groups before finally residing together, making fires and creating dwellings. Their life became more sheltered from the extremes of nature, and, as a result, they began to lose their former strength and stature, developing a more recognizably modern form. The new communalism constituted the first society and so marked the transition from no culture to culture. Such a turning point entailed mental transformations as dramatic as the physical ones. Fostered by the social need to communicate among themselves, language emerged as the most important of these changes, and it marked a departure from the absolute concreteness of the giants' psychology. The use of language implied an ability to think about and refer to objects that were not immediately present to the senses. It demonstrated a new capacity, however rudimentary, for abstract thinking, including the ability to see similarities between particular objects and to make generalities about them. Where the lonely giant saw two unique trees, the linguistic primitive would see two versions of the same type of tree. As primitive societies developed, this ability grew and eventually led to systems of laws, forms of wealth, and the first rulers.

The early capacity for abstraction had other consequences as well. It led to the birth of superstition.[16] Belief in the existence of supernatural beings followed from the rudimentary ability to imagine something that was not tangibly present. The first gods were conceived as explanations for the events of nature, such as the change of seasons, storms, lightning, and celestial events. "What sorry creatures!" Lucretius laments,

> Unhappy race of men, to grant the gods
> Such feats, and add bitter vindictiveness.
> What sighs and groans they gave themselves, what wounds
> For us today, what tears for our descendents! (193)

The belief that supernatural beings controlled nature was a fundamental mistake, Lucretius insisted, but he thought that, for primitive humans, the new superstitions served an important function. As they were elaborated over time, they eventually turned into the belief, familiar in Epicurus's time as well as that of Lucretius, that humans lived in a world of providential rewards and punishments: "the assertions of the many concerning the gods," Epicurus writes, "are conceptions grounded not in experience but in false assumptions, according to which the greatest misfortunes are brought upon the evil by the gods and greatest benefits upon the good" (62). Humans anthropomorphized natural events in the attempt to explain nature to themselves. "Men being always at home with their own virtues, they embrace those like themselves and regard everything unlike themselves as alien" (62–63). Thus, as early as Epicurus, the second key ingredient of primitive fetishism had been spelled out: psychological projection.

In *De Rerum Natura*, Lucretius questions "the state in which all men / Must dwell forever and ever after death," concluding that death is followed by nothingness, and so "[d]eath / is nothing to us," and need not be feared.[17] More explicitly than Epicurus, he analyzes beliefs about the afterlife as psychological projections of lived experience. He illustrates this premise in book 3 with a rich poetic catalog of characters from Roman mythology who were punished for their sins in the afterlife; he then explains each one as the reified expression of everyday anxieties.

> The story says that Tantalus, the wretch,
> Frozen in terror, fears the massive rock
> Balanced in air above him. It's not true.
> What happens is that in our lives the fear,
> The silly, vain, ridiculous fear of gods,
> Causes our panic dread of accident. (114)

Similarly, there is no Tityos, eternally pecked at by vultures, but

> We do have
> A Tityos in ourselves, and lie, in love,
> Torn and consumed by our anxieties,
> Our fickle passions. . . . (115)

The Danaids vainly filling leaking vessels with water, Cerberus, the Furies, and

> Tartarus, belching blasts of heat—all these
> Do not exist at all, and never could.
> But here on earth we do fear punishment
> For wickedness, and in proportion dread
> Our dreadful deeds . . . . (115)

Thus the answer to the basic question of how the belief in an afterlife became universal was a psychological one: the Romans explained death in terms of themselves.

Lucretius told the story of a human mind that began in global concreteness and gradually developed a capacity for abstract thinking, as the state before culture receded into the distance and culture progressed towards his own time, the first century BCE. Even as he described the process by which abstractions led to a mental imprisonment in an oppressive supernaturalism, he also continued the narrative to a further stage in which abstract thinking would become the means of liberation from such fantastic illusions. This future stage represented the triumph of his own philosophy. *De Rerum Natura* exemplified the ultimate ability of rational thought to critique the false belief in deities and the afterlife, identifying both as projections of human fears. Ultimately, in the story Lucretius told, the human mind began in primitive concreteness, moved to supernaturalism, and finally entered the utopia of Epicurean rationalism.

Medieval theologians resolved the problem of Greco-Roman polytheism along very different lines from the pagan Lucretius.[18] While viewing the ancient myths as heretical, they reconciled them to the orthodoxy of primitive monotheism by reading them allegorically as prefigurations of Christianity. They used a similar logic to account for Egyptian polytheism, though in the latter case they had to overcome the difficult stumbling block posed by animal worship. The practice of deifying brutes was antithetical to the belief in the Chain of Being, and interpreters could not easily accept the heresy that God created humans who worshipped beings below themselves. In *Oedipus Aegyptiacus* (1652–54), the German Jesuit Athanasius Kircher (1601–80) produced the interpretation that reconciled the evidence from antiquity with seventeenth-century Christian orthodoxy. He argues that the Egyptians had learned the basic truth through direct revelation, and through an elaborate and contrived system of analogy, those masked truths could be revealed. Each figure has a "concrete scientific or theological significance."[19] Thus, for example, the Egyptian gods Isis, Osiris, and Horus prefigured the Holy Trinity. By redefining the animal images as figurative, he was able to maintain that they were not literal representations of brute worship but had instead symbolically affirmed Christian truths.[20]

French philosopher Pierre Bayle (1647–1706) was one of the earliest to make the case for what might be called a "Genesis-free" account of primitive society. He took the then unusual step of comparing the classical texts with Renaissance travel literature on African "savages," and so was able to suggest correlations between primitives, then and now. In *Réponse aux questions d'un provincial* (1704–7) he draws heavily on William Bosman's newly published *Voyage de Guinée* (1705) to compare the African fetishist with the Greek temple priest. He echoes the arguments of the Epicureans by characterizing primitive thought as a "pristine materialism."[21] Bayle also extends the primitive net beyond social groups that were literally primitive, using it to encompass modern peasants and the lower class as well, there finding more evidence for the prevalence of superstition among the less developed classes.

Bayle's compatriot Bernard le Bovier de Fontanelle (1657–1757), a nephew of the dramatist Corneille, made a similar argument, but where Bayle conceptualized the relationship between primitive and advanced states as fixed and ahistorical, Fontanelle added the principle of gradual cultural development. In *Digression sur les anciens et les modernes* (1715) and *Discours sur l'origine des fables* (1724), he describes a distinct primitive mind that characterized the original stage of all human society, including his own. He further identifies the primitive mind with the Greeks, contemporary savages, the vulgar mass, and children. With the addition of this last category, the primitive mind could account for the first stage of development within the individual as well as society. Its leading characteristic was psychological: the primitive mind perceived the world differently from that of developed human beings, like Fontanelle and his contemporaries, because it projected its own experiences outward, transforming them into imaginary independent divinities, and this led inevitably to the initial stage of polytheism found in the evidence from classical antiquity. As the human's ability to synthesize specifics into generalities improved, the diverse gods combined with one another, and this eventually led to the most advanced stage of all, Christian monotheism. Fontanelle's argument constituted heresy because it described an original polytheism, but this was finessed by beginning his narrative after the Biblical flood; this allowed for a discontinuous, antediluvian state that may have been monotheistic. Thus he could describe a progression that began with polytheism without overtly contradicting Genesis. The same window-dressing strategy was adopted by later philosophers in Catholic countries.[22] A second principle to appear in subsequent writing concerned the origination of the supernatural. In an argument similar to the late-Victorian debate between the evolutionists and diffusionists, he insisted that the universal belief in supernatural beings did not spread by historical contact between societies. He held the primitive mind to develop its religious ideas naturally; the original mental impulse toward spiritual belief was an autonomous development caused by an inborn quality, and so was innate rather than acquired.[23]

For Bayle and Fontanelle, the defining feature of primitive religion was its polytheism, in contrast to the orthodox assumption of original monotheism. All forms of polytheism were included in this concept, including idol worship, the belief in oracles, and the particular fetishism that remained linked with African object worship. Thus at this time fetishism proper was only one among many

superstitious practices. However, in a more general sense, fetishism already under-
lay all the other manifestations of primitive religion. First, all of the variations took
for granted a consciousness that was immersed in the concreteness of its own
experience, much like the early humans of Lucretius. Second, that consciousness
unwittingly projected its own psychological state outward, investing the material
world with anthropomorphic meanings that it then took for real, as Lucretius had
also claimed. Even though primitive religion was most often termed idolatry or
polytheism in the Enlightenment, it contained the two basic elements of primitive
fetishism within these other terms. This assumption of a fundamental fetishism
would soon be made explicit in the work of Charles de Brosses.

Giambattista Vico, de Brosses, and David Hume all belonged to a group of
mid-eighteenth-century writers on primitive religion and mythography that
stressed the effect that the physical condition of the early earth had on the psychological state of its first inhabitants.[24] And it is in the work of this group that the
association between the primitive and the concrete became foremost. Like
Fontanelle, they accepted the concept of a distinct primitive mind, but, unlike
him, that mind's original religious impulse was not innate. Instead, the universal
appearance of religious ideas resulted from the primitive mind's interaction with
the material environment. All three writers worked within the sensationalist tradition of Locke, who rejected the theory of innate ideas in favor of the impact of
experience. And so it remained to these mid-century mythographers to explain
how the earliest human societies all arrived independently at the concept of supernatural beings, without inheriting the concept. They accomplished this by proposing an environmental cause, arguing that the physical characteristics of the
primitive earth were both unique and radically different from those of the modern
world. These conditions gave rise to religious beliefs among all primitive societies.
The young earth was volatile, prone to quakes, eruptions, and catastrophic storms,
and the interaction between this dramatic geography and the blank slate of the
primitive mind led to the emergence of the first beliefs in the supernatural.[25]

In the third and last edition of *Scienzia Nuova*, or *New Science*, published in
1744, Giambattista Vico (1668–1744) tells a particularly dramatic story of the
young earth. He produces a detailed timeline of earth's history in which he allows
a century for the earth to dry out after the biblical flood. During that time, the
descendents of Noah scattered and "wandered like brutes," living a Hobbesian
existence and growing to enormous stature, similar to Lucretius's lonely giants.[26]
Vico's giants were "stupid, insensate, and horrid beasts," with no capacity for
thought (144). "Their minds were in no way abstract, refined, or intellectualized;
rather, they were completely sunk in their senses, numbed by their passions, and
buried in their bodies" (147). The concreteness of their mental process made it
scarcely possible for the modern person to comprehend them, since "countless

abstract expressions"—language, writing, counting—distanced moderns from their sense experiences (146). In the interaction between this concrete imagination and the unstable environment lay the birth of mythology, marking the second phase of primitive existence. As the earth dried out from the flood, alterations in weather produced the first thunder and lightning, and these new phenomena terrified the giants. They "imagined its cause as a god. And at the same time, whatever aroused their wonder they endowed with a substantial being based on their own ideas. This is the nature of children, whom we see picking up inanimate objects in play and talking with them as if they were living persons . . ." (145). Over time, the giants came to imagine the entire heavens as having passions and emotions like their own, and they named this great being "Jupiter." Ultimately, "they endowed all the universe and its parts with the being of an animate substance" (147). The significance he gives to the act of anthropomorphism cannot be overestimated. In his list of 141 axioms, it stands at number one: "By its nature, the human mind is indeterminate; hence, when man is sunk in ignorance, he makes himself the measure of the universe" (75).

Vico viewed myth as the first poetry, and the oracles and sibyls of antiquity who transformed natural events into mythology were the first poets. As he explains, "the proper subject of poetry is a believable impossibility. Thus, while it is impossible that physical objects have intelligence, people believed that the thundering heavens were Jupiter" (149). This view of mythology led Vico to a new insight: because they were psychological projections, ancient myths constituted a historical record of early human perceptions. It reflected experience as it was shaped by the volatile earth. This concrete analysis of myth put Vico profoundly at odds with the older, orthodox view that had found Christian mystical truths allegorically represented in Greek myths and Egyptian hieroglyphics. He was certainly blunt in his dismissal of this older scholarship, calling it "absurd," and specifically labeling Kircher's allegories "madness" (149, 269).

His examination of the "poetic wisdom" in pagan mythology was only the beginning of his broader narrative of cultural development (148). Like the later evolutionists, he saw cultural changes as occurring in an invariable, universal sequence, such that all nations "begin, develop, and end in the same stages" (154). That sequence had three stages: the Age of Gods, Age of Heroes, and Age of Men.[27] Each was defined by the particulars of its sign system, with each reflecting a different capacity for abstraction. He associated the first, the language of the gods, with hieroglyphs, "gestures or objects naturally related to their ideas."[28] In the second stage, Heroes spoke using symbols, or "heroic emblems like those *mute similes*" of Homer (177). Finally, the Age of Men employed "epistolary" language, which "distant persons used to discuss the common needs of everyday life" (178).

Although relatively ignored in his own day, there was renewed interest in *New Science* after 1770, first by German historians and then by French historian Jules Michelet, who published a popular series of abridgments and translations of Vico, beginning in 1827 with his *Discours sur le système et la vie de Vico*. As a result, the early-eighteenth-century Italian became a more well-known figure in the nineteenth century than he had been while alive. Indeed, both Comte and Marx read and admired the *New Science*, and their subsequent theories of evolutionary periodization owed much to Vico's three stages.[29]

Scottish philosopher David Hume took a different, ahistorical approach to the birth of religion, in *The Natural History of Religion* (1777). He also expanded the concept of the primitive mind to include not only children and peasants but the entire female sex. "What age or period of life is the most addicted to superstition? The weakest and most timid. What sex? The same answer must be given."[30] Like the earlier Bayle (and the later Matthew Arnold), Hume imagined society as alternating between two states, rather than developing linearly. "It is remarkable, that the principles of religion have a kind of flux and reflux in the human mind, and that men have a natural tendency to rise from idolatry to theism, and to sink again from theism to idolatry" (46–47). Hume's principal argument was against the orthodoxy of primitive monotheism and specifically against natural theology. Spelled out by the English theologian John Ray (1628–1705) in *The Wisdom of God Manifested in the Works of the Creation* (1691), natural theology was based on the logical belief that humans, when contemplating the infinite complexity of nature's interlocking design, would have understood that a design must have a designer and so inferred a single creative intelligence behind it. Nonsense, says Hume: "The savage tribes of America, Africa, and Asia are all idolaters. Not a single exception to this rule" (23). Repeating the anthropomorphic trope seen in writing from Lucretius to Vico, he argues that, far from a rational contemplation of nature, "the first ideas of religion arose . . . from a concern with regard to the events of life, and from the incessant hopes and fears, which actuate the human mind" (27). The primitive mind began in the rudest state of immersion in its own concrete experience, but it eventually developed a capacity for abstraction, and with it came illusions of deities. "The mind rises gradually, from inferior to superior: By abstracting from what is imperfect, it forms an idea of perfection: And slowly distinguishing the nobler parts of its own frame from the grosser, it learns to transfer only the former, much elevated and refined, to its divinity" (24). In this early state, the concept of "an invisible spiritual intelligence is an object too refined" for apprehension, and so "men naturally affix it to some sensible representation" (40). The polytheist, he writes, "deifies every part of the universe, and conceives all the conspicuous productions of nature, to be themselves so many real divinities. The sun, moon, and stars, are all gods according to his system: Fountains are inhabited by nymphs, and trees by hamadryads: Even monkeys, dogs, cats, and other animals often become sacred in his eyes, and strike him with a religious veneration" (38). This description could have been written by Comte. The similarity between the two writers is particularly noticeable when Hume says: "There is an universal tendency among mankind to conceive all beings like themselves, and to transfer to every object, those qualities, with which they are familiarly acquainted, and of which they are intimately conscious" (29). Already, in Hume, Vico, and Fontanelle, we see the basic concepts emerging that later define the nineteenth-century European theory of the primitive: an immersion in the concrete, combined with anthropomorphic projection.

These two attributes finally became labeled "fetishism" in 1760, when the minor philosophe and French magistrate Charles de Brosses (1709–77) published *Du culte des dieux fétiches*. Later uses of the term derive from this book: a young Karl Marx read it in German translation as a student in 1842–43, and Comte knew it, directly or indirectly, as well.[31] *Dieux fétiches* was an interpretation of ancient Egyptian figures found on mummies, papyri, and obelisks. Writers who interpreted these objects allegorically or symbolically were wrong, he argued. In fact the objects were fetishes, objects whose supernatural quality coincided with their material quality. Like Bayle and Fontanelle, de Brosses employed an early version of the comparative method. He drew analogies between the ancient objects and observations of existing "primitive" societies, again using firsthand reports of African fetish worship in travelers' accounts. He was certainly well prepared to do so. While his colleagues in the Academy were poring over the evidence from classical antiquity, he read the accounts of travelers in the Southern Hemisphere, which he gathered together and published in his *Histoire des navigations aux terres australes* (1756). He knew the major accounts of seventeenth- and eighteenth-century explorers to Western Africa, including Bosman's *Voyage de Guinée*, and knew they described primitive cults that worshipped objects and animals as gods, and so he was able to argue that the Egyptian figures of animal worship represented exactly what they appeared to depict.[32]

De Brosses committed heresy by positing an initial stage of fetishism, contradicting the orthodoxy of primitive monotheism, but he preserved himself from prosecution by employing a version of Fontanelle's window-dressing strategy and proposing an early stage of monotheistic star-worship.[33] Nonetheless, as in the case of Fontanelle, his fundamental progression began with fetishism. While vague on the stages themselves, he proposed a uniform universal sequence so that all religion went through a process of historical development, which might take longer in one place than another but was ultimately inevitable. Since fetishism was universal in the earliest stage, it had to stem from some quality inherent to human beings, and he argued that it reflected their primordial psychology. As a "natural" element of human psychology, fetishism was evident in the early development of the individual as well as that of society. He compared children to primitives and asked why anyone should be surprised to see fetishism in savages when all children imagine their dolls to be alive. In the same vein, he drew parallels between religious development and the evolution of languages, a field he discusses further in *Traité de la formation mécanique des langues et des principes physiques de l'étymologie* (1765).[34] Children and primitives alike, he reasoned, have only rudimentary language abilities because they lack a capacity for abstract concepts, and this linguistic deficiency contributes to their fetishistic mode of thought. Through de Brosses, the two crucial psychological elements of concreteness and projection, which had been firmly linked throughout eighteenth-century writing on the primitive, became jointly signified as fetishism. At the same time, fetishism was now understood as a universal attribute of primitive life, rather than a localized practice of the West Africans.

De Brosses was a member of the *Académie des inscriptions et belles-lettres*, but his doctrine of an original fetishism was controversial enough that *Culte des dieux fétiches* was rejected when he proposed it to the *Académie* in 1760. He had to have it printed secretly, which may explain why his book received so little notice at the time. It was mentioned in *Mercure de France* and was reviewed in *Monde primitif*, but by and large his idea of primitive fetishism "created no great stir," according to Manuel.[35] It was not until the end of the eighteenth century that the doctrine of fetishism as the earliest state of religion became a more established part of European intellectual culture. At the turn of the century, two German historians of religion, Christoph Meiners and Philipp Christian Reinhard, wrote at length about a primitive state of fetishism, as did the French writers J. A. Dulaure and Charles Dupuis.[36] Even then, it was not until 1835 that de Brosses's neologism, *fétichisme*, was accepted by the French Academy, fully three-quarters of a century after he first published *Culte des dieux fétiches*.

In England early in the nineteenth century, de Brosses's name was notable in its absence from the most influential ethnological work of the time, Prichard's *Researches into the Physical History of Man*.[37] Relying on linguistic as well as physical evidence, Prichard defended the historical accuracy of Genesis at a time when the literality of the Bible was subject to intense scientific skepticism. By marshalling an impressive array of evidence to support his claim that the human race was no more than six thousand years old, Prichard gave a new lease on life to biblical anthropology in Britain. But in an omission of "critical diagnostic importance," he ignored studies by anyone that could be connected to the French

Revolution, leaving out all references to the philosophes, encyclopédistes, and idéologues, including de Brosses.[38]

———

The theory of the primitive fetish achieved its greatest prominence in the mid-nineteenth century, largely due to the work of Auguste Comte. More well known in Britain than France, his doctrine of primitive fetishism is definitively explained in *Cours de philosophie positive*, published 1830–42. His relationship to subsequent thinking within British ethnology and post-Darwinian anthropology was of a broad, ideological kind; he was known as a philosopher of social science, not an anthropologist. As the philosopher of positivism, he articulated the model of accumulated knowledge that Victorian science and social science took as axiomatic, and he contributed to a new emphasis on the role of hypothesis and verification, a point that differentiated him from the earlier inductive method of Bacon and Descartes. His case is one of singular significance to the understanding of Victorian anthropology because his work served as an important bridge between the nineteenth century and the earlier developmentalism of Fontanelle, Vico, and de Brosses, and in this respect it contributed to the eclipse of Prichard's biblical anthropology. The path from the Enlightenment to Victorian anthropology was through Comte. As Stocking notes, "it was the successive volumes of Comte's *Positive Philosophy* . . . that offered the most systematic and influential model for an ostensibly *scientific* study of human progress in civilization."[39] In *Cours*, primitive fetishism was the first moment in the universal pattern through which societies developed from infancy to adulthood; it was the opening sentence in Comte's developmental narrative, which was subsequently absorbed into British ethnology. "The Comtian framework was widely adopted," notes Ellen, and more than any other writer Comte established the scientific framework within which a professional Victorian anthropology could emerge from the gentleman's hobby of amateur ethnology.[40]

Comte's objective in *Cours* was to establish a new science of society founded on the history of large-scale social transformations arranged into stages. The changing human brain, with its concomitant psychological growth, was the engine powering social development. The mind came to comprehend the world in radically different terms over time, evolving from the subjective explanations of primitives to the scientific explanations of the present. The promise of positivism was that the social scientist "could understand the changes that had occurred and would occur in the human mind and thus in the social system."[41] The law of three stages explained those changes. He argued that all humanity was subject to the same law of continuous development. This was a scientific law of human nature reflecting both subjective and social factors, and so he saw himself as a scientist engaged in the discovery of natural laws and not a metaphysician. The law of three stages was as fundamental to social phenomena as Newton's law of gravity was to physics. Of the many fields of human knowledge, several had eliminated the conjectural imprecision that plagued medicine, history, and physics before Newton. Mathematics (and physics after Newton) yielded results that were definite and verifiable, rather than speculative or dogmatic. Comte, his older contemporary Henri de Saint-Simon, and others at the time called these the "positive" sciences because their results were certain, and this distinguished them from fields that relied on a priori concepts or guesswork. Positive science relied solely on established facts and was thereby able to establish explanations for other facts that could be tested and verified. Comte's title, *Positive Philosophy*, meant "scientific philosophy." That philosophy was based on the history of the sciences he detailed in his narrative of social development. The law of three stages was the established fact on which the most complex of all sciences, that of society itself, was to be based.

He first outlined his three stages in 1824, in his fundamental opuscule, *Plan des travaux scientifiques nécessaires pour réorganiser la société*.[42] The "theological," "metaphysical," and "positive" stages existed in a progressive sequence. The first and last represented completely distinct modes of comprehending the external world, while the middle was transitional; the metaphysical stage combined elements from both the theological and the positive.

In the theological stage, people were ill equipped to understand the world scientifically. They engaged in magical thinking, similar to the primitives and poets in Lucretius and Vico. Plagues, storms, bad harvests—all were explained through supernatural agency as responses to human actions or otherwise products of supernatural events. Such accounts explained the vagaries of the environment through projection, using internal feelings to account for external events. The theological stage itself had three subdivisions, and Comte associated each with a specific historical period. The first, primitive fetishism, typified the period of prehistory. It was followed by the second phase, polytheism, in classical antiquity. Monotheism defined the third phase and dominated the medieval centuries, particularly 1000–1300 CE.

The metaphysical stage was transitional in that the supernatural explanations of the theological era were replaced by fantastic secular ideas. Like so many George Eliot-style Casaubons, metaphysicians imagined they had discovered the key to unlocking the mysteries of nature. Abstract principles came first, facts second, so deductive reasoning from assumed truth was the characteristic feature. For Comte, the shift from the theological to the metaphysical was largely a transposition of historical causation from one kind of abstraction to another, and the power previously attributed to the gods was reassigned to a priori concepts. But the metaphysical stage also had elements of the positive. It included an increased emphasis on empirical observation, and with that came the first glimmer of interest in the possibility of scientific verification. While the substitution of abstract themes onto different concepts was a backward-looking remnant of the theological, the developing interest in observation was a revolutionary trait leading forward to positivism.

The positive stage was the grand finale of the sequence and was yet to be fully realized. It was characterized by inductive thinking, in which the observer began with facts and then constructed a theory to account for them, rather than the other way around. Thus a familiar way of distinguishing between the three stages was by focusing on the basic method people use to explain historical causation, or why things happen. The English positivist George Henry Lewes summarizes the difference in his description of the three stages:

> In the first, man explains phenomena by some fanciful conception suggested by the analogies of his own consciousness.

> In the second, he explains phenomena by some à priori conception of inherent or superadded entities, suggested by the constancy observable in phenomena, which constancy leads him to suspect that they are not produced by any intervention on the part of an external being, but are owing to the nature of the things themselves.

> In the third, he explains phenomena by adhering solely to these constancies of succession and co-existence ascertained inductively, and recognised as the laws of nature.[43]

The positive stage could not be reduced to induction alone. Comte himself argued against this, placing more emphasis on verification than induction, and this was part of the novelty of Comte's definition of the scientific method.[44] Science previously had been defined as certainty of knowledge, but Comte rejected this view. Instead, he thought it impossible ever to know anything with finality, and thus the degree of knowledge was relative to what had been known before and what would be known in future. Rather than certainty, he defined science as having a predictive power that was capable of being tested. Hypotheses should be tested through both inductive and deductive processes before they become scientific theories. He argues in *Cours* that "*science* is essentially destined to dispense with all direct observation—as much as the diverse phenomena allow—by making it possible to deduce from the smallest possible number of immediate data the greatest possible number of results."[45] By placing more emphasis on hypothesis than observation, Comte dramatically increased the role of imagination in the scientific process. In volume 3, he discusses the art of hypotheses, or "scientific fictions," and likens them to poetic invention.[46]

The stages transitioned gradually from one to the next and elements from all three mingled in each. Thus Comte argued that the positive revolution was initiated in the metaphysical stage, by Bacon, Descartes, and Galileo. He also argued that positivism had in fact existed since the theological stage, first appearing in the philosophy of Aristotle.[47] Rather than sharp, absolute distinctions, the three stages were composites of competing forces, and Comte, like Marx, differentiated those tending toward the future and those harking back to the past.

While many of his fundamental ideas were entirely original, others were borrowed from writers with whom he had collaborated, especially Saint-Simon, or writers whom he had read. From Baron de Montesquieu (1689–1755), whom he first studied in 1816, he seems to have absorbed the basic idea that human society could be studied scientifically, as a sequence of three stages.[48] But his most important early influence was the ideologue Marquis de Condorcet (1743–94), whom he read in the following year of 1817.[49] Condorcet viewed the progress of history as more dynamic than did Montesquieu. For Condorcet, progress centered on the gradually growing power of human reason, accompanied by a related growth of political freedom. History was the continuous story of social evolution through a sequence of ten historical epochs, each with distinct changes in the arts, economics, and sciences. Changes in any one field inevitably had repercussions in the others, and so he defined social progress as both continuous and organic, two qualities that reappeared in Comte's philosophy.[50]

⁓〰⁓

The writing of *Cours* was a drawn-out process, to say the least. Its central concepts were earlier articulated in six opuscules, smaller works he published between 1819 and 1828 in journals associated with Saint-Simon, his mentor and employer from August 1817 until March 1824. In the late 1820s, he needed to supplement a meager income, and he designed a series of lectures on positive philosophy that could be taught by subscription. The scheme had the added benefits of promoting his philosophy and attracting potential followers. His course was first taught in 1828–29, consisting of seventy-two lessons in all. No records survive of its contents, but the following year he taught it again in an abbreviated format of fifty lectures. That course attracted two hundred students and met twice weekly at the Athénée, from December 1829 to November 1830. While teaching this second course he negotiated a contract with Roen Brothers to publish the original seventy-two lessons. Paired lessons were to be issued in weekly numbers, bound into volumes as they went along. The original plan called for four volumes completed in two years. Unable to keep up with the weekly deadlines, he nonetheless completed the first volume quickly, and it was published in July 1830 with a total of eighteen lessons.

The aim of *Cours* was to establish a new science of "social physics," the positive science for the study of society. A topic of interest throughout the nineteenth century, social science culminated in the establishment of sociology as a discipline, using the term Comte later coined as an improvement on "social physics." Volume 1 begins with two introductory lessons outlining these ideas and explaining how the sciences related to one another. All sciences can be arranged hierarchically, from the more fundamental bodies of knowledge to the most advanced. The simpler sciences, like mathematics, generate the essential tools on which other sciences depend; for example, mathematics is an essential component of all the other sciences, while it depends on none of them for its own practice, and thus it comes first in the arrangement. Next come the inorganic sciences— astronomy, physics, and chemistry—followed by the organic sciences—physiology (a term that at first included biology) and social physics. This sequence was also a historical progression: the history of science, and indeed of society, was the stepwise development of new forms of knowledge, beginning with the most fundamental and advancing as each new science successfully built on the established older ones. Thus Comte's law of the three stages was essentially a succession of steps in the evolution of scientific knowledge. Because it was the most advanced of the natural sciences, social physics was therefore the latest to develop. However, it could not be understood properly without grasping each of the earlier sciences on which it depended, from mathematics to biology. Consistent to a fault, he therefore planned the four volumes to begin with an explanation of all the sciences, beginning with the simplest and concluding with social physics. In volume 1, then, apart from the two introductory lessons on positivism and the classification of the sciences, he explains the principles of mathematics.

Historical developments intervened when the July Revolution that same year put Roen out of business, leaving Comte without a publisher for volumes 2, 3, and 4. To make matters worse, the first volume had not sold well, and other publishers were not rushing forward. In the meantime, he taught his course again at the Athénée the following year, 1831. It was two more years before he successfully negotiated a deal with a new publisher, but finally on 3 March 1833 he signed a contract for the last three volumes with Bachelier, a publisher of scientific literature. It took two more years to finish the second volume, which continues the study of the inorganic sciences, with sections on astronomy and physics. After a hiatus of nearly five years, volume 2 appeared in April 1835. Writing for the third volume went more smoothly, and it was published 2 January 1838. Divided into two parts, the first covers chemistry, the last of the inorganic sciences. The second part initiates the review of organic science with an explanation of biology, which contains his theory of milieu, the concept that organisms must be understood in the context of their environment.[51]

He waited until the end of 1838 to begin writing the fourth volume, in which he planned to cover social physics. Replacing the term with a neologism of his own, "sociology," he subdivided the volume into two parts. Social statics focused on the complex structure of the social body and how it was organized. Social dynamics studied the growth and development of society and so examined historical changes structured around the law of three stages. The volume grew to an unmanageable length and, to avoid another long delay between volumes, he issued volume 4, "Part 1," on 26 July 1839. Devoted almost entirely to social statics, it includes an introduction to social dynamics as the last lesson. The topic of social dynamics also grew in size; it occupied all of the new volume 5 and most of an additional volume 6, which proved to be the final volume. The fifth volume was penned quickly, and when it was published in May 1841, less than two years had passed since the previous installment. It contains a comprehensive description of the first two stages, the theological and metaphysical. The three phases of the theological (fetishism, polytheism, and monotheism) are discussed first, and the last and longest chapter covers the metaphysical stage. The writing for volume 6 was soon completed, on 6 July 1842, and the volume was published five weeks later, fourteen months after volume 5. It contains the progress of positivism from the fourteenth century to 1838. In the final three lessons, he reviews the positive method, the positive doctrine, and discusses the future.

With those lessons *Cours* was at last finished. Expected to take two years and fill four volumes, it had ultimately taken Comte thirteen and one-half years to complete and had grown in size by half.

—◁◁◁◁—

On the nature of earliest society, Comte is straightforward. "The theological period of humanity could begin no otherwise than by a complete and usually very durable state of pure Fetishism" (*PP*, 545). While Fontanelle, Vico, and de Brosses had left open the possibility of an earlier monotheism, Comte, who had grown up in the changed environment of post-Revolutionary France, made no such concession. In *Cours*, fetishism was the beginning of the beginning: the first phase of the first stage in the immutable development of human culture and was thus the seed from which civilization grew.

In describing fetishism, he focuses on psychological projection. When humans encounter inexplicable events, he argues, they "conceive of the production of unknown effects according to the passions and affections of the corresponding being regarded as alive; and this is the philosophical principle of fetichism" (*PP*, 547). In a state of "gross fetichism," humans imagined everything as "animated by passion and will" (*PP*, 546). The primitive perspective was dominated by this global fetishizing activity, which populated the material world with magical life in every tree, every animal, every storm, every rock, and every twig, as the primitive passively yielded "to his propensity to transfer to outward objects the sense of existence which served him for an explanation of his own phenomena, and therefore for an absolute explanation of all out of himself" (*PP*, 547). Thus the external world for Comte's primitive consisted entirely of fetishes, and this global fetishism made the chaos of daily experience meaningful.

Society under fetishism lacked any real cohesion because its members were necessarily isolated within their separate psychological experiences. Primitive individualism was the order of the day, accompanied by social disunity and an absence of moral or political leadership. In the state of pure fetishism, "gods were individual," making centralized authority neither possible nor desirable (*PP*, 549). The result was a leaderless state resembling anarchy. "The worship . . . when every act of a man's life had its religious aspect, was of a kind that required every man to be his own priest" (*PP*, 550). For the same reason, knowledge was in a similar condition. "The fetich gods had little power to unite men, or to govern them. Though there were certainly fetiches of the tribe, and even of the nation, the greater number were domestic, or even personal; and such deities could afford little assistance to the development of common ideas" (*PP*, 550).

In a world where "every object is a divinity with a will of its own," unifying abstractions about natural laws are not just unnecessary; they would contradict the view of each object as unique (*PP*, 551). Instead, "[i]maginary facts wholly overwhelm real ones," and the world becomes transformed by the primitive mind into "a kind of permanent hallucination" (*PP*, 551). This stunted condition of knowledge was accompanied by a flourishing of artistic activity. "It is evident that a philosophy which endowed the whole universe with life must favour the expansion of imagination, which was then supreme among the faculties. Thus, it is certain that the origin of all the fine arts, not excepting poetry, is to be referred to the fetich period" (*PP*, 551). Vico had arrived at a similar conclusion, and his logic also reemerged in Comte's juxtaposition of art and science as inversely related.

The three stages were each subdivided so that they contained smooth, logical steps through which one stage gradually blended into the next. Like Condorcet, Comte described development as the consequence of organic processes, rather than external forces. Gone were the cataclysms of the young earth that figured largely in the account of Vico. In their place, Comte substituted the psychological maturation of the primitive mind. The engine driving social change was a new capacity for abstract thinking. As primitives began to abstract, the multitude of separate fetishes began to merge into unified categories that conflicted with the unique status of each object:

> Thus, when the oaks of a forest, in their likeness to each other, suggested certain general phenomena, the abstract being in whom so many fetiches coalesced was no fetich, but the god of the forest . . . . Each god took the place of a troop of fetiches, which were thenceforth permitted, or reduced, to serve as his escort. (*PP*, 559–60)

This new tree god was no longer a fetish because it was no longer embodied in the tree. Like de Brosses, Comte insists that the supernatural quality of the fetish is "inseparable from the one object in which it resides" (*PP*, 559). A fetish must be a particular thing, meaningful in and of itself, but this concreteness disappears when the object is understood instead as merely one instance of a general class of objects. The type exists apart from the object, so the particular loses its meaning as a singularity. The tree ceases to be a fetish when it becomes a synecdoche for the god of the forest. Polytheism emerged out of this conflict between the concrete and the abstract. The emphasis is perhaps clearest in Lewes's explanation of *Cours*: "All the great successive modifications of the religious spirit have been determined at first by the development of the scientific spirit. The insensibly increasing generalization of the diverse observations upon Humanity must necessarily have led to analogies in corresponding theological conceptions, and thus determined the transformation of Fetichism into a simple Polytheism."[52] The birth of representation lay within this new development. In the new form of worship, the tree represented a god that resided elsewhere, apart from the object in which it was once immanent. Instead of worshipping the thing itself, polytheist worship was characterized by "the adoration of images," objects that represented an absent spirit (*PP*, 546).

This shift to more abstract gods and the concomitant emergence of representation produced further changes, like the necessity for an intellectual elite. Under pure fetishism: "the residence of each deity in a material object left nothing for a priesthood to do, and therefore gave no occasion for the rise of a distinct speculative class" (*PP*, 550). However, under polytheism, the gods were invisible "and distinct from the substances which they ruled," so a new intellectual class, a "real priesthood," emerged to mediate between the "worshipper and his deity" (*PP*, 550).

With the growing capacity for abstraction, polytheism became monotheism, and then the theological passed into the metaphysical. However, as society evolved it retained elements of each earlier stage, and thus fetishism never wholly disappeared. Like Charles Darwin's later "rudiments," or Edward Tylor's "survivals," fetishism persists within advanced civilization as the residue of the past. All ages have "very marked traces . . . of the original fetichism, however it may be involved in metaphysical forms in subtle understandings" (*PP*, 547). Comte illustrates his point by silently reworking the metaphor made famous in William Paley's defense of natural theology. If a person who had never before encountered a watch were to stumble across one and inspect it closely, Paley claims, "the inference, we think, is inevitable; that the watch must have had a maker; that there must have existed, at some time and at some place or other, an artificer or artificers who formed it for the purpose which we find it actually to answer; who comprehended its construction, and designed its use."[53] So, too, he thought, the primitive contemplating nature infers a maker. Comte turns Paley's figure on its head. When a man discovers his watch malfunctioning, he imagines that it has a capricious devil inside (*PP*, 547). Thus fetishism remains active in nineteenth-century life as an anti-scientific attitude that ambivalently coexists with the new scientific inclination.[54]

Comte was not finished with religious fetishism upon the completion of *Cours*. From his earliest writing, he demonstrated a nostalgic attitude towards fetishism as preferable to pure rationalism. "Impatient with pure theorizing, he praised primitive man's interest in the 'concrete,'" and emphasized utility, according to Pickering.[55] "Let us leave the beautiful," Pickering quotes Comte; "let us seek the good, let us return to nature, never to leave it again. May the faculty of abstraction be employed only to facilitate the combination of concrete ideas; in short, may it no longer be the abstract which dominates, but the positive" (108). In *Cours*, he tried to paint a sympathetic picture of fetishism as a fundamental part of human psychology. In an almost Romantic manner, he "admired the fetishist stage because it represented the period when religious beliefs were most intense . . . . During this time, people's emotions were also the strongest. Moreover, Comte respected fetishism for its overriding concern with concrete reality" (698). Like Vico, he believed that fetishism was the basis for artistic creation, and so it remained a necessary part of developed civilization. But *Cours* was "merely a preamble to the redemption and regeneration of humanity," and in *Système de politique positive* (1851–54) and *Catéchisme positiviste* (1852), written near the end of his life, he proposed a return to fetishism as an integral part of the positivist stage.[56] *Cours* focused on the processes of social and mental development, but positivism needed to address the moral aspect of human existence before political change was possible. Positivism could "draw the attention of all members of the community to a single concrete reality—that of humanity," and yet in order to fulfill human desires and inspire a broader sense of purpose, this reality had to be experienced morally; it had to be felt as well as understood.[57] Comte addressed this deficiency by returning to fetishism and broadening the role of the positivist to include that of quasi-spiritual guide, transforming the abstract concept of humanity into something concrete. Fetishism and the Religion of Humanity "rest on one and the same fundamental principle, a principle adopted by the instinct of the race and then by its reason; they agree, that is, in proclaiming the constant predominance of feeling over thought and action."[58] The positivist philosopher "was to become, not a king, but a priest, a member of . . . a spiritual power, a priesthood, serving not some theological fiction, but Humanity itself."[59] Comte thus laid out the principles for a Religion of Humanity, complete with its own churches, priesthood, and ceremonies to satisfy people's emotional needs, such as the "Great-Fetish" rituals he describes in *Système de politique positive*. Comte's priests (much like Coleridge's clerisy) would be an elite group guiding the less-informed masses in the moral development that Comte believed must precede social and political change. The return of fetishism would unify society through the common worship of humanity itself.[60]

When considered as a whole, Comte's theory of primitive fetishism has four decisive characteristics. Two of these reiterated ideas seen as early as Lucretius. Like the ancient atomist, Comte represents primitives as immersed in materiality; where every object is alive, the lived experience is of continuous interaction with a densely populated, vital, material world. *Cours* also emphasizes the boundless imaginative activity of the primitive, who endlessly projects his or her psychology outward, resulting in a dense material world populated by endless unacknowledged versions of himself or herself. In addition to these two familiar traits, Comte added two new qualities. One was the pronounced individualism of the primitive, who lived in a world of his or her own fantasy; where Lucretius saw independence in the early giants, Comte saw solipsism. The other was that primitives did not synthesize multiplicity by combining like with like. The profusion of the material world, its sheer density of objects, stemmed from this inability to think abstractly, since all objects were comprehended individually, rather than subordinated as similar representatives of larger essences. These four features constituted the basic terms of Victorian fetishism in action, and they appeared again and again in Victorian thinking about what it meant to be primitive, on the one hand, and on the other about what it meant to be the opposite of primitive, or, to be Victorian.

The reception of Comte's philosophy in Britain and France could hardly have been more different. The erratic publishing schedule for *Cours* cost him most of his audience in France, but that was not the only reason he was largely forgotten there by the time his signature work was complete.[61] The primary source of interest in the work initially was his new philosophy of social physics. It proposed a wholly original science that held out the promise of making sense of French life and culture at a time in its post-Revolutionary history when little seemed to make sense. If society could be studied scientifically through the neutral objectivity of detached investigators, then anything might happen. Such hopeful expectations were inevitably frustrated by Comte's decision to put social physics at the end of *Cours*. In this choice, he went against the advice of others, who were ultimately proven correct.[62] By the time volume 3 appeared, in 1839, few readers remained to slog through the last of his history of the natural sciences. The author would not get around to discussing his central topic, social dynamics, until May 1841, eleven years after volume 1, and by then it was too late.

His ideas met with a better fate in Britain.[63] A lengthy delay in first noticing *Cours* meant that his theories were presented in a fuller and more compressed form there than in France, and thus the later circulation in Britain proved distinctly advantageous. One of the first English intellectuals to embrace positive philosophy was John Stuart Mill.[64] A student of Comte, Gustave d'Eichthal, knew Mill and, in 1828, supplied him with a copy of Comte's fundamental opuscule.[65] This piece summarized all of the main principles of positivism, and, in a letter introducing himself to Comte thirteen years later, Mill describes its effect on him:

> It was in the year 1828, Sir, that I read for the first time your treatise of Politique Positive; and this reading gave to all my ideas a strong jolt, which along with other causes, but much more than they, brought about my definitive exit from the Benthamist section of the revolutionary school, in which I was brought up and I can almost even say in which I was born.[66]

He later minimized the influence of Comte on his early philosophical ideas, claiming, in the final revision to his *Autobiography*, that "the amount of these obligations is far less than has sometimes been asserted."[67] However, Pickering has shown that his attitude in an earlier draft of the *Autobiography* was more consistent with the enthusiasm he described in his letter to Comte; she also points out that his subsequent letters to d'Eichthal, which expressed his thoughts at the time, substantiate the idea that he was more influenced by Comte's theories than he was later willing to acknowledge.[68]

In 1837, Sir Charles Wheatstone brought the first two volumes of *Cours* to England, and Mill read them while writing *A System of Logic* (1843).[69] Journalist David Brewster also used Wheatstone's copies to write the first significant account for British readers of Comte's ideas: a thirty-seven-page review of *Cours* published in the *Edinburgh Review* in July 1838.[70] Mill read the later four volumes of *Cours* as they came out. In October 1842, when he finished the last volume, he wrote to Comte that he had anticipated a "sort of intellectual voluptuousness [*volupté*] in the idea of savoring this last volume."[71] Having read it, he "completely revised the last section of *A System of Logic*" to devote more space to positivism.[72] When first published in 1843, Mill's *Logic* had nearly one-hundred references to Comte, including long passages from *Cours,* and, for this reason, *Logic* became the basic introduction to positivism for most British intellectuals.[73] Mill later points out in his *Autobiography,* "In consequence chiefly of what I had said of him in my Logic, he had readers and admirers among thoughtful men on this side of the Channel at a time when his name had not yet in France emerged from obscurity."[74] Certainly, after the publication of Mill's *Logic,* "intellectual Englishmen no longer had any excuse for not knowing the philosophy of Auguste Comte."[75]

Other writers who disseminated Comte's ideas in the early years were William Molesworth, the Benthamite founder of the *London Review,* and a youthful Lewes, who corresponded with Comte, visited him in Paris, and first came to public notice as a popularizer of Comte's ideas. His *Biographical History of Philosophy* (1845–46) is structured as an example of Comte's three stages, culminating in an account of *Cours.* Written as an accessible primer to philosophy and published in "Knights's Weekly Volume Series," its inexpensive one-shilling installments reached an audience well beyond the English and Scottish intellectual circles that knew Mill's *Logic.* Lewes prided himself on this fact and wrote to Comte, "My book is read at Oxford and Cambridge as well as by artisans and even women."[76] By 1857, when a revised edition appeared, it had already sold forty-thousand copies.[77] In 1852 Lewes also published a series of articles on Comte in *The Leader;* in revised form a year later, these became his comprehensive explanation of positivism, *Comte's Philosophy of the Sciences: An Exposition of the Principles of the "Cours de Philosophie Positive."* More than just an explanation, it also updated Comte's history of sciences, which stopped at 1838, to bring in "the very latest facts and ideas of 1853."[78]

By the early 1850s, there was a growing circle of people who were familiar with Comte's ideas; how large, exactly, is unknown. Cashdollar notes that Comte had no absolute disciples then, but his ideas were widely used, often without acknowledgement. In many situations, it was politic to conceal Comte as the source of an idea. Because of his atheism, *Cours* was anathema in clerical settings, as candidates for academic posts sometimes learned the hard way.[79] In England, interest at Oxford was greater than at Cambridge, though still not especially large. Interest in London centered on the group of intellectuals that orbited John Chapman's *Westminster Review.* Scottish interest was not as restricted, a point that explains why so many of the articles on positivism at the time appeared in Scottish journals. "By the early 1850s throughout Britain, but especially in Scotland, a fair foundation had been laid."[80] Nonetheless the daunting task of working through six volumes of awkward French necessarily limited the potential audience.

In 1853 that situation changed with the publication of Harriet Martineau's *Positive Philosophy of Auguste Comte*. Martineau came late to positivism, relatively speaking. She first read *Cours* in April 1851. Almost immediately she began planning a translation that condensed the six volumes into two. Chapman agreed to publish it; more than that, he also sought out a wealthy benefactor, who underwrote the project with £500, enough to keep the final cost low for buyers. Martineau began translating in June 1852, finishing sixteen months later, and by November 1853 the volumes were in print. In the preface to her "freely translated and condensed" version, she explains that "M. Comte's work, in its original form, does no justice to its importance, even in France; and much less in England."[81] In addition to his repetitiveness, "M. Comte's style is singular. . . . Every sentence is full fraught with meaning; yet it is overloaded with words" (4). Regardless of their opinion of positivism, reviewers agreed that Martineau had done her job well.[82]

The Martineau and Lewes volumes contributed to the increasing interest in positivism that continued through the 1860s.[83] There were other factors as well. One was the stir caused by the publication of *Système de politique positive* (1851–54) and *Catèchism positiviste* (1852).[84] Another was Comte's death in 1857, which led to a further volubility in discussions of positivism, and it was soon followed by Richard Congreve's translation of the *Catechism of Positive Religion*. In 1859, when Congreve became a neighbor of George Eliot and Lewes, he founded his positivist church in London, whose members included John Henry Bridges, Edward Spencer Beesly, and Congreve's former student at Wadham College, Frederic Harrison. By 1860 the center of gravity for interest in positivism had shifted from Scotland to England.[85]

While his earlier theory of social science remained a respected one, Comte's later works clearly lessened the enthusiasm of many in Britain for the philosopher himself, revealing him to have feet of clay. Mill was particularly appalled by Comte's anti-democratic political philosophy. In 1859, he asserted that Comte's political philosophy "aims at establishing (though by moral more than by legal appliances) a despotism of society over the individual surpassing anything contemplated in the political ideal of the most rigid disciplinarian among the ancient philosophers."[86] Lewes redefined his own relation to Comtism, calling himself "a reverent heretic" and explaining, "I profoundly admire the greatness and sincerity of the thinker, although he seems to have attempted a task for which the materials were not ready."[87] Comte thus fell from his lofty perch as the demigod philosopher, the High Priest of the Religion of Humanity, but by then the historical narrative of *Cours* had already been thoroughly absorbed by British intellectuals.

—*∿*—

Use of the term *fetishism* for universal, primitive object worship became commonplace after *Cours,* but Comte's choice of the term seemed novel at the time. Pickering points out that *fetishism* "does not seem to have been used very often in the late eighteenth and early nineteenth centuries," and it was "almost never used" when *Cours* was first being written.[88] His most likely source was Benjamin Constant's *De la religion considérée dans sa source, ses formes, et ses développements* (1824–25). He was reading this work in 1825, during the same month in which he wrote the fourth opuscule, "Considérations philosophiques sur les sciences et les savants." There he first describes fetishism as prior to polytheism and as the initial state of religion.[89] Constant, who probably picked up the term from de Brosses, uses it to refer to "the 'material divinities' worshipped by primitive people during the infancy of humanity. In adoring concrete objects and animals, primitive man believed that he could persuade the power animating them to act for him."[90] Constant also described three stages in the development of religion that probably influenced Comte: fetishism, polytheism, and theism.

Evidence suggests a similar scarcity of usage in Britain prior to Comte's work. As a term for a specifically African religious practice, *fetishism* was still used in ethnography and travel literature, as it had been since the Renaissance. Thomas M. Winterbottom, a physician in West Africa, thus writes of "the greegree, or fetish, hung round their neck" in *An Account of the Native Africans in the Neighbourhood of Sierra Leone* (1803).[91] The term was also used to reference the religious practices of diasporic Africans, such as in narratives describing slavery in the New World. In "The Grateful Negro" (1802), Maria Edgeworth describes life among the slaves on a Jamaican plantation, where the old religion reemerges: "I have administered to Hector and his companions the solemn fetish oath, at the sound of which every negro in Africa trembles!"[92]

The meaning of *fetish* expanded by 1810, when Coleridge used it as a simile for European behavior: "As well might the poor African prepare for himself a fetisch by plucking out the eyes of the eagle."[93] Similarly, he critiques natural history by likening it to African fetish worship: "From the fetisch of the imbruted African to the soul-debasing errors of the proud fact-hunting materialist we may trace the various ceremonials of the same idolatry" (518). Coleridge, like Thomas Carlyle, was steeped in German literature and philosophy, and it may be there that he encountered the term.[94]

By the 1830s, if not earlier, the term was familiar enough to be used without glossing it as an African practice. Writing in 1837, Ralph Waldo Emerson uses it as a figure of speech for anything irrationally revered: "Some great decorum, some fetish of a government, some ephemeral trade, or war, or man, is cried up by half mankind and cried down by the other half, as if all depended on this particular up or down."[95] On the other hand, Carlyle retained the African connection but used it figuratively, as an ancient form of the sublime that was implicit in the power and terror of any uncompromised faith. In discussing the power of the writer in *Sartor Resartus*, published 1831, he applies the term to writing itself: "In Pagan countries, cannot one write Fetishes? Living! Little knowest thou what alchemy is in an inventive Soul; how, as with its little finger, it can create provision enough for the body (of a Philosopher); and then, as with both hands, create quite other than provision; namely, spectres to torment itself withal."[96] Unlike the other writers considered here, Carlyle embraced fetishism as a real, rather than false, form of worship. His faith in the power of fetishism reappeared a decade later, in *On Heroes, Hero-Worship, and the Heroic in History*. In this instance, the African fetishist serves as a desirable model of unbounded faith:

> The poorest mortal worshipping his Fetish, while his heart is full of it, may be an object of pity, of contempt and avoidance, if you will; but cannot surely be an object of hatred. Let his heart be honestly full of it, the whole space of his dark narrow mind illuminated thereby; in one word, let him entirely believe in his Fetish,—it will then be, I should say, if not well with him, yet as well as it can readily be made to be, and you will leave him alone, unmolested there.[97]

Fetishism here is a metaphor for an older authenticity, figured as a connection with the real that is absent in the sham of modern life. Carlyle also employed the idea of fetishism to suggest the related idea of a universal, primitive past, one that industrial Britain has lost touch with, to its infinite detriment. He complains that, in modern religious faith, "[s]ouls are no longer *filled* with their Fetish; but only pretend to be filled, and would fain make themselves feel that they are filled. 'You do not believe,' says Coleridge; 'you only believe that you believe'" (141). In this passage, he drops the figurative reference to an alien African fetishism, much as Emerson had, and substitutes a primitive fetishism that is an integral part of English ancestry as an inheritance from the universal past.[98]

The Coleridge and Carlyle references remain the most frequently cited examples of the use of the word in English during the early century, but usage at this time was far less common than after the half-century mark.[99] As an illustration, we can compare two major nonfiction prose writers: Carlyle, who uses the term twice in *Sartor Resartus* and three times in *Heroes and Hero-Worship*, with Matthew Arnold. The term appears seventeen times in *Culture and Anarchy*, written in the late 1850s and published 1860.[100] In this escalation, Arnold was going with the historical tide. A review of titles from periodical literature during the nineteenth century demonstrates the shift. Between 1802 and 1907, forty-eight articles had some variation of the term *fetish* in the title, according to *Poole's*, but none predated 1864.[101] For *Wellesley*, the earliest was 1878.[102] In a search of all words in nine-hundred periodicals published in English from 1790–1919, the first identified usage was 1852.[103] A sprinkling of earlier articles by missionaries in religious periodicals and travelers in popular science journals can also be identified, from the 1830s and 1840s, as would be expected.[104] A similar search of the text in 250 works of prose fiction by 102 authors from the period 1782 to 1903 produces a list of seventeen works, all from 1849 or later.[105] For nondramatic verse written in English between 1800–1899, twenty-nine poems had some version of the term in the text. Of these, twenty-seven were later than 1870 while the remaining two were from the 1820s.[106]

Ultimately Pickering's general claims about French usage apply to English as well; while references are relatively rare before *Cours*, the term *fetish* is commonplace after it. Thus, even though it had been in use since the Renaissance, it only became popular enough to enter the general lexicon at the middle of the nineteenth century. It is impossible to say with certainty what role Comte's *Cours* might have played in this linguistic shift, but it is equally impossible to imagine that it did not contribute directly to the new Victorian interest in primitive fetishism.

2

Matthew Arnold's Culture

Arnold was a vocal critic of positivism, but he also relied on certain of Comte's ideas. The theory of the primitive fetish is particularly significant in this regard because it formed the assumed ground for his social criticism of Victorian life. On the far side of his familiar call for objectivism lies a world of fetishism. His phrase, "to see the object as in itself it really is," responds to a vision of the social body as particularly in need of objectivity. And because it lacks this quality, Arnold's Victorian society is one that sees the object as in itself it really is not.[1] This mode of perception is the other side of Arnold's writing: a world of biased, idiosyncratic, illusory, introverted, personal, unobjective views, where fictions are taken for fact and facts for fiction. Among the many possible types of unobjective perceptions, fetishism is the preeminent bugbear in Arnold's writing.

Illustrative is the stanza in his dramatic poem, "Empedocles on Etna," when the Greek philosopher describes what happens when a child is injured, and then compares it to the normal condition of social life:

> Scratched by a fall, with moans
> As children of weak age
> Lend life to the dumb stones
> Whereon to vent their rage,
> And bend their little fists, and rate the senseless ground.[2]

Attributing "life" to a stone or to the ground is a case of seeing the object as a fetish. It involves an imaginative attribution of power to the object, and this active investing then goes unrecognized by the child. Instead, the child believes that the object's power exists independently, in the external world. The passage continues by expanding the simile of the child's reaction into an account of how society as a whole reacts to the unknown:

So, loth to suffer mute,
We, peopling the void air,
Make Gods to whom to impute
The ills we ought to bear;
With God and Fate to rail at, suffering easily. (1.2.277–81)

Lucretius had described exactly the same pattern in *De Rerum Natura*, a poem Arnold knew well. He read Epicurus and the Atomist philosophers closely in 1845, as preparation for a long-projected tragedy on Lucretius, in whose writing he discerned what he called a "modern feeling."[3] As his concept for the incomplete "Lucretius" grew, it became "Empedocles on Etna: A Dramatic Poem," in which Lucretius and Empedocles are the two classical sources for his ideas.[4] The importance of Epicureanism to the classicist Arnold is well known; it impacted his writing throughout the late 1840s.[5] It is only with difficulty that we can identify the difference between Epicurean materialism and Arnoldian humanism in this passage from "Empedocles"; Lucretius had argued that the invention of gods increased human suffering, while Arnold's speaker views it as false comfort.

Arnold's writing against the arbitrariness of evaluation in England's social, religious, and literary thought regularly adopted anti-fetishistic rhetoric, and this mode of critique led to an Arnoldian vision of England as a society defined by an essential fetishism. He imagined false gods being worshipped everywhere in Victorian England and claimed that England's fetishism set it apart from all other nations. Representations of England as a society of the fetish show up throughout his critical essays, but *Culture and Anarchy* provides his most comprehensive treatment of the topic. It also provides a problematic solution to it, for in proposing his version of a detached and theoretical culture, he enters into a new form of fetishism and one that is classically Victorian in its own cultural values. I argue that Arnold's *Culture and Anarchy* reproduces the fetishistic practice it critiques, so that his attempt to reform the society of the fetish paradoxically reintroduces fetishism at a higher level of abstraction.

This paradox needs to be considered in relation to Arnold's thought, but it has other implications as well. Because Arnold holds the nominal position as the initiator of the discipline of literary criticism, the paradoxical quality in his thought helps to explain the radically different ways he is regarded within the discipline.

—⁓—

Arnold long identified Victorian England as culturally crippled by its isolation from the rest of Europe, and he attributed its lack of objectivity to that insularity. He preached against the dangers of English provincialism both before and after writing *Culture and Anarchy,* and this attitude persisted throughout his life.[6] His first sustained engagement with the topic appears in *On Translating Homer*, the four 1860–61 lectures that mark the beginning of Arnold's practical criticism.[7] In the second lecture of the series, he reaches a climax in critiquing his main target, Francis W. Newman's Victorian translation of the *Iliad*, for its over-intellectualized artifice.[8] Expanding on the subject, he views the translator's shortcomings as quintessentially English. "The eccentricity too, the arbitrariness, of which Mr. Newman's conception of Homer offers so signal an example, are not a peculiar failing of Mr. Newman's own; in varying degrees they are the great defect of English intellect, the great blemish of English literature" (*CP*, 1:140). Arnold maintains that England's provincialism has led to its "eccentric and arbitrary spirit," leaving it in a state of cultural deficiency. English intellectual work ranks only third in Europe, behind the works of France and Germany, where intellectual production exhibits "the endeavour, in all branches of knowledge—theology, philosophy, history, art, science,—to see the object as in itself it really is" (*CP*, 1:140).

In the fourth and final lecture, "Last Words," Arnold expands on the nature of England's intellectual defect. The English intellectual is blind to the "flagrant misdirection" of thought, and this tendency toward error is perversely encouraged by the intellectual atmosphere: "I think, even, that in our country a powerful misdirection of this kind is often more likely to subjugate and pervert opinion than to be checked and corrected by it. Hence a chaos of false tendencies, wasted efforts, impotent conclusions, works which ought never to have been undertaken" (*CP*, 1:140). Newman's translation thus becomes an illustration of the more general problem of the English intellect; Arnold's larger critique aims at the national condition which Newman represents: "False tendency is, I have said, an evil to which the artist or the man of letters in England is peculiarly prone" (*CP*, 1:140).

Three years later, he returns to the topic of England's cultural deficiency, in "The Literary Influence of Academies."[9] Again comparing the literature of France with England, his own country becomes "the native home of intellectual eccentricity of all kinds," and he traces this flaw to its lack of a corrective center for cultural authority (*CP*, 3:243). "Educated opinion exists here as in France; but in France the Academy serves as a sort of centre and rallying-point to it, and gives it a force which it has not got here," resulting in a lack of sophistication (*CP*, 3:241). "There is observable a *note of provinciality*" in English literature, a note that sounds as a distorted or eccentric judgment.[10] In a line of argument influenced by the earlier writings of John H. Newman, Arnold explains that this distortion is caused by valuing objects in isolation, rather than in a comprehensive, relational manner.[11]

> The provincial spirit, again, exaggerates the value of its ideas for want of
> a high standard at hand by which to try them. Or rather, for want of

such a standard, it gives one idea too much prominence at the expense of others; it orders its ideas amiss; it is hurried away by fancies; it likes and dislikes too passionately, too exclusively. Its admiration weeps hysterical tears, and its disapprobation foams at the mouth. (*CP*, 3:249)

In its more extreme forms, this overvaluation can even lead to a qualitative transformation in the relationship between the evaluator and the evaluated object. John H. Newman puts it this way: "Men, whose minds are possessed with some one object, take exaggerated views of its importance [and] are feverish in the pursuit of it."[12] Arnold is more dramatic, making the fever into a bizarre auto-possession: "it is a note of the provincial spirit not to hold ideas of [merit] a little more easily, to be so devoured by them, to suffer them to become crotchets" (*CP*, 3:250). For Arnold, provincialism initiates a dialectic through which the cultural object takes on a life of its own and, as if autonomous, turns and consumes its producer. Like Empedocles's complaint about his society, England's provincial spirit leads to "peopling the void air" through magical acts of unaware self-projection.

In *Culture and Anarchy*, Arnold produces his most comprehensive analysis of this national eccentricity, and he describes it as taking two contradictory forms. Arnold's England is famously dominated by convention, the "blind following of certain stock notions as infallible" (*CP*, 5:219). Thus the first requirement for addressing England's need for social reform is a necessary paradigm-shift in cultural values, away from "Hebraic" conventionality and toward "Hellenic" innovation.[13] Such a movement, Arnold insists, is already underway in Victorian England: "is not the close and bounded intellectual horizon within which we have long lived and moved now lifting up . . . ?" he asks. (*CP*, 5:92). This openness provides a fertile ground for innovation "to flourish in," and it gives Arnold hope: "we are sure that the detaching ourselves from our stock notions and habits . . . is the master-impulse even now of the life of our nation and of humanity,— somewhat obscurely perhaps for this actual moment, but decisively and certainly for the immediate future" (*CP*, 5:92, 5:229). With this new impulse comes a new problem, according to Arnold. The primary danger used to be the tyranny of convention, but that is no longer the case: the "danger now is, not that people should obstinately refuse to allow anything but their old routine to pass for reason and the will of God, but . . . that they should allow some novelty or other to pass for these too easily . . ." (*CP*, 5:92). With the decline of an enforced system of values, a new threat comes from the appealing novelty of ideas and the desire to enact them. In the age of intellectual freedom, innovation takes on a seductiveness of its own. "A current in people's minds sets towards new ideas," and the danger of this "new current" is typified by the popularity of the novel social "systems" Arnold abhors, Comte's positivism in particular (*CP*, 5:109–10). Thus Victorian England simultaneously faces two contradictory dangers: a reliance on convention and a fascination with innovation.[14]

There are two different ways to resolve this contradiction in Arnold's account of England's provincial essence. Viewed diachronically, or in its historical dimension, Arnold's argument assumed that England was still dominantly Hebraic, but that currents of Hellenism were beginning to shift the historical teeter-totter.[15] However, when viewed synchronically, or as a conflict within a snapshot of the present age, both convention and innovation—stock notion and novelty—instead represented variations of the same underlying impulse. While conventionalists enforced "a rigid invincible exclusion of whatever is new . . . simply because [it is] new," at the other extreme, "the lovers of new ideas" were attracted by the same novelty and saw it as a mark of value (*CP*, 5:93, 5:227). Both responded to subsidiary traits (in Arnold's terms) of the cultural object, its conventionality or novelty, rather than the primary trait, its ideational content. In this sense, both examples represented the same problem: an identical seduction of form.

Arnold explores the problem of form and false value at length, using instead the word *machinery*, and whether old ideas or new, the problem is the same: "Faith in machinery is, I said, our besetting danger; often in machinery most absurdly disproportioned to the end which this machinery, if it is to do any good at all, is to serve; but always in machinery, as if it had a value in and for itself" (*CP*, 5:96). Industrial output, democracy, individual freedom—"England is accustomed to speak of these things as if they were precious ends in themselves," but to Arnold these are rather means to an end, and related as form to content.[16] Arnold repeatedly distinguishes between the culturally valueless object and the false value that the English project onto it. The middle class believes "that the increase of houses and manufactories, or the increase of population, are absolute goods in themselves, to be mechanically pursued," but Arnold emphasizes that these "are not, like perfection, absolute goods in themselves, though we think them so" (*CP*, 5:215, 216). Because the problem of machinery is present within both Hebraism and Hellenism, it exists outside Arnold's historical narrative.[17] While the West will always be in a state of transition between one or the other of these two phases of human existence, there will always be a need to differentiate between the presence and absence of value, regardless of the historical moment. Thus there is a trans-historical need to counter the pervasive frequency with which absence is taken for presence. "The mass of mankind," Arnold borrows from Aristotle, "follow seeming goods for real" (*CP*, 5:225). Arnold's text explores the transformational process through which this happens and explains why Victorians consistently confuse nothing with something.

In clarifying what he means by this transforming process, Arnold explains: when "mechanically pursued by us as ends precious in themselves," such artifacts "are worshipped as what we call fetishes" (*CP*, 5:210). He describes, for example, the "fetish of the production of wealth and of the increase of manufactures and population" (*CP*, 5:218). The "fetish . . . of the Nonconformists," he tells us, "provokes the counter-employment of other fetishes or mechanical maxims on the opposite side" leading to "the apparition of such fetishes as are beginning to be set up on the Conservative side against the fetish of the Nonconformists" (*CP*, 5:195). Arnold applies the label of fetishism to describe what happens whenever a politician, journalist, academic, clergyman, or social reformer—in short, any middle-class commentator—attributes excessive value to cultural objects, whether social reform schemes or established conventions. And since that happens often, he uses the term "fetish" often. He defines it precisely, too: rather than a synonym for *machinery, fetish* refers to the result of the overvaluation which transforms machinery into an object of worship.[18] The fetish is the afterlife of convention or innovation when it ceases to be a means to an end and becomes a living god, suddenly meaningful as if it had a value in and for itself. Thus the call for objectivity in Arnold's writing is a response to a particular problem. When Arnold asserts that England is "peculiarly prone" to "false tendency," and when he calls it "the native home of intellectual eccentricity," he is identifying Victorian England as the center for fetishism in the West. His was the society of the fetish, and it is this process of deification that Arnold's critical method was designed to combat.

—*~~*—

Arnold derided positivism more than once. Probably his most well-known remark is the warning against "abstract systems of renovation applied wholesale, a new doctrine drawn up in black and white for elaborating down to the very smallest details a rational society for the future," as proposed by "Mr. Frederic Harrison and other disciples of Comte" (*CP*, 5:109). He then prescribes open-mindedness as the antidote: "Culture tends always thus to deal with the men of a system, of disciplines, of a school; with men like Comte, or the late Mr. Buckle, or Mr. Mill" (*CP*, 5:111). Mill was Comte's leading early proponent; the historian Henry Thomas Buckle had a "system" of his own but was generally seen as a sympathizer with positivism.[19] While Comte is only directly mentioned three times in *Culture and Anarchy,* the English positivist Frederic Harrison is mentioned there more often than any other individual—twenty times in all—and he holds the same position in *Friendship's Garland,* which was written in tandem with it.[20] This quantity of references has attracted notice by modern critics, but it was actually toned down from what appeared in earlier drafts; the longest passage omitted from *Culture and Anarchy* is a lengthy response to Harrison that Arnold included in "Anarchy and Authority," a sequence of five essays he wrote in 1868 and revised as part of *Culture and Anarchy*.[21]

With such pronounced protests, Arnold's own theory should be easier to differentiate from positivism than it is. Broad similarities between Comte's philosophy and Arnold's theory of culture were first noted by Harrison in 1867.[22] His "Culture: A Dialogue" responded to early installments in the series of the essays that became *Culture and Anarchy* by having the imaginary philosopher Arminius expose parallels between Arnold's thought and Comte's: "there seems very much in which the higher Culture may be said to coincide with this philosopher."[23] Harrison repeated the sentiment years later, after Arnold's death, when he noted Arnold was "constantly talking Comte without knowing it."[24]

In describing the condition of unculture, *Culture and Anarchy* certainly did reproduce Comte's *Cours*. Some of the resemblance may be owing to the overlap in each writer's influence by the vision of primitive life in *De Rerum Natura*, as discussed in the previous chapter. But others clearly have more in common with Comte's two innovations. The defining problem in Arnold's treatise is individualism, or "doing as one likes," and like Comte's primitives this behavior stems from each person worshipping their own gods. In Arnold's discourse, these become the many forms of "machinery" he cites, such as the insistence on the amount of coal produced as the measure of national greatness, or the blind faith in democracy, or the Malthusian attribution of all social ills to overpopulation. These household gods are ideas, rather than discrete material objects, but in the language of primitive fetishism the two categories were indivisible because the primitive's incapacity for abstraction made it impossible to differentiate between ideas about objects and objects themselves. Ideas, in short, are quickly reified—transformed into an illusion of concrete existence—and so take on the immediacy of things, as Marx described in defining commodity fetishism.[25] Arnold highlights this illusion by referring to these abstract concepts with the metaphor of machinery, an image that reinforces the sense that he is discussing tangible things rather than concepts.

The evolution of primitive culture beyond fetishism was connected by Comte with the rise of a priestly class that could mediate between the primitive worshipper and the new abstract gods, as we have seen. In Arnold's writing, this speculative class reappears as the idealized man of culture, more oriented toward Hellenic abstractions than Hebraic practice and more able to comprehend the complexities of social problems. In the end, the principle difference between the two writers on the topic of fetishism was that when Arnold transposed Comte's fetishistic stage onto the stage of Victorian life, he was no longer describing a residual trait but rather the essential Victorian condition.

※

While he was not the first to metaphorically connect ethnological fetishism with modern civilization, Arnold gave the new primitivism an unusual prominence. It became more emphatic in *Culture and Anarchy* than in either Carlyle or Coleridge, but Arnold of course had the advantage of following, rather than preceding Comte; in 1869 the primitive fetish had a greater cultural currency than in the first half of the century. The centrality of the metaphor can be seen by considering his treatment of the most recognizably Victorian aspect of national life, the economic system and its effect on the perceptions of his contemporaries.

According to Arnold, the prototypical Victorian fetish was the worship of free trade. At the time, laissez faire was still one of the "unshakeable pillars of the mid-Victorian state,"[26] so he was clearly swimming against the current of the 1860s. But that current was shifting: by the 1880s, complaints about the "fetish of free trade" were widespread.[27]

Arnold first explains that he is not opposed to free trade per se; he readily accepts the principle of eliminating taxes and tariffs that "interfere with the natural flow of trade and commerce" (*CP*, 5:210). This policy "seems clearly right," and in this regard he is more accepting of the free-trade principle than many in the next generation would be (*CP*, 5:210). But he clearly distinguishes between free trade as a mechanism and free trade as a transforming magic that makes nothing into something. He objects to the fetishistic added value that is ascribed to both the machinery of free trade and the Victorian policy of laissez faire, as if each had value in and of itself. While acceptable as a mechanism, in "the policy of our Liberal friends free-trade means more than this, and is specially valued as a stimulant to the production of wealth, as they call it, and to the increase of the trade, business, and population of the country" (*CP*, 5:210). The Liberals see free trade "as an instrument of national happiness and salvation," and in it "think they have found the secret of national prosperity" (*CP*, 5:210, 5:216). According to Arnold, this fetishization has led to a social hallucination similar to that described by Comte, in which imaginary facts substitute for real ones: pointing to the poverty in London's East End, Arnold argues that, far from increasing national happiness and prosperity, the opposite is the case. Free trade has created "those vast, miserable, unmanageable masses of sunken people," and the only answer the "appointed doctors of free-trade" provide is to gloss over poverty as an inevitable side effect of laissez-faire economics (*CP*, 5:216, 5:211). He concludes that the Liberals, "mechanically worshipping their fetish of the production of wealth and of the increase of manufactures and population," are incapable of objectivity because they have confused the means of free trade with the end of a better general quality of life (*CP*, 5:218).

Arnold traces the fetishization of free trade beyond the economic sphere, of course, and follows it into the arena of ethics as well. In terms of social actions, laissez-faire values lead to the "prevalent notion . . . that it is a most happy and important thing for a man merely to be able to do as he likes," and this has resulted in an English right to free behavior every bit as unregulated as free trade (*CP*, 5:117). While taking many forms, the variants of ethical laissez faire are interchangeable manifestations of the same paradigm, in which one comes to see "free play in bodily exercises, or business, or popular agitation," or anything else, as "all-sufficient" (*CP*, 5:187). Ultimately, he poses the big question: "What is freedom but machinery?" (*CP*, 5:96). This question has led at least one Arnold scholar, rightly, to the conclusion that "his best treatment of a stock notion is his discussion of Freedom."[28] The fetishization of freedom becomes Arnold's ultimate example of the dangers that follow from confusing means with ends. "Freedom, I said, was one of those things which we thus worshipped in itself, without enough regarding the ends for which freedom is to be desired. In our common notions and talk about freedom, we eminently show our idolatry of machinery" (*CP*, 5:117). Whether analyzing ethics through his critique of individualism, or political economy in his comments on free trade, the adoration of freedom remains Arnold's central illustration of how Victorians worship the object as it is not.

Given the clarity with which he critiques the fetish of freedom as the central problem in Victorian life, his position on the relationship between freedom and culture is striking in its contrast. Freedom is the center of Arnold's theory of culture. A "more free play of consciousness" is the basis of culture (*CP*, 5:229). This is a slight variation on his earlier phrase, "a current of fresh and true ideas," from "The Function of Criticism"; another version appears in the later *St. Paul and Protestantism*, when Arnold praises "the natural, spontaneous, free character of true development" in religion (*CP*, 3:282, 6:89). This same free play is of course also implicit in his call for Hellenic "spontaneity of consciousness" (*CP*, 5:175). In one of the most widely repeated phrases in *Culture and Anarchy*, Arnold recommends "turning a stream of fresh and free thought upon our stock notions and habits" as the answer to anarchy (*CP*, 5:233). Thus he contrasts the desirability of intellectual free play with its apparent opposite, the absence of free play in the adherence to convention in societies like his own.[29]

In fact, however, the contrast is less clear-cut. While intellectual free play is situated as antithetical to "stock notions, " the most prominent among these is the stock notion of freedom as valuable "in itself" (*CP*, 5:117). Arnold's formula thus rhetorically masks its most problematic aspect, but it can be clearly seen when his statement is understood to recommend "turning a stream of fresh and free thought upon" the notion of freedom, a recommendation that calls into question its own premise. Thus when Arnold writes that ideas in this free play "try the very ground on which we appear to stand," this can theoretically hold true for all grounds except the ground on which the proposition itself stands, the ground of intellectual free play (*CP*, 5:181). Arnold's biographer has expressed this same concept, although in the form of an endorsement rather than a critique: "Culture, then, is a psychological attitude which implies a refusal to be locked in, finally enrolled, or seduced by any idea except the idea of mental freedom."[30] Intellectual free play is thus the one necessary exception to Arnold's critique of freedom as machinery. And because of this exception, Arnold's theory of culture rests on an apparent paradox: the fetishization of freedom in one arena is to be remedied by freedom in another.[31]

That Arnold was a Philistine, of course, he readily admitted. And by now it is axiomatic that he "was in no sense an outsider: he belonged, by upbringing and style of life, to the most comfortable stratum of the Victorian professional class."[32] He was a product of the same middle-class values that he also critiqued, as Williams notes.[33] Recognizing the conflict within this self-reflexive position helps in understanding the problematic treatment of freedom within Arnold's theory of culture, for it draws attention to the historical position that intellectual exchange played within the logic of free trade. The historian J. G. A. Pocock has shown that the valorization of intellectual freedom was a key element in the early rhetoric of free trade.[34] The commercial branch of the emerging middle class in the eighteenth century included the bankers, shippers, and speculators; the eventual dominance of laissez-faire economic practices was a triumph for this same branch. Unlike the manufacturers of the productive branch, who used the rhetoric of self-reliance to defend their interests, the commercial branch developed a defense of commerce that transformed free trade, and the mutual dependencies it created, into the foundation of all social virtue. Trade brought isolated populations into better communication. Commerce between nations allowed them to learn about other cultures and about the broader world as a whole. Exchanges of goods encouraged diplomatic relationships and discouraged war. The widest exchange of books and information expanded scientific and historical knowledge, and it was crucial to the exchange of ideas between societies. In the rhetoric of the commercial branch, free trade was the engine behind a progressive history, in which civilization improved humans from their primitive origins. Commercial ideology thus promoted the view that free trade produced social value.

It is undoubtedly true that Arnold's economic criticism was anachronistic, as others have pointed out; it responded less to "the novelty of industrialism" in his own day than "to the older and broader conception of 'commercial society.'"[35]

And it is equally true that Arnold's emphasis on the dangers of provincial isolation, on the improving aspects of the free exchange of ideas, on the importance of the broad circulation of literature between nations, on the accumulative process of knowledge—all recapitulated the commercial defense of free trade. Thus, by looking at the place of learning and intellectual development within the rhetoric of that older conception, we can understand generally how Arnold's attitude toward freedom could take such a paradoxical form.

In a more specific way, the paradox becomes practically unavoidable when we look at Arnold's interest in establishing the grounds for a new profession of criticism and a new, professional breed of critic. This same commercial ideology was a necessary historical component in the nineteenth-century rise of the professions. Privileging the idea of a specialized knowledge base was a key element in establishing legalized rights to perform specific services and to exclude others from performing them, as Waddington shows.[36] Arnold was concerned with establishing a professional base for literary criticism, and he needed to rely on the same premise of free trade in the realm of ideas. He articulates this view throughout the *Essays in Criticism*, where he first comprehensively asserts the basic value of literary criticism that continues to be used as a self-justification by professional critics today. In his essay on the Academy, for example, values are comparative; the "best" is not an ultimate accomplishment, fixed for all time, but is the "best" within a given pool. Expanding the pool from small to large or provincial to European, raises the standard by expanding the competition and allowing a stronger comparative basis for evaluating literary productions. The professional critic's role is essentially to master this larger, nonprovincial knowledge base and promote the circulation of the best to the provincials. As Bell notes, in the 1890s Arnold's rhetoric of disinterestedness and learning "was constantly being invoked . . . because it conveniently served to legitimize the function of the reviewing establishment."[37] Despite its lack of an identifiable professional association, criticism as a profession created an economic incentive for its practitioners that had not existed before. "Whereas the 'high brow' had at mid-century been the domain of the independently wealthy man of letters, by the 1890s it had become the posture of the professional 'bookman,' the new arbiter of literary taste who now lived by the journalistic pen" (158).

Arnold's cultural theory owed a profound debt to commercial ideology, and one that ultimately extended into the heart of his theory: its logic as a system of cultural evaluation. This is most evident in the way he recapitulated the logic of the free market within his assumptions about the role of "spontaneity of consciousness" in cultural evaluation.[38] Arnold situates intellectual free play as the arena in which all critical evaluation takes place; he then assumes that objective cultural value will spontaneously align with cultural objects in the arena. This assumption was not original to Arnold, though he may be the first writer to apply it to the theory of cultural value. In its more well-known form, the logic of spontaneous evaluation within an arena of free play appears in economic theory as the basic justification for the unregulated market.

In *The Wealth of Nations* (1776), Adam Smith argues famously that free competition insures that the appropriate value attaches to a specific commodity through the self-regulating mechanism of the market.[39] Left to its own devices, the free play of the market regulates value through the balancing forces of self-interest and competition. Government efforts to regulate and control trade only hinder the appearance of appropriate economic value, which would otherwise emerge spontaneously in the free market. This argument was succinctly made in Smith's well-known discussion of the relationship between two different forms of value, the natural and the market price of a commodity. While the *natural price* is "what it really costs the person who brings it to market," the price at which it is sold is the *market price,* and what concerns Smith throughout *The Wealth of Nations* is explaining the forces that cause a disparity between these two values.[40] Indeed, he insists, the two naturally tend to equivalence:

> The natural price, therefore, is, as it were, the central price, to which the prices of all commodities are continually gravitating. Different accidents may sometimes keep them suspended a good deal above it, and sometimes force them down even somewhat below it. But whatever may be the obstacles which hinder them from settling in this center of repose and continuance, they are constantly tending towards it. (58)

This tendency is the fundamental mechanism through which the market regulates itself. When the mechanism is genuinely free to work, "the market price naturally comes to be . . . the same with the natural price" (57). In looking at what happens when it is not free to work, Smith identifies the factors that "keep up the market price, for a long time together, a good deal above the natural price."[41] While some are accidents of nature, such as the possession of a rare soil that exists nowhere else, most factors are socially caused. High profits may be hidden from competitors; well-preserved trade secrets may lead to "extraordinary gains" (60). "A monopoly granted either to an individual or to a trading company has the same effect as a secret in trade or manufactures," he adds and then expands the same logic to regulations of apprenticeship and labor (61). By preventing rival commodities from coming into the market, these and other exclusionary forces lead to sustained market prices in excess of the natural price.

Arnold confronts the same problem of evaluation in his theory of culture. In "The Literary Influence of Academies," he takes up, as his central thesis, the claim that provincialism inhibits the free circulation of literary works; it thus causes a disparity between the "objective" value of a work and the "eccentric" or popular value it fetches in a provincial environment. The difference between these two forms of literary value recapitulates Smith's distinction between natural and market values. Arnold's essay asserts that intellectual protectionism causes a disparity between the "objective" and popular values of literary objects, and in this regard his concept of provincialism mimics the protected environment of Smith's regulated marketplace. In *Culture and Anarchy*, mental free play offers the best chance of insuring the spontaneous alignment of "objective" and popularly assigned values, so long as they circulate in what one Arnold critic refers to as "a sort of free zone for the market of ideas."[42] In Arnold's spontaneity of consciousness, as in the free marketplace, value inherently tends toward the "natural" value of ideas. He attacks stock notions because they function like monopolies in the arena of ideas; Hebraic "strictness of conscience" is an intellectual over-regulation that inhibits the full exchange of ideas. In every case, Arnold's logic promotes a deregulation of the intellectual playing field, so that ideas will be comparatively valued as freely as possible. In an age of too many stock notions, "what we want is Hellenism, the letting our consciousness play freely and simply upon the facts before us, and listening to what it tells us . . ." (*CP*, 5:218). Freed of the constraints of ideational monopolies and top-down regulations, the "best" ideas will receive their natural price through the laws of competition in the market of ideas. Thus Arnold's comparativism transposes Smith's model of economic competition onto the sphere of intellectual evaluation, and because of this transposition, Arnold's concept of free play with its spontaneous assignment of value functions like an ideational free market.

Arnold's emphasis on disinterest in the man of culture is as familiar today as Smith's opposite emphasis on self-interest in the man of business, and so the two theories might appear incompatible. In fact, however, the concept of "interest" plays an identical role in both schemes.[43] Each promotes the same faith in the efficacy of spontaneity within a structure regulated only by its internal logic. Smith's target is not the individual producer but the government that controls relationships within the marketplace. His argument is for an end to legislated monopolies, tariffs, and other legal embodiments of the state's self-interest in controlling the market. Instead he reassures the state of the real value of governmental disinterest, allowing market relations to adjust themselves spontaneously. Smith's *Wealth of Nations*, because it argues for governmental non-interference, argues for a state disinterest that resembles Arnold's disinterested "best self" rather than his self-interested "ordinary self."

Arnold's larger argument thus hinges on the paradoxical formula that the problems created by free trade are to be resolved by free thought; the fetish of economic free play is to be answered by intellectual free play. His own language regularly juxtaposes free trade with free thought: he advocates, "instead of worshipping free-trade . . . we turn the free stream of our thought upon" it; he urges that "we Hellenise a little with free-trade" (*CP*, 5:209). But is his mental free play a fetish? In Arnold's terms, as we have seen, free trade and its social manifestation of free behavior are not in themselves problems. But the uncritical faith in their efficacy is a problem. The excess of value attached to them by zealots, who view freedom of speech, or doing as one likes, as somehow sacred, transforms them into fetishes, valued as ends in themselves rather than as means to an end, so that machinery becomes conflated with the goal it is meant to attain. Within these terms, Arnold fetishizes mental free play. "Turning a stream of fresh and free thought upon our stock notions and habits" becomes a goal in itself, quite apart from the end this fresh stream is supposed to attain. And this is why free play is the one exception to his rejection of an *unum necessarium*. When he writes, "In all those cases what is needed is a freer play of consciousness upon the object of pursuit," or argues, "What we want is . . . a free play of thought upon our routine notions, spontaneity of consciousness," Arnold is conflating his machinery of mental free play with the epistemological goal of objective assessment (*CP*, 5:186, 191). Because of this, the Arnoldian free play machine seems to take on an immediate attractiveness in and of itself, as if free play had a life of its own and were intrinsically valuable apart from the results this machine is supposed to produce. He sums up the source for his own practical solutions to Victorian social problems by explaining, "Plain thoughts of this kind are surely the spontaneous product of our consciousness, when it is allowed to play freely and disinterestedly upon the actual facts of our social condition . . ." (*CP*, 5:219–20). In this well-worn phrase, he asserts his faith in the efficacy of intellectual free play as a means to an end, but at the same time he elevates this means—this machinery of free play—into an object of worship, making a deity out of the void.

Nevertheless—in fact, precisely because of its fetishistic quality—Arnold's theory of culture deployed a reassuring social symbolism. While challenging the middle-class faith in unrestricted trade as productive of value, his theory rewrote the basic logic of that faith onto the arena of ideas and its production of intellectual value.[44] In a society that already accepted Arnold's underlying premise of free play as an item of faith, this was not a radical step or a revolutionary concept so much as a familiar or even a comfortable one, no matter how uncomfortable some were—and Arnold certainly was—with the material consequences of the government's laissez-faire policies.[45] This theory of culture even provided a way to criticize those policies overtly, while staying well within the basic structure of commercial ideology. And so, while Arnold represents free play as a means of combating the fetishism of his society, it was also a product of its age, a particularly Victorian idea, even in its fetishism. The Arnoldian culture idea was a compelling expression of Victorian cultural values, rather than an escape from them, and it was most expressive of its Victorianism in the instance of its imagined flight from it to the laissez-faire world of intellectual free play.

———ᴠᴠᴠ———

"There is surely a danger of allowing Culture also to become a fetish," Williams warned years ago, in his discussion of *Culture and Anarchy*.[46] That danger is clearest in Arnold's later essays, where he shifts from his explicit rejection to tacit acceptance of fetishistic practices. In his 1880 essay, "The Study of Poetry," he reinscribes fetishism in the theory of poetic value that produces his "touchstones."[47] In stark contrast to *Culture and Anarchy*, where his insistence on rational explanation for his political evaluations dominates the chapter on "Our Liberal Practitioners," and in contrast to both the 1853 Preface to *Poems* and *On Translating Homer*, where the system of poetic values is explicitly spelled out, his later stance relies entirely on an appeal to experience, as he pointedly refuses to explain the rational basis for his evaluative process:

> Critics give themselves great labour to draw out what in the abstract constitutes the characters of a high quality of poetry. It is much better simply to have recourse to concrete examples . . . . But if we are asked to define this mark and accent in the abstract, our answer must be: No, for we should thereby be darkening the question, not clearing it. (*CP*, 9:170–71)

A similar reticence appeared two years later, in "Literature and Science." His definition of the role of science in education limits instruction to the conclusions of science rather than focusing on the scientific method: "The great results of the scientific investigation of nature we are agreed upon knowing, but how much of our study are we bound to give to the processes by which those results are reached?" (*CP*, 10:60). For the "great majority of mankind," the answer is very little (*CP*, 10:61). This was a significant change from the insistence in *Culture and Anarchy* that the Victorian era is particularly in need of Hellenic theorizing, the same theorizing that he dismisses in "Literature and Science" as "instrument-knowledges," and in "The Study of Poetry" as "darkening the question" (*CP*, 10:63). In both of these late essays, he abbreviates the cultural object into a fragment—whether scientific result or poetic touchstone—that he then uses to substitute for the whole. Denuded of the abstractions that underlie it, stripped of its rational justification, the cultural fragment suggests a place in Arnold's later writing for the same conceptual shorthand that he had earlier denounced as "stock notions." And so his familiar complaint about the Puritan and his stock notions—"he then remains satisfied with a very crude conception of what this rule really is and what it tells him, [and] thinks he has now knowledge . . ."—is equally applicable to his own defense of cultural fragments, twenty years later (*CP*, 5:180). Presented by Arnold simply as predetermined values, to be assimilated by rote rather than questioned, these fragments recapitulate the fetishistic trope of worshipping machinery as if it had value in and of itself. *Culture and Anarchy*, we have seen, critiques the process of fetishization even as it recapitulates it in its methodology. By comparison, these later writings consciously employ that trope in the service of promoting predetermined cultural values.

In 1982, Bromwich noted that Arnold's critical principles "still seem to me the dominant assumptions in the teaching of literature."[48] Given the continued prominence of his critical method in literary studies, the contradiction between the fetishistic and anti-fetishistic Arnold has been writ large, in a historical sense, within the discipline that he helped to found. Arnold's own writings hold a peculiarly unstable and politically charged position within literary studies today.[49] He can serve "as an awkward ally (for those who want criticism to be centered on the play of interpretation) or as a chosen one (for those who want it to be centered on the work of guarding a permanent canon)."[50] More recently, research on Arnold's critical reception shows that "there were a number of Matthew Arnolds at the close of the nineteenth century," and that the "question of who owned Arnold would become ever more urgent as the twentieth century progressed."[51] Perhaps alone among Victorian authors, Arnold has a major critic who can say, as DeLaura does, that "we still do not know how to 'read' Arnold and why we should read him."[52] The irony here is evident: scholars writing on the founder of the objective method in criticism have never agreed on what he meant.[53] Because of the contradictions within Arnold's work, this foundation for a discipline will always be more Jell-O than bedrock, more water than ground. While this instability shows up starkly in the changing of Arnold's ideas over time, it is never far away at any point in his writing; it is implicit even within *Culture and Anarchy*, as we have seen, in the manner in which Arnold's concept of intellectual free play depends on the simultaneous acceptance and rejection of its underlying concept. Thus even *Culture and Anarchy* embodies the simultaneous acceptance and rejection of fetishism that becomes inescapable in viewing Arnold's ideas over time. Although long acknowledged as "the father of criticism" in the English-speaking world, Arnold has always represented a foundational paradox, rather than a foundational premise.[54]

Because of the instability that his writings reflect, Arnold's adoption by American cultural conservatives in the late twentieth century as a standard-bearer for stable cultural values was necessarily premised on eliding this instability.

Treated in shorthand fashion, he was reduced to a stable cultural fragment based on the fetishistic values of the late essays. This fragment—in which Arnold is transformed into his own touchstone—has served as fodder for a cultural myth, an outsized Arnold who, far from embodying paradox and instability, could be invoked as the defender of stable cultural values.[55] Stripped of his inconsistencies, the mythic Arnold became "a talisman against the evil demons" of relativism.[56] And thus he was finally made into a household god, though in this case the creation was less conjuration from the void than banishment to the void of substantial parts of his writing. Invested with a spirit of its own, the remaining fragment became transformed into the Arnold Fetish.

This Arnold Fetish was famously invoked in the 1984 "Report on the Humanities in Education," issued by William J. Bennett, Chairman of the National Endowment for the Humanities under Ronald Reagan. "Expanding on a phrase from Matthew Arnold," Bennett writes in his opening, "I would describe the humanities as the best that has been said, thought, written, and otherwise expressed about the human experience."[57] In an argument frequently repeated in the writing of cultural conservatives, he explains that the humanities curriculum was once coherently structured around "the best," but it has since fallen into "irrelevance" because of the new relativism in cultural values: "the humanities are declared to have no inherent meaning because all meaning is subjective and relative to one's own perspective."[58] To Bennett, this relativism represents a fundamental surrender to the encroaching forces of unculture, and so he situates himself as a defender of Arnoldian cultural value. He targets a new provincialism, for example, when he complains about teachers who use specialized texts, chosen because they fit the professor's research or because they cater to the student's interest. Canonicity in the classroom—and Bennett offers specific suggestions—guarantees the practice of professional disinterest and thus makes intellectual free play possible.[59] While Bennett deploys Arnoldian catch phrases and concepts, his usage also becomes Arnoldian in an ironic fashion. The "Report" demonstrates the wholesale transformation of Arnold's paradoxical and unstable theory of cultural evaluation into precisely the kind of fetishized values he had opposed. Arnold's own anti-provincialism was premised on expanding the body of texts to include the largest possible pool, within which "the best" would spontaneously emerge. Bennett, however, like one of Arnold's neo-Puritans, exists in a world in which "the best" is predetermined. And so he argues against globalizing the curriculum, defending instead Western cultural exclusivity: "the core of the American college curriculum—its heart and soul—should be the civilization of the West, source of the most powerful and pervasive influences on America and all of its people" (A21). While Arnold's cultural value was premised on the inclusivity of an open intellectual market, the Arnold Fetish defends cultural exclusivity. In the hands of such a disciple, Arnold, for whom all values were comparative, becomes his own worst enemy.

Bennett's vision of a lost Arnoldian Eden has been called the "humanist myth."[60] In his history of English as an institutional entity, Graff shows how this complaint has continually surfaced, ever since research scholars first made the discipline acceptable as a separate department in the American university. Rather than an earlier age of Arnoldian dominance, Graff argues, "Arnoldian humanism has been the outlook of singular individuals, individuals who have exerted a powerful and still-present influence on students and followers, but who have repeatedly failed to make their values visibly characteristic of the totality" (6). Historical signs of an Arnoldian heyday in literature departments are indeed difficult to find. T. S. Eliot's prominent remark that Arnold "was rather a propagandist for criticism than a critic, a popularizer rather than a creator of ideas," illustrates his own, vexed relationship to Arnold's work as well as the vexed position Arnold held in 1920, as the "father" of English criticism.[61] In an overtly antagonistic assessment, written in 1957, William K. Wimsatt and Cleanth Brooks express pronounced "dissatisfaction" with Arnold's commitment to the social function of culture.[62] It led Arnold into the deadly sin of creating a "didactic theory" in which he suffers "the embarrassment of equating poetry with some kind of quasi-philosophic discipline" (447). Arnold's second prophecy, that poetry would one day replace religion and philosophy, would lead to a "didactic function for poetry" that Wimsatt and Brooks call "appalling."[63]

While Graff challenges the humanist myth of a lost Arnoldian ascendancy, other critics take issue with the present-day implications of the same myth, that is, the implication that Arnold has actually disappeared. Focusing on the persistence of several key Arnoldian concepts in critical theory, Arac argues, that "Arnold is everywhere" in contemporary critical debate because Arnold today is the unremarked founder whose premises are taken for granted.[64] Arac assembles a diverse group of contemporary critics, including Graff, to demonstrate how their work inevitably recapitulates Arnoldian principles, even in the process of challenging Arnold's ideas. Thus, like most narratives of a lost Eden, the humanist myth of the lost Arnoldian age sheds more light on the political power of rhetoric, particularly in Bennett's hands, than on Arnold's past or present reputation in the humanities.

In its usage today, Arnold's theory of culture has finally come to operate at the level of meta-commentary. His supposedly stable justification for high culture has itself been made an object of worship, as Bennett's "Report" demonstrates. There may be nothing unusual in this, as merely one among many efforts to legitimize a political movement by appealing to an admired author's name. But as a household god for the sanctity of fixed cultural values, the Arnold Fetish is an uneasy spirit. It is uneasy because it talks about itself and, above all, about the fate of its own vision of culture and of the role of the "speculative class." Arnold's logic, as Arac shows, established the broad terms through which academics continue to think about and to value critical work. Academics in the humanities still act out in earnest Arnold's ideal of mental free play as a mechanism for establishing cultural value, and in this sense Collini is clearly right in arguing that Arnold has become "an unavoidable cultural reference-point."[65] For Arnold, that mechanism was ideal only insofar as it was uncontaminated by the consequences of life within a limiting social environment. He insisted that there was a neutral "outside," or an ideology-free zone, into which the intellectual could escape, and the maintenance of this Victorian premise underpins much of the humanities today. However, while Arnold promised an escape from ideology, the Victorian social world he represented was populated by subjects for whom escape was unavailable. Arnold's examples in "Our Liberal Practitioners," the least read chapter of *Culture and Anarchy*, exemplify the failure of objectivism that underlies his representation of Victorian society as a society of the fetish. Trapped within a pattern of worshipping the thing that is not, his Liberals can be read as case studies of subject formation through interpellation.[66] Arnold represents their escape as always deferred; culture itself is never finally attained, "Not a having and a resting, but a growing and a becoming," and so his subjects remain contaminated by ideology to some extent, unable fully to enter the neutral "outside" (*CP*, 5:94). This ambivalence is one of the reminders of Arnold's paradoxical base: this most prominent defender of academic freedom from the pressures of commerce premised that defense on the logic of free trade. Today, when Arnold is fetishized, this marked instability drops out, and he becomes instead the new "stock notion" that gets in the way. As the promoter of intellectual free play, he becomes at the same time an intellectual jailer, one who developed the institutional language in which humanities professionals learn to feel imprisoned but cannot communicate without. In short, the Arnold Fetish has become the ground that Arnold warned against. More precisely, the Arnold Fetish is a cultural construction that defends the concept of free thought while making it impossible.

Arnold's writing also describes the process of fetishization and because of this can be interpreted as describing the social practice by which his reputation was to be later transformed. To take this literally, of course, would be to credit Arnold with a third prophecy, rather than the usual two.[67] In this proposed third prophecy, Arnold foresees his own future as the fetish god of culture. He prophecies the days of his transformation from an 1860s novelty into a future stock notion and finally into the Arnold Fetish itself. Viewed in this perspective, however, Arnold's writing does not succumb easily to its fate because the Arnold Fetish continues to argue against fetishism, and in this unstable, liquid element of contingency and self-negation, it perseveres.

Arnold represents a similar moment at the climax of "Empedocles on Etna," the production about which he was, more than any other, militantly ambivalent. Empedocles presents a litany of the illusions that plague society, including the simile of the injured child. But just before he leaps into the crater, he turns the question of illusion on himself, as the critic of illusions:

> Slave of sense
> I have in no wise been;—but slave of thought? . . .
> And who can say: I have been always free,
> Lived ever in the light of my own soul?—
> I cannot; I have lived in wrath and gloom,
> Fierce, disputatious, ever at war with man,
> Far from my own soul, far from warmth and light.
> But I have not grown easy in these bonds—
> But I have not denied what bonds these were. (1.2.391–98, ellipses
>   original)

It is his only moment of hope and affirmation in the poem. His understanding is contingent, for while not "free," he at least knows he remains—in ways of which he is unaware—subject to ideology, and this contingency is his consolation. It gives him the courage to act, and so he leaps and is glad. Empedocles employs a different sense of the word "free" than the "free play" of *Culture and Anarchy*. To this speaker, freedom is not available as an option except in the contingent form of negation, or knowing he is not free, and so he focuses at the last on his bonds and finds a comparative freedom in that moment. While Arnold is not Empedocles, Arnold's writing needs to be interpreted similarly. When we see Arnold as trapped within the Victorian ideology he critiques, then the question becomes whether or not he has "grown easy in these bonds." The answers depend ultimately on whether we view him as the Arnold Fetish or consider him historically as the anti-fetishist who argues against his own future. The choice between the two Arnolds is less a question about Arnold's fetishism than our own, and that is ultimately why the question needs to be posed.

3

George Eliot's Realism

On 29 May 1856, while at the English seaside village of Ilfracombe, North Devon, Marian Evans watched the local celebration of the end of the Crimean War.[1] In her account of the incident, she describes a parade, an outdoor tea, and other examples of local eccentricities, and then refers to the event as a "bit of primitive provincial life."[2] Her association of provincialism with primitivity was a studied one, and in this instance it has several different registers. She and her partner, George H. Lewes, were in the middle of a naturalist expedition to collect specimens of mollusks and anemones, biological forms of primitive life. Her observations of the Ilfracombe natives reflect this preoccupation by combining zoological imagery with comments on village life; she describes the village houses as "barnacles clustered on the side of a great rock," and comments on "the strong family likeness between ourselves and all other building, burrowing house-appropriating and shell-secreting animals" (*Letters*, 2:242). The primitivity of provincial life was much on Evans's mind at that particular moment for nonzoological reasons as well. She encountered the village celebration as she was writing an article for the *Westminster Review* on a recent cultural study of German peasant life. She had only begun reading Wilhelm Heinrich von Riehl's *Die bürgerliche Gesellschaft* and *Land und Leute* four weeks earlier, and on 13 May 1856 she was not at all confident in the outcome: "Began my article on Riehl this morning with rather despairing prospects."[3] Three weeks later, on 5 June 1856, she was done, not quite a week after the village celebration. So her comment on provincial primitivity occurred while she was immersed in the problems and promise of Riehl's ethnography, which she describes in full in the final article, "The Natural History of German Life," published the following month.[4] Through the lens of Riehl's peasant study, Ilfracombe and its barnacle cottages became a living example for present-day ethnography and thus came to be seen as primitive provincial life.

Evans's comment on Ilfracombe is an illustration of domestic primitivism, in that she sees provincial life as if it were a less-developed form of her own advanced culture. As the novelist George Eliot, she regularly used this form of domestic primitivism, most familiarly in her portrayal of the Dodsons and Tul-livers, in *The Mill on the Floss*.[5] The practice continued throughout her novel-writing career. More than a decade after the Ilfracombe expedition, she wrote on 22 March 1868 to Sara Hennell, "I am reading about savages and semi-savages" (*Letters*, 4:424). Her notes at the time demonstrate an immersion in the study of primitive culture: she transcribed quotes from John Lubbock's *Pre-Historic Times* (1865), which she read in 1868, and from Edward B. Tylor's *Researches into the Early History of Mankind and the Development of Civilization* (1865).[6] In her "Notes for Felix Holt and Other," she annotated a reference to Tylor's *Researches* with the blunt comment, "for savage customs and ideas."[7] Evidently she was studying up on the basic attributes of primitives, intending to bring that information to bear in her representation of provincial life in *Middlemarch*, the "other" of the notebook's title. In part, Eliot's realism was thus a domestic form of Victorian ethnography. "Instead of faithfully copying the circumstances of external life, George Eliot arranged reality to make it substantiate her moral values," observes Knoepflmacher.[8] Similarly her research led her to substantiate assumptions about the moral values of uncultured society in her representation of English life, and we see an early variant of the same process at work in the Ilfracombe passage.

Like Matthew Arnold, Eliot demonstrated a fundamental ambivalence toward fetishism in her writing. As different as the two writers were, such a similarity might seem unlikely. Arnold rejected positivism outright, whereas Eliot viewed it sympathetically. While Arnold wrote polemically on the theory of culture, Eliot wrote novels describing English culture that studiously avoided polemic. She detested novels in which she perceived a thinly veiled argument, a point she made in her periodical writing, specifically in her reviews of Charles Kingsley and Geraldine Jewsbury, and in her essay, "Silly Novels by Lady Novelists." She repeats the point a decade later, in response to an 1866 letter from Frederic Harrison suggesting she compose a poem or tale to illustrate positivist principles; she answers, "I think aesthetic teaching is the highest of all teaching because it deals with life in its highest complexity. But if it ceases to be purely aesthetic—if it lapses anywhere from the picture to the diagram—it becomes the most offensive of all teaching."[9] Arnold's theory was abstract, while Eliot's realism was concrete. Nonetheless, both were prominently engaged with culture as a concept. He represented the central nineteenth-century theory of culture; she represented culture in the central narrative form of the nineteenth century. On the topic of culture, particularly its social function, they were in close accord: Eliot's hope for realism to improve social understanding was consonant with Arnold's insistence that culture was the only way out of Victorian Britain's difficulty.

Different genres produce different theoretical problems, and it was the status of the realist novel as a cultural object that complicated Eliot's treatment of domestic primitivism in ways that did not apply to *Culture and Anarchy*. What kind of object was the Victorian realist novel? And what did Eliot mean to accomplish with it? She developed her theory of realism early in her career, in the essays and reviews she wrote during the 1840s and 1850s, before attempting fiction. In that luminous body of material, she consistently values those works that expose rather than reinforce stereotypes, superstitions, and other forms of a priori thought. In this respect, her realism was essentially anti-fetishistic; it demystified the kind of illusions that made fetishism possible. But fictional realism also depends on illusion, and this poses a paradox. While fetishism in Eliot's fiction regularly serves as a negative sign—as when indicating a character's immaturity—it also holds a positive place in her critical essays on the mechanics of realism. Her realism necessarily relied on fetishism to accomplish its anti-fetishistic goals. This paradox can be understood as a basic conflict between form and content; while realist literary form relies on illusion, its content seeks to undo illusion. By recognizing this distinction, we can see the way in which her novels comment on themselves, in an ongoing dialogue between anti-fetishist content and fetishist form. These are self-reflexive artifacts, then, and Eliot's ambivalent attitude towards fetishism surfaces in their self-commentary.

Like many English intellectuals in the 1850s, Eliot was enthusiastic about the new ideas in Comte's *Cours de philosophie positive*. Her irregular marriage with Lewes—though not officially recognized, they considered themselves husband and wife—began in 1853, just months before Lewes collected his periodical essays on positivism and published them as *Comte's Philosophy of the Sciences*. That she was well versed in positivism by this date is certain, but it is also clear that her familiarity with Comte's philosophy predated the relationship with Lewes by several years.[10] In a letter to Charles and Cara Bray on 20 September 1849, she mentions having lent out her copy of the volume that introduced the English to positivism, Mill's *A System of Logic*, which the Brays had inquired about, and suggests they retrieve it for themselves.[11] Two years later, in a letter to Cara from London (3 October 1851), she asks Charles to return it to her, explaining, "I shall be glad to have it by me for reference" (*Letters*, 1:363). She moved to London from Coventry in January 1851, when she changed her name from Mary Ann to Marian Evans, and during that first year she was actively promoting Comte's writing; we know, for example, that she urged Herbert

Spencer to read Comte.[12] Her interest in positivism is particularly evident after 1859, when she became a neighbor in Wandsworth to Richard and Maria Congreve, with whom she and Lewes became lifelong friends. She read Comte's *Catèchism positiviste* that October, which Congreve, the high priest of English Comtists, had translated the previous year (*Journals*, 81). In her journal entry for 9 July 1861, she notes reading "Comte on the middle ages," from *Cours*, vol. 5; she was writing *Romola* at the time, her only novel set in the Middle Ages, which she followed with *The Spanish Gypsy*, a novel-length poem set in the same time period.[13] She and Lewes read *Cours* together in the mid-1860s and visited Comte's house in Paris; in 1867 they attended the first four of Congreve's nine Sunday-morning lectures to the Positivist Society, an organization to which she gave a minor sum annually for the rest of her life.[14] In August 1868, she read *Système de politique positive*; two years later, she read the newly published volume of Comte's letters.[15] By 1871, her engagement with positivism was so well-known that the writer John Morely, himself a positivist sympathizer, could chide the more orthodox Comtist, Harrison, "There is not a Positivist among you. There are only two in England—Mill and George Eliot."[16]

Many attempts have been made to minimize her historical affinity for positivism, but these have proven untenable in light of much evidence to the contrary.[17] None of this means that she was an orthodox Comtist. Certainly, aspects of the Religion of Humanity appealed to her, but she was not one to subordinate her judgment to another's, nor did she endorse blind adherence to doctrine by others, notwithstanding her conservatism. When asked, later in life, about her attitude towards Comte, she reportedly explained, "I will not submit to him my heart and my intellect."[18] Distinctions need to be made between true believers—like Congreve and Harrison—and the many others who sympathized with Comte's general principles, while disagreeing with his late extensions of them into the terrain of politics and religion. Mill and Lewes both fit this second category.[19] So did Eliot, with one exception. Comte's Religion of Humanity resonated with her own views on the fundamental dignity and nobility of humanity as a whole. This similarity was not lost on Harrison; in a retrospective of Eliot's work, written five years after her death, he noted the connection:

> With the cardinal ideas of Positivism—the cherishing and extension of all true religious sentiment, and the direction of that sentiment toward the collective well-being of mankind—not only was George Eliot in profound sympathy, but no one else in our time has expressed those ideas with such power. . . . [S]he may be said to be the greatest believer in humanity as a religious inspiration whom our country and time have produced.[20]

While many members of the public viewed her as a leading English positivist, the central figures in that group were frustrated, even disillusioned, at her unwillingness to commit her talents to their cause, seeing her as sympathetic but detached.[21] In the end, Eliot's relationship to positivism can only be described as ambivalent. She admired its English advocates, particularly Maria and Richard Congreve and Frederick Harrison, subscribed to its daring proposal for a science of social bodies, and agreed with the elevated position positivism assigned humanity. At the same time, she disagreed with the authoritarianism of Comte's later works (as did most of her contemporaries) and had ideas about art that put her at odds with important positivists.[22] We need to appreciate the multifaceted complexity of her beliefs—a complexity that makes the wide range of subsequent opinions about her positivism feasible—while recognizing that both her embrace of positivist history and her rejection of its politics speak volumes about her intellectual independence.

Her first published reference to Comte appears in the first paragraph of the first article she wrote for a London periodical, her review of Robert William Mackay's *The Progress of the Intellect*, published in the January 1851 *Westminster Review*.[23] She wrote this piece in the fall of 1850, while still in Coventry, and it demonstrated a working knowledge of the intricacies of Comte's three stages even before her move to London. The journal's selection of her as Mackay's reviewer was logical: she knew the German higher criticism well, and Mackay was almost alone among British biblical scholars in embracing its historical view of the Bible.[24] She introduced her review topic with an opening paragraph on the regrettable lack of interest in history, generally, among present thinkers. Many powerful English intellectuals, she explains, "are prone to under-rate critical research into ancient modes of life and forms of thought," in deference to addressing the immediate needs of the present (*Essays*, 27). "Holding, with Auguste Comte, that theological and metaphysical speculation have reached their limit, and that the only hope of extending man's sources of knowledge and happiness is to be found in positive science . . . they urge that the thinkers who are in the van of human progress should devote their energies to the actual rather than to the retrospective" (*Essays*, 28). Although Comte would be one of the last people to propose the insignificance of historical study, Eliot does not explicitly correct their mistaken understanding. Instead she responds to their position with one more in line with the philosophy of Positivism itself. It "would be a very serious mistake to suppose that the study of the past and the labours of criticism have no important practical bearing on the present," she points out; contemporary life is littered with survivals from antiquity, "lifeless barbarisms" or "petrifactions from distant ages" (*Essays*, 28). The scientific study of the past makes it possible to recognize them and thus to gain a clearer understanding of the present. As she explains, "We are in bondage to terms and conceptions which, having had their root in conditions of thought no longer existing, have ceased to possess any vitality, and are for us as spells which have lost their virtue" (*Essays*, 28). Such "*idola theatri*" militate against the very possibility of spreading the "enlightened ideas" that the progressive English thinkers value (*Essays*, 29). Within this intellectual context, Mackay's developmental study becomes singularly important.

While generally admiring *Progress of the Intellect*, her review takes issue with several points in it, including its assumptions about the earliest religion. In Mackay's scheme of intellectual evolution, she notes, "mythical conception, instead of being a step in advance of fetishism, is a decadence of the religious sentiment from that monotheistic or pantheistic impression to which it leaps by its first impulse."[25] Such a view recapitulates biblical doctrine, of course, and she criticizes the very idea of an initial monotheism, describing as more likely a psychological condition among primitives that sounds remarkably similar to Comte's primitive fetishism: "To the uncultured intellect, a plurality of divine agencies, analogous to the human, would seem by their conflicting wills and influences, a natural explanation of physical and moral vicissitudes" (*Essays*, 38). At this early stage of her career, Eliot was restating some of Comte's most basic ideas, including the role of anthropomorphic projection in primitive society, with little modification.

We can identify the primitivism of Ilfracombe's celebration in its own *idola theatri*: the "melancholy foot-races" and "feeble fire-works" that she described on her visit there five years later (*Letters*, 2:248). In contrast to these listless residues, she notes how "fine" it was to see the bonfires, which "made one think of the times when such fires were lighted as signals to arm—the symbol of a common cause and a common feeling" (*Letters*, 2:248). Their vitality lies in the past, however, and they survive only as fetishized petrifactions, keeping the Ilfracombe natives in bondage to their stunted state of culture. "It seems scarcely too much to assert, once for all," Tylor writes in *Primitive Culture*, "that meaningless customs must be survivals, that they had a practical, or at least ceremonial, intention when and where they first arose, but are now fallen into absurdity from having been carried on into a new state of society, where their original sense has been discarded."[26] Eliot's similar sense of the connection between present and past predates Tylor, not because she is prescient, but because both she and Tylor drew on Comte, who had articulated the idea.

Her early positivist ideals were substantially modified by her translation of Ludwig Feuerbach's *Das Wesen des Christenthums*. She took on this project in late 1853, when she gave up the editorship of the *Westminster Review*. In July 1854, less than a year later, *The Essence of Christianity* was published, marking the only time the author "Marian Evans" appeared in print. Eliot's affinity for Feuerbach's philosophy is well known, but by looking briefly at his ideas, we can see that his anti-theological humanism was premised on a radical critique of religious fetishism in modern life.

Compared to Comte, Feuerbach dramatically widened the reach of fetishism. Instead of a holdover from the most distant stage of social development, it became, in his hands, the essence of modern Christianity. Feuerbach reinstated fetishism at the center of religious life in even the most developed societies, thus elevating it into an immediate and pressing concern. In this respect, his attitude toward fetishism resembled Comte's less than that of Marx, for whom fetishism was an essential part of industrial capitalism.[27] With Marx, Feuerbach shared a base in German materialist philosophy and a shared objection to the idealism of Hegel. "I do not generate the object from the thought, but the thought from the object . . . . I attach myself . . . only to *realism*, to materialism," he writes.[28] And this engagement with realism can account for Feuerbach's interest to the translating Marian Evans, then in the process of defining her own realist values. The two authorial voices—her translation, his original—intermingle in this text, becoming inseparable as the single voice of two consciousnesses. As Beer explains, referring to another passage, "These are Eliot's words as well as Feuerbach's," and the same can be said here.[29] This intertextuality was underscored by Eliot herself, in what is now her most frequently cited comment on Feuerbach. "With the ideas of Feuerbach I everywhere agree," she notes in a letter to Sara Hennell, written as she finished the translation (*Letters*, 2:153).

The Essence of Christianity begins with the position that "[r]eligion is the dream of the human mind."[30] However, this illusory quality is no reason to dismiss it. On the contrary, "in dreams we do not find ourselves in emptiness or in heaven, but on earth, in the realm of reality; we only see real things in the entrancing splendour of imagination and caprice, instead of in the simple daylight of reality and necessity" (xix). Illusions are meaningful as a guide to the qualities of the beings that imagine them. Like Epicurus, Feuerbach argues that religious belief is a projection of human ideals onto an imagined, external being; once again, people anthropomorphize, creating a deity in their own, self-reflecting terms. Were a bird to imagine God, then God "would be a winged being: the bird knows nothing higher, nothing more blissful, than the winged condition" (17). Furthermore, as human culture develops, the anthropomorphic image goes through an "identical" change: "So long as man is in a mere state of nature, so long is his god a mere nature-god—a personification of some natural force. Where man inhabits houses, he also encloses his gods in temples" (20). In broad terms, the changing image of God reflects the fluid values of cultural progress, and this malleability is one of the proofs that the deity originates in the human mind.

Having thus historicized the underlying issue of projection, Feuerbach complicates matters: humans reverse the pattern of projection and imagine that God created them, rather than the other way around. They begin to think of themselves as creations of the all-powerful being they invented, and, in doing so, they define themselves as subordinate to God.

> Man—this is the mystery of religion—projects his being into objectivity, and then again makes himself an object to this projected image of himself thus converted into a subject. (29–30)

The creator becomes the created. In Feuerbach's terms, the subject man first creates the object God, and then redefines God as the subject who created the object man. Indirectly, then, and without realizing it, the human "thinks of himself [a]s an object to himself," because he has become "the object of an object, of another being than himself" (30). Thus humans make themselves subordinate to an alienated image of themselves, defined as God. This pattern has been nicely summarized by Simpson, not in relation to Feuerbach (whom he does not discuss), but in providing his own readers with a general definition of *fetishism*. He writes, "fetishism occurs when the mind ceases to realize that it has itself created the outward images or things to which it subsequently posits itself as in some sort of subservient relation."[31] This definition describes the central claim of *The Essence of Christianity*, whose history of religion followed the same vein mined by Epicurus and named *fetishism* by de Brosses, whose work influenced German and French historians of religion at the turn of the nineteenth century.[32]

The relationship between humans and God involves an economy of exchange. As humans attribute their best qualities to God, few positive traits remain that they can call their own. Over time, as the image of God becomes idealized, the self-image of the human is impoverished, consisting of only the remaining attributes, attributes that are necessarily ignoble. Lucretius viewed the human invention of gods as oppressive, causing misery and unhappiness, and Feuerbach describes similar consequences, evident in the negative view humans take of their own character.[33] Rightfully, he argues, they can lay claim to all of the positive qualities they imagine in God, but unhappily they see humanity in the most negative terms. A realistic assessment of humanity would need to include all of the highest qualities attributed to God as essential human traits, and in this assessment, humanity as a whole becomes a wonderful and noble concept, something to be celebrated and valued in itself.

If a writer were to unmask this illusory sequence for a broad audience, her readers could see the positive qualities that are the essence of their own humanity. Those attributes that most define God as the ideal moral being—sympathy, compassion, love—are ultimately human qualities: "God is love," Feuerbach (and Evans) writes.[34] Eliot's realism engages in the project of restoring those attributes to their rightful owner. Realism demands that the values of love and compassion be represented as human values, rather than falsely attributed to an imaginary external object. Both Feuerbach's and Eliot's humanism springs from this basic imperative. The idea of God in *The Essence of Christianity* comes about in three stages: (1) humans project their own qualities onto an external object, (2) forget that it was a projection, and (3) perceive the object as actually possessing those qualities. This is, of course, the process of fetishism in action, as described by Comte, and so we can see that Feuerbach's materialist critique of religion defines realism as the antidote to religious fetishism.

This anti-fetishistic critique featured prominently in Eliot's essays and reviews. In some she unmasked the fetishist; in others she praised writers who unmasked fetishistic beliefs. The first can be seen in her last extended article, "Worldliness and Other-Worldliness: The Poet Young," published in January 1857. It challenged the reverence with which Edward Young's poem, *Night Thoughts,* was held at the time. In discussing the poet's life, she charges him with the narcissistic quality of unknowingly worshipping an image of himself: "Young has no conception of religion as anything else than egoism turned heavenward" (*Essays*, 378). Because she wrote this article simultaneously with her first story, "The Sad Fortunes of the Reverend Amos Barton," the two were both on her mind at the time: on the one hand, actively unmasking the system of fetishistic projection in Young, while, on the other, working through her initial process of learning how to write fiction.[35]

She heaped praise on writers who unmasked modern fetishistic assumptions, never more so than when commenting on writers practicing higher criticism of the Bible. Her 1851 review of William Rathbone Greg's *The Creed of Christendom* lauds it for countering religious fetishism with a healthy dose of realism. Calling it "an introductory manual of biblical criticism," she argues that, by treating the canonical writings as historical documents, rather than revelations "dictated or suggested by God," Greg clears "away the dazzling haze with which the inspiration dogma invests the biblical writings."[36] This historicist move defetishizes scripture, and it pointedly defetishizes the supernatural person of Jesus, the living god whom she redefines in Feuerbachian terms as "'humanity in its divinest phase'" (292).

Eliot similarly praised the work of social commentators who questioned religious-like beliefs. In her 1855 review of works by two feminist writers, "Margaret Fuller and Mary Wollstonecraft," she contrasts the ideal of Victorian womanhood, the "doll-Madonna in her shrine," with the reality of women's ignorance in an age that discounts female education (*Essays*, 205). While Feuerbach describes humans as diminishing themselves in the process of projecting their best qualities onto God, Eliot describes women as diminished by the deification of the Angel in the House, arguing that men worship this deity in order to avoid "looking up to our wives" (*Essays*, 205). Deification in domestic relations becomes a form of disempowerment:

> *Sit divus, dummodo non sit vivus* (let him be a god, provided he be not living), said the Roman magnates of Romulus; and so men say of women, let them be idols, useless absorbents of precious things, provided we are not obliged to admit them to be strictly fellow-beings, to be treated, one and all, with justice and sober reverence. (*Essays*, 205)

Instead of this doll-worship, she proposes the realistic treatment women receive in Fuller's and Wollstonecraft's two works; for both authors, their "ardent hopes of what women may become do not prevent them from seeing and painting women as they are" (*Essays*, 205). Thus, in addition to defetishizing Jesus, she protests the deification of women.

In Eliot's early novels, her critique of fetishism is less censorious than in the nonfiction. Typical is the compassionate description of Mrs. Tulliver weeping over her "Teraphim, or Household Gods," in *The Mill on the Floss*.[37] Mrs. Tulliver sits alone in the storeroom, where "her linen and all the precious 'best things'" are spread out before her (177). "'But I shouldn't ha' minded so much if we could ha' kept the things wi' my name on 'em,'" she explains, referring to the table cloths she had marked with "a particular stitch" (179). In Feuerbachian fashion, Mrs. Tulliver grieves not only for her household gods, but for a god that bears the marks of her own invention. Within this episode, her daughter Maggie occupies the position of antifetishist by taking the stance of the critical observer in the fetishistic triangle. She upbraids both her mother and brother for caring more about "table-cloths and china" than about her invalided father, "who was lying there in a sort of living death" (179). The first, then, are reevaluated as simple, inert material objects, while the second—her paralyzed father, himself transformed into a material object—has his animation reasserted. By contrasting the paralyzed Mr. Tulliver with Mrs. Tulliver's vibrant household objects, the novel sets up a reversal of value, in which objects appear alive and the living appear lifeless. These are opposite manifestations of the same fetishistic pattern, described by one writer as the "paradox of moving statues, of dead objects coming alive and/or of petrified living objects" that comes into play when "the barrier which separates the living from the dead is transgressed."[38] That paradox is always implicit within fetishism, and both versions of it—objects that become beings, beings that become objects—are evident in *The Mill on the Floss*.

Eliot's most familiar reference to fetishism occurs earlier in the same novel, in a scene whose dramatic structure is identical to the incident of Mrs. Tulliver, alone in her storeroom. This time, the little girl Maggie is alone and sobbing in her attic-sanctuary, engaging in her own ritualized object worship: "here she kept a Fetish which she punished for all her misfortunes."[39] The object is her doll, "now entirely defaced by a long career of vicarious suffering" for the sins others have committed toward Maggie. In this instance, it is occupied by the spirit of her overbearing Aunt Glegg (*Mill*, 23–25). Accustomed to driving nails into the doll's head, Maggie needs to moderate her revenge; she "reflected that if she drove many nails in, she would not be so well able to fancy that the head was hurt when she knocked it against the wall."[40] Rather than a living fetish, the doll is on the threshold of being reduced to its sheer materiality, as splinters of wood, so the child resorts to less violent methods of punishment. She "soothed herself by alternately grinding and beating the wooden head" (25). Also present in this incident is the counterstance of the critic, which appears this time in the narrator's voice, rather than in the perspective of another character. As is usual for Eliot's narrators, that voice is compassionate while also detached. The narrator's language suggests an indulgent humor in the representation of Maggie: to be "soothed" by the violent actions of "grinding and beating" is an image of primordial catharsis, one well suited to expressing the irrational passions of a child-fetishist. This passage, along with the previous one, contrasts the highly developed, well-educated narrator's voice with the domestic primitivism of the underdeveloped Tulliver family, and in the two scenes, we see Maggie play both roles, the fetishist and the critic. Commenting on the beliefs of the Tullivers in general, the narrator epitomizes the objectivity of the outsider in the fetishistic triangle, and thus that voice can also resemble the kind of paternalism characteristic in other contexts as that of the colonizer for the colonized, the advanced society for the undeveloped, or even the Ilfracombe tourist for the primitive provincial.

While it is the most well-known example, Maggie's fetish doll was neither Eliot's first reference to fetishism nor her last. Much earlier, in her Coventry days, a twenty-four-year-old Mary Ann Evans used the term to describe herself. In November 1843, she attended the marriage of Charles Hennell, the brother of her neighbor, Cara Bray, and author of *Inquiry Concerning the Origin of Christianity*.[41] Hennell was marrying Rufa Brabant, who was in the process of translating D. F. Strauss's *Das Leben Jesu* into *The Life of Jesus*, a project which she soon turned over to Eliot.[42] Following the wedding in London, Eliot went for a six-week stay in Devizes with Rufa's family, beginning 7 November. While there, she flirted with and was flattered by Dr. Robert Brabant, then in his sixties. Mrs. Brabant was blind, but evidently not so blind that she could not see what was going on. She became jealous and, by the time Rufa returned from her honeymoon, matters were uncomfortable enough that her visitor left for home two weeks early, on 4 December. The exact nature of Eliot's feeling for Dr. Brabant is unknown, but the incident caused concern at the time to both Cara Bray and her sister, Sara Hennell. Three years later, in a letter to Sara, Eliot reflected on her behavior:

> I begin to be of your and Cara's opinion anent Dr. B. . . . If I ever offered incense to him it was because there was no other deity at hand and because I wanted some kind of worship pour passer le temps. I always knew that I could belabour my fetisch if I chose, and laughed at him in my sleeve. Even that degree of inclination toward mock reverence has long since passed away . . . . (*Letters*, 1:225)

Like the narrator of *The Mill on the Floss*, the narrating subject of the letter positions the younger fetishist at a distance and frames her worship of the fetish object as the product of immaturity. But the example is, of course, much closer to home, in the relationship it asserts between critic and worshipper, than in the case of her later novel. Here, interpreting subject and fetishist are one and the same. Her letter recognizes this uncomfortable proximity in its hint of defensiveness, as if to deny that this was true infatuation but was rather a consciously-created artifice for her own entertainment.[43] Nonetheless, at the time the entertainment had been serious enough to lead to real consequences, so in this letter the mind of the fetishist and critic are close to being two aspects of the same consciousness.

———◊———

Because of the anti-representational status of the fetish, fetishism and representation are inimical to one another.[44] This opposition can magically evaporate when representation ceases to be pure representation—a disembodied set of abstractions—and begins to take on the quality and status of an object in its own right. Such is the case in the realist novel. The rise of realism in philosophy is a familiar story, in which classical generality yields to realist particularity.[45] In the epistemology of realism, particulars are significant in relation to an assumed overarching design, and so particulars become meaningful as a way to access that larger general truth. Ian Watt's definition of formal realism, for example, holds that the novel "works by exhaustive presentation," in order to "make the words bring [the] object home to us in all its concrete particularity."[46] Through this generous heaping of details, fiction produces the illusion that "the novel is a full and authentic report of human experience" (32). The realist use of particularity thus encourages the reader to attribute a kind of life to the narrative, to imagine that behind or within this inert body of words resides a living spirit. The rhetoric used by major critics of realism in Watt's generation emphasized this illusion of life. Hardy insists that the critique of realism hinges on the extent to which the novel succeeds at becoming "the imitation of life."[47] Kettle writes that novels "must give us a sense that what is being conveyed across to us by the words on the page is life or, at any rate, has something of the quality of life."[48] Such phrases refer to the mimetic capabilities of representation, of course, but the same words describe an object that succeeds only by coming to life. Thus Harvey, whose criticism centers on "the question of mimetic adequacy," writes that "Dreiser . . . still has the power of deeply moving the reader because the life he has imagined is indeed alive."[49] In each of these evaluations, the novel becomes a form of prosopopeia. As a criterion of aesthetic evaluation, this requirement ties the success or failure of the object to a form of hypostatization, in which the critic must come to regard the (successful) object as a self-existing being. The critic can avoid the problem of fetishism by retaining the distinction between a representation and its subject matter, or between the object and its effects. But the underlying assumption remains that it is the business of realism in the novel to obscure that distinction through its heaping of particulars, so that a "report of human experience" can become "full and authentic," even when there is no historical experience to report. In this branch of twentieth-century theories of the novel, realism works by creating an illusion of life, and in this function, the realist object is defined as one that strives to attain the status of the fetish.

The language of fetishism in nineteenth-century appraisals of realist novels is, if anything, even more emphatic. "A novel is a living thing, all one and continuous, like any other organism," wrote Henry James in 1884.[50] The source of this trope can be assigned earlier in the century to the criticism of John Ruskin, whose ideas shaped the basic theory of Victorian realism to which Eliot and her contemporaries subscribed. In reviewing Ruskin's *Modern Painters*, for the April 1856 *Westminster Review*, Eliot explains: "The truth of infinite value that he teaches is *realism*—the doctrine that all truth and beauty are to be attained by a humble and faithful study of nature, and not by substituting vague forms, bred by imagination on the mists of feeling, in place of definite, substantial reality."[51] Most of her commentary centers on Ruskin's definition of the "Grand Style" in painting and his insistence, there, on the importance of detailed particularity in art. Ruskin writes: "Nearly *every* other rule applicable to art has some exception but this. This has absolutely none."[52] Neither fuzzy nor hazy, art is to have a crystal clarity in its treatment of details, and thus, "all *great* drawing is *distinct* drawing" (62).

Theorists of erotic fetishism, from Alfred Binet forward, regularly identify an obsession with detail as, itself, a form of fetishism, and it is easy to confuse Ruskin's claims with a similar interest in the individual detail.[53] Certainly, when viewed in isolation, particular details can be perceived as aesthetic singularities, and thus eroticized. However, Ruskin's treatment of detail is fundamentally different because he does not value details as isolated particulars; instead he focuses on the aggregate effect of many, combined details. For example, he argues that an artist's selection among available details is made by choosing "the most necessary first, and afterwards the most consistent with these, so as to obtain the greatest possible and most harmonious *sum*."[54] As his argument develops, he consistently emphasizes quantitative accumulation, and from this aggregate perspective, detail takes on a new importance. Rather than individual representations, details become presentations in the "*sum*" that they make. He talks about details as if they were units of embodied Truth (now with a capital *T*), Truths so concrete that one could actually count them: "great art . . . includes the largest possible quantity of Truth . . ." (60). Thus, he continues, "the difference between the great and inferior artists . . . may be determined at once by the question, which of them conveys the largest sum of truth?" (62) That sum is not only quantitatively greater, but also qualitatively different from its parts, and the key element in that qualitative distinction is the hypostatization of art: through aggregation, realist particulars foster the illusion of concreteness that transforms them from a representation to an embodiment of truth.

That sum of truth is directly associated with the spirit world. Ruskin defines truth as fidelity to nature, so that details can be true or false "while the picture is considered as a statement of facts" (57n). However, Ruskin's nature is a providential one, rather than a sheer materiality. Objects in the natural world have meaning as signs, however unclear, of the hidden providential design.[55] The value of incorporating the greatest amount of detail in art is that the artist represents a providential text, and the more of that text that can be included, the greater the possibility of getting it right. In this sense, Ruskin's call for the "largest possible quantity of Truth" is a prescription for the greatest potency of a supernatural presence in the realist object.

What happens, then, when the viewer or reader comes in contact with this inspired object? In defining the technical qualities of greatness in art, he explains "why the word 'Great' is used of this art. It is literally great. It compasses and calls forth the entire human spirit, whereas any other kind of art, being more or less small or narrow, compasses and calls forth only *part* of the human spirit."[56] This doctrine centers on a universal spirit, rather than the ancestral spirits of West African religious beliefs, and yet the relationship he asserts between the spirit and the object is identical. The fetishistic quality of the object is evident, first, in the claim that the object "compasses" the spirit, so that it becomes a residence for a spirit that is now "in" the object. But that fetishism is also implicit in the active power Ruskin attributes to the object, as able to "call forth" the spirit within the viewer. In the interaction between viewer and object, the providential spirit of nature is housed within the art object and, through it, acts on the viewer, whose own spirit reacts in an ethereal vibration to the spirit in the object. This language posits art as an active object, rather than a passive image for reception. It seems to radiate supernatural force, as if through a halo effect that influences all who come in contact with its great spirit. In the eyes of an imaginary primitive who steps out of Comte's book, Ruskin's "great art" would seem a powerful fetish indeed. And this is precisely the point because the Victorian theory of realism was premised on the fetishization of the art object.

This same hypostatization is widespread in Eliot's own writing on realism. It becomes most pronounced when she comments on the effect of art on its audience. In these remarks, the value of realism is routinely premised on its ability to transform the book object into an object of quasi-supernatural powers.[57] Her 1849 review of J. A. Froude's novel, *The Nemesis of Faith*, was the second review she ever wrote, and in it she describes this function dramatically and unambiguously:

> On certain red-letter days of our existence, it happens to us to discover among the *spawn* of the press, a book which, as we read, seems to undergo a sort of transfiguration before us. We no longer hold heavily in our hands an octavo of some hundred pages . . . but we seem to be in companionship with a spirit, who is transfusing himself into our souls, and is vitalizing them by his superior energy . . . .[58]

Froude's novel and others like it carry "this magic in them," and it is this attribution of spirit to object that transforms *The Nemesis of Faith* into a fetish, whose "influence" can be used "for good or evil" (15). A similar statement comes later, in her 1855 review of Thomas Carlyle. The review begins with the same structure as the previous one and many other Eliot reviews. It opens with a broad observation (generally about books), and then concludes that the subject under review is (or is not) such a book. In the cases of the Froude and Carlyle reviews, her broad observation focuses on an affective distinction similar to De Quincey's theory of the literature of knowledge and the literature of power.[59] There are two types of educators, she notes in introducing Carlyle, the instructive and the inspirational: "He is the most effective educator . . . who does not seek to make his pupils moral by enjoining particular courses of action, but by bringing into activity the feelings and sympathies that must issue in noble action" (*Essays*, 213). The same holds true for writers, and she values an author who does not simply give practical instruction to readers but instead "inspires their souls with courage and sends a strong will into their muscles" (*Essays*, 213). In the second case, the "influence of such a writer is dynamic. . . . He does not, perhaps, convince you, but he strikes you, undeceives you, animates you" (*Essays*, 213). This visceral quality changes the viewer or reader. As she explains in "The Morality of *Wilhelm Meister*," written the same year, Goethe's work has an active force, a distinct spiritual power that can reform its audience because it can "call forth our best sympathies" (*Essays*, 146). A similar moment occurs in her 1856 review of Robert Browning's *Men and Women*. Eliot praises his "Art-criticism," and remarks, "we would rather have 'Fra Lippo Lippi' than an essay on Realism in Art."[60] The poem, which she extracts at length, dramatizes the desired effect of realist representation most clearly when it describes the "pious people" who, on seeing Lippi's realist fresco of St. Laurence's martyrdom, immediately "scratched and prodded to our heart's content," defacing the image of the torturers.[61] The image transforms the pious parishioners into enraged actors, as if it were real. And, on a small scale, this active power embodies the dream of all mid-Victorian realism, by picturing the power of representation to change the thing it represents.[62]

The most familiar formulation of this expectation in Eliot's work appears in that essay she labored over during her visit to Ilfracombe. In "The Natural History of German Life," she explains: "Art is the nearest thing to life; it is a mode of amplifying experience and extending our contact with our fellowmen beyond the bounds of our personal lot" (*Essays*, 271). This imposes a moral responsibility on the artist that makes the artist's task "[a]ll the more sacred" (*Essays*, 271). As Stang observes, this insistence on the sacred function of the novelist was a particularly nineteenth-century belief, and one that is more typical of mid-Victorian writers than those of the late Regency.[63] By the time of modernism, it was an anachronism. In retrospect, this quasi-religious attribute was the defining quality of the Victorian realist novel; thus Stang long ago appropriated Eliot's phrase to characterize the general attitude of realist novelists toward writing as "The Sacred Office." As the sense of a spiritual imperative suggests, the social function of realism—the effect it proposes to have on its readership—is not limited to a simple, factual information exchange. In any event, such information is already available in non-fiction social studies, like the volumes of Riehl's study of German peasant life that she was reviewing. Eliot differentiates between realism in art and the realism of social science by pointing to the unique ability of art to alter its audience's moral condition. As she explains:

> Appeals founded on generalizations and statistics require a sympathy ready-made, a moral sentiment already in activity; but a picture of human life such as a great artist can give, surprises even the trivial and the selfish into that attention to what is apart from themselves, which may be called the raw material of moral sentiment. (*Essays*, 270)

The effect described in these familiar words is premised on moral magic. She attributes a transformational power to fictional realism in the assumption that it can fundamentally charge even "the selfish" with a new selflessness, never before present. The "trivial" person's inward focus will change to an outward focus, so what is being described is a capacity to transform the reader or viewer morally, and this transformation occurs through an undefined and indefinable quality in art that is distinct from simple information, of the kind Riehl's own book conveys. "Art is the nearest thing to life," hovering at the border line between a representation of life and life as such (*Essays*, 271). This liminal quality—unique to realist art, among all forms of created objects and discourses—is what differentiates it from information: it creates an illusion of being alive, and its transformational power resides in this illusion, so that realism's power is premised on a singular *as if*: the subject is transformed by realist art *as if* art were life.[64]

Such a comparison raises the question of where, exactly, to situate the border between reforming influence and supernatural, fetish effect. For a Victorian novelist to imagine that her production would reform its readership is one thing. But at what point does it become an attribution of supernatural power to the object? In broad terms, the border between moral influence and supernatural transformation was a porous one in Victorian culture, and one that was crossed and recrossed with regularity. When Eliot refers to the "doll-Madonna in her shrine," she points to the most pervasive example of that border crossing, the Angel in the House, an image of the power of moral influence that rapidly became fetishized. Even Coventry Patmore's name for this linchpin of domestic ideology posits a relationship between a spirit and a residence that mimics the structure of the primitive fetish, as a spirit that becomes coterminous with its material embodiment. In Ruskin's essay, "Of Queen's Gardens," he describes "the woman's true place and power."[65] That place is less concrete than the "house" of Patmore's label, being a purely figurative term for the domestic sphere. But the "power" is palpable, described as a radiant emanation influencing everyone it touches:

> And wherever a true wife comes, this home is always round her. The stars only may be over her head; the glow-worm in the night-cold grass may be the only fire at her foot: but home is yet wherever she is: and for a noble woman it stretches far round her, better than ceiled with cedar, or painted with vermilion, shedding its quiet light far, for those who else were homeless. (85–86)

This language describes an active energy radiating outward from the idealized woman, and in that sense of the Angel as a radiant body, possessed of an active power to affect others, Ruskin's Queen crosses the borderline and enters the terrain of the supernatural. The figure of the Angel in the House is one of the most ubiquitous of Victorian fetishes; she becomes, quite simply, a body inhabited by domestic ideals, a residence for a benevolent spirit.

Eliot's periodical reviews attribute the same active, radiant power found in Ruskin's Queen to her favorite realist writers, and this leads to a conflict, within Eliot's writing, between representations of fetishism, like the doll-Madonna, and its inverse, the fetishism of representation. We can see this conflict play out in her praise of Carlyle, for example, when she borrows her terms from the sentimental language of domestic ideology: "It is not as a theorist, but as a great and beautiful human nature, that Carlyle influences us," she begins; he "warms your heart by the pressure of his hand, and looks out on the world with so clear and loving an eye, that nature seems to reflect the light of his glance upon your own feeling" (*Essays*, 214). While the gender terminology is male, the mode of influence is undistinguishable from Ruskin's definition of the Queen's power, a writer's "clear light" that alters everyone who comes within range of it (*Essays*, 214). One has to stop oneself for a moment to remember, in every essay and review, that Eliot is actually describing the effect of a book, rather than a person. And in this case, it is a book that seems as if it were a person, as if it contained Carlyle's spirit within its covers and could have the same effect.

This fusion of object and spirit is consistent with Eliot's stated goals as a writer, which she describes as grappling with the difficulty of accomplishing their merger. In the same 1866 letter to her friend Harrison, mentioned above, she notes: "[I] have gone through again and again the severe effort of trying to make certain ideas thoroughly incarnate, as if they had revealed themselves to me first in the flesh and not in the spirit."[66] This line of thought in Eliot's writing found its clearest expression in her translations of Spinoza, but it was also an important part of Feuerbach's examination of God as a fetishistic projection of human feeling. And in this second work, in addition to a philosophy of religion, we find an account of the psychological mechanism through which ideas become conceived as material objects. "All religious cosmogonies are products of the imagination," and this fact leads to the suggestion that there is value in harnessing that human tendency to project feelings onto imaginary objects, making them seem alive.[67]

> And the task of philosophy in investigating this subject is to comprehend the relation of the imagination to the reason,—the genesis of the image by means of which an object of thought becomes an object of sense, of feeling. (81)

Feuerbach's emphasis on the means of transforming thoughts into objects is precisely what Eliot means about making "ideas thoroughly incarnate." There are artistic reasons why a realist novelist, in particular, would want to comprehend this subject, to learn in detail how ideas can be attached to images that seem to take on the solidity of objects of sense and feeling. Within that genesis lies the psychological process through which representation becomes incarnate, taking on the appearance and solidity of flesh. Understanding how humans unintentionally generate such images is the task of philosophy, but it must also be the task of a writer interested in the intentional creation of images that can draw upon that preexisting psychological mechanism. Feuerbach's philosophy thus holds the promise for the artist of making "ideas thoroughly incarnate" through a better understanding of the machinery of fetishism, and this is ultimately the promise that Eliot labors over in her writing. In Feuerbach she found much more than a realist's voice with which to critique the fetishism of everyday life. She also discovered a means of tapping into the power of that ubiquitous fetishism and putting it to use in her own realist mode of representation.

⁓〰⁓

The fetishistic goal of realism—to create an object that succeeds by seeming to come to life—gives it a counterintuitive resemblance to the discourse of fantasy, that narrative mode familiarly hinging on a fetishistic dream. In Carlo Lorenzini's *Pinocchio*, published in 1883, a stick of wood talks back to the carpenter Gepetto, as he transforms it into a puppet. No sooner are its legs carved than the disobedient puppet runs out of the carpenter's shop and into the street, pursued by the fiery-tempered Gepetto. The puppet is quickly surrounded by the bustle of midday city life. At first astonished at the spectacle, the crowd soon sympathizes with the wooden boy and, fearing its fate at the hands of Gepetto, helps him to escape. The scene, as illustrated by Attilio Mussino, shows the wooden boy in the middle of the social hodgepodge of everyday, commercial life (see fig. 1). The puppet is the same size as the boys who chase him, and he adopts a posture of alarm as dogs bark and an angry Gepetto gesticulates close behind. The crowd's reactions are as varied as the people: a large lady with a shawl points and laughs, a scowling gentleman in a cape waves his cane, a child leans forward to touch the puppet. Mussino's image is of a particular type of artifact, a piece of wood that is shaped as a boy, but is clearly yet a piece of wood, that is vibrantly engaged with the social world of everyday life, while exhibiting qualities that have gone beyond the control of its maker.

In this illustration, we can read a parable about Eliot's realism. The image of the object that comes to life in the middle of the crowd is a literalization of the dream of the realist author. In this dream, her own products, carved delicately and laboriously into "the nearest thing to life," are immersed in the social, and, like Pinocchio, they inspire wrath in some and humor in others. Pinocchio calls forth

Fig. 1. Detail from an illustration by Attilio Mussino, for Carlo Collodi, *Le avventure di Pinocchio* (1911).

the sympathy of the crowd, in the end, which protects the wooden boy from Geppeto's wrath, and in this we see the same moral transformation that the realist novelist hopes her artifact will produce in her audience.

Pinocchio is an unambiguous fetish, a fairy-tale for primitives and children alike—the two conjoined Victorian figures of unculture—which no self-respecting, "civilized" adult would confuse with the real. The Victorian realist novel, on the other hand, is a more complex cultural object. But by understanding its sibling relationship with Pinocchio, we are able to see the paradox of Eliot's realism. We can formulate that paradox in simple terms: realism's effect depends on the primitive fetishism that it critiques. Eliot's imagined readership, we might say, is always in the position of the Ilfracombe native—a subject of "primitive provincial life," who tends to invest inert objects with an independent existence. This tendency is unmasked as a social problem by the novelist, who assists her readers to develop beyond the superstitions and prejudices endemic to primitive fetishism. However, the novelist simultaneously appeals to the willingness of her readers to fetishize objects to get them to believe that what they read is, in fact, real. Only in this way can they be affected by her social realism, in the manner she describes. In the novel's content, it operates as an antidote to fetishism, while in its formal technique, it exploits fetishism in the service of the realist mimetic effect.

To note this paradox is not to carp about Victorian realism. It is a means of indicating how Eliot's fictional representations of uncultured life are complicated by the role of primitivism within her theory of realism, so that they appeal to the same tendency they seek to correct. In this respect, Eliot is no more and no less self-contradicting than the other Victorian writers examined here, all of whom engaged the topic of fetishism in a serious manner. There is no reason to suppose that, in terms of the fetishistic triangle, one subject cannot simultaneously occupy both positions, fetish and critic. In fact, because of the fetish dialectic, there is every reason to suppose that it is impossible to occupy only one of the two. Once we accept, as a given, that the realist novel is going to have to be both fetish and its critique, then Eliot's complicity is unavoidable. The only thing that matters is the remarkable self-awareness she brings to the problem of ambivalence in writing about fetishism—her acknowledgment that fetishism is both a problem, as social presence, and a power, as aesthetic device. The skill with which she manages to navigate those two contradictory uses should merit our own, unambivalent wonder.

4

Edward Tylor's Science

When Matthew Arnold and George Eliot refer to culture, they describe an ideal. Culture is a desideratum, the "one thing needful" to improve the existing condition of society. Rather than "things as they are," culture gestures toward "things as they might be." As Arnold's prescriptive theory of culture was first appearing in periodical form in the 1860s, his contemporary, Edward B. Tylor, was writing his most well-known work, laying out the descriptive theory of culture that became identified with anthropology.[1] *Primitive Culture: Researches into the Development of Mythology, Philosophy, Religion, Language, Art, and Custom* was published in two volumes in 1871, two years after *Culture and Anarchy* appeared. It begins with the definition of culture credited with establishing anthropology as a science:

> Culture or Civilization, taken in its wide ethnographic sense, is that complex whole which includes knowledge, belief, art, morals, law, custom, and any other capabilities and habits acquired by man as a member of society.[2]

Tylor's use of *culture* and *civilization* as synonyms suggests how distinct his concept of culture is from our contemporary sense.[3] For Tylor, culture develops through a regular sequence, beginning with the complete absence of culture, followed by the three stages of savagery, barbarism, and finally civilization proper. His use of *civilization,* rather than *culture,* in the titles of two of his other anthropological works reflects the degree to which he saw the terms as synonymous.

Initially, Arnold's and Tylor's definitions seem similar because both focus on culture as a psychological quality, not a state of material development. Tylor refers to learned capabilities and habits, while Arnold defines culture as existing "in an inward condition of the mind and spirit, not in an outward set of circumstances"

(*CP*, 5:94–95). However, while both locate culture in an internal state, they make opposite connections between that state and the social world in which people exist. Tylor's culture is "acquired by man as a member of society," that is, as an internalized product of the world without. Arnold specifically excludes any "outward set of circumstances," suggesting that culture comes from within. The two types of culture emphasize opposite roles for social determinism, a force that is central to Tylor's culture but anathema to Arnold's, in which the paradigmatic cultural type is that of the extrasocial alien. For Arnold, culture is a form of transcendent morality, but for Tylor, morality develops through the process of social evolution, not apart from it.[4]

Arnold prescribes cultural values; Tylor describes cultural facts. In actual practice, this binary distinction is oversimplified. Arnold's culture is also a description of his own social values and of the middle-class commercial ideology he naturalized as "common sense." Similarly, Tylor's nominally descriptive approach contains more than a hint of idealized schematics masquerading as factual description. Thus, the distinction between prescription and description is not absolute. In fact, it applies less to the cultural practice of either the humanities or social sciences than it does to the different ways the two discourses think about themselves and the different rhetorical strategies they deploy to represent their findings, with Arnoldians appealing to idealized truth, Tylorites to empirical fact.

Tylor worked in the era of the armchair anthropologist, when a division of labor existed between the practical ethnographer, who got dirty in the field, and the theoretical ethnologist, who, stereotypically, analyzed ethnographic data from the comfort of a study in Victorian Britain.[5] This may account for Tylor's emphasis on solving the problem of cultural bias in ethnographic observation. He notes how subjectivity colors the observer's reports, and he also complains that, even when a behavior or belief is accurately recorded, its meaning is often misconstrued. No one today would see Tylor himself as successful in overcoming subjective bias; in fact, he has been regularly held up as an example of precisely the opposite. However, for this very reason, his interest in the problem of accuracy and his efforts to counteract bias in ethnography present us with a conundrum that goes to the essence of his project.[6] How could a writer so clearly preoccupied with avoiding bias also be so patently guilty of it?

We could dismiss the question of bias here with an easy answer: bias is inescapable. So it is, but this response proves overly reductive when the problem of fetishism is involved. Like Arnold, Tylor also defined culture in relation to an assumed primitive condition marked by fetishism. In itself, this is not surprising. He worked firmly within the tradition of Comte's assumptions for most of his life; notwithstanding his novel substitution of the term *animism*, Tylor's first stage of culture is a mirror image of Comte's primitive fetishism. However, the problem of bias in Tylor's method leaves it in the unenviable position of recapitulating the psychological subjectivism he claims to find in primitive culture. "Mr. Tylor's Science," to use Max Müller's term, is an example of a self-defining fetishism in which Tylor, while looking at primitive fetishism and considering the problem of looking, is also talking about himself and the limitations of his own science. In other words, Tylor's scientific anthropology bears a marked resemblance to the primitive culture it describes. Furthermore, by considering his scientific method in detail, it becomes clear that this self-reflexivity—far from being an accidental byproduct of writing on fetishism—is an element he acknowledges as necessary to cultural science.

Tylor was one of a minority of prominent anthropologists in his generation whose family had manufacturing backgrounds.[7] He was born in 1832 into the Quaker family of Harriet Skipper and Joseph Tylor, who owned a successful brass foundry.[8] Educated at a school in Tottenham run by the Society of Friends, Tylor's Quaker status made him ineligible to enter Oxbridge, and so, at the age of sixteen, he went to work in the family business. He began showing signs of consumption around 1852, and, in accordance with medical advice, he traveled to a warmer climate, touring part of the United States in 1855 before visiting Havana. There in 1856 he met Henry Christy, a collector of ethnographic artifacts and a fellow Quaker, and together they made a four-month expedition to Mexico to visit Aztec ruins, sparking Tylor's interest in ethnography. He returned to England and in 1858 married Anna Fox. This turned out to be a fortuitous partnership, as Andrew Lang notes in his 1907 tribute to Tylor, whom he describes as "favoured by the . . . long companionship of the lady who shares his interest and aids his researches."[9] When signs of illness reappeared, he convalesced on the French Mediterranean, at Cannes, where he organized his observations on Mexican life into a manuscript, published in 1861 as *Anahuac*. He read widely in ethnography and linguistics, two interrelated fields, leading him to the study of sign language at the Berlin Deaf-and-Dumb Institute. He saw such "gesture-language" as offering significant evidence of the earliest forms of language (*PC*, 1:164). His reputation as a major voice in the study of primitive cultures was established when he published the results of his further studies in 1865, *Researches into the Early History of Mankind and the Development of Civilization*.

Primitive Culture came six years later, and it was followed by a new wave of academic recognition. In a case of poetic justice, Oxford awarded him the honorary degree of Doctor of Civil Law in 1875. In 1883, he was made Keeper of the University Museum at Oxford, then Reader in Anthropology the following year.[10] He became Professor of Anthropology in 1896, the first holder of an academic chair in the discipline. His last completed book was *Anthropology: An Introduction to the Study of Man and Civilization* (1881), an overview of the "new science" for the "heavily-pressed student" that became anthropology's introductory textbook.[11]

Tylor hoped to establish anthropology on a professional footing that would make it impossible to confuse the new science with the haphazard practices of the amateur past. Above all, this meant that he had to define the discipline's object of study by delineating the boundaries of the field. At the same time, he also had to create and justify the most basic processes governing the collection and analysis of ethnographic information that his science would use as its primary data. These were his basic goals in *Primitive Culture*. The first chapter is titled "The Science of Culture," and there he lays out his basic program. He acknowledges that culture as a whole is too complex to study scientifically, which has led to the collapse of many previous attempts. The subject "is as yet only susceptible of divided study. The present comparatively narrow argument on the development of culture at any rate avoids this greatest perplexity. It takes cognizance principally of knowledge, art, and custom, and indeed only very partial cognizance within this field, the vast range of physical, political, social, and ethical considerations being left all but untouched" (*PC*, 1:32). By focusing on distinct segments of the ungovernable culture concept, he immediately makes its study seem more feasible. The problems presented by ethnographic data are further reduced through a second narrowing process, one designed to tame the mountains of extant ethnographic material. Even a single traveler's account might include a plethora of information on particular aspects of one society's life: notes on diet, clothing, speech, or weapons, for example. While such accounts contain potentially valuable scientific data, digging factual nuggets from the mass of available ethnographies and discerning valid details from fanciful embellishment is a difficult task. Tylor defines the problem as one of taxonomy. He argues, "the ethnographer's business is to classify such details," separating them into categories by type; after classifying the separate parts, the scientist could begin the process of analysis, by "making out their distribution in geography and history, and the relations which exist among them" (*PC*, 1:8). He detaches fragments of a culture from their historical surroundings and considers them within the imaginary context of all objects of the same type in all societies combined. These global categories are the basic unit of study in his science of culture, rather than specific groups of people. Weapons, textile arts, myths, tools, rites and ceremonies—each is considered separately and subdivided into further variations (type of weapon, theme of myth). "To the ethnographer the bow and arrow is a species, the habit of flattening children's skulls is a species, the practice of reckoning numbers by tens is a species. . . . Just as the catalogue of all the species of plants and animals of a district represents its Flora and Fauna, so the list of all the items of the general life of a people represents that whole which we call its culture" (*PC*, 1:8). The botanist has plants; the anthropologist has objects, behaviors, and beliefs.[12]

Objects can be validly compared in this way because, for Tylor, there is ultimately only one culture, shared by all races and societies. His Quaker upbringing gave him a strong commitment to the doctrine of human unity, and thus he holds it necessary "to eliminate considerations of . . . races of man, and to treat mankind as homogenous in nature, though placed in different grades of civilization" (*PC*, 1:7). Tylor nonetheless sees himself as a relativist who accepts cultural differences, but the differences are variations on an underlying similarity, like different sets of clothes on the same person.[13] His science of culture is thus precisely what it sounds like: the study of *culture* in the universal singular, not *cultures* in the plural. Nowhere in his work does the word *cultures* appear.[14]

While universal, culture is not uniform. It exists in time, developing the way individuals develop from infancy to maturity, with the earlier stages inferior to the later stages. Rejecting degeneration in favor of progressive development, he notes that: "the general tenour of the evidence goes far to justify the view that on the whole the civilized man is not only wiser and more capable than the savage, but also better and happier, and that the barbarian stands between" (*PC*, 1:31). As this remark illustrates, Tylor prefers the older terminology of Montesquieu to that of Comte for the three stages, but the sequence of stages is in fact uniform and progressive, as in Comte.[15]

Tylor also needs to explain how and why so many similarities appear to exist between cultures at different times and at widely different points of the globe. In his earlier *Researches*, he outlined the possibilities:

> Three ways are open, independent invention, inheritance from ancestors in a distant region, transmission from one race to another; but between these three ways the choice is commonly a difficult one.[16]

At this point, he clearly favors inheritance and transmission caused by contact between societies, but in *Primitive Culture* he is more committed to the other possibility, independent invention.[17] For instance, in discussing language he challenges the received wisdom about why the first words of children in the most far-flung societies commonly resemble the syllables *pa* and *ma* (*PC*, 1:223). Linguists generally viewed this as evidence that the languages had common origins, an explanation predicated on cultural inheritance or transmission. Instead, Tylor turns to physiology: "children's language," he argues, has a "common character . . . due to its concerning itself with the limited set of ideas in which little children are interested, and expressing these ideas by the limited set of articulations suited to the child's first attempts to talk" (*PC*, 1:225–26). Physical similarity, and not cultural interaction, is the cause. This explanation assumes independent invention, rather than transmission, illustrating, "the recurrence of a similar but independent process of mental development among various races of man" (*PC*, 1:247).

Independent invention became a cornerstone of British evolutionary anthropology. It rested on the further assumption of psychological universality: "the uniformity which so largely pervades civilization may be ascribed, in great measure, to the uniform action of uniform causes . . ." (*PC*, 1:1). The doctrine of psychic unity assumed that human psychology is universal, operating through "imaginative processes recurring with the evident regularity of mental law" (*PC*, 1:282). *Primitive Culture* includes examples of all three causes, and it acknowledges the difficulty of distinguishing, in any particular case, "how far this wide distribution is due to independent growth in several regions, how far to conveyance from race to race, and how far to ancestral inheritance," but the first of the three options is more frequently appealed to than either of the others (*PC*, 1:103–4).

Tylor's theory was of a piece with the other evolutionary developments of mid-century: the discovery of geological strata, the newly found fossil record, the expansion of time. In an 1889 paper delivered to the Anthropological Institute, "On Method," Tylor makes the comparison himself, and he gives his clearest summary of the key elements of evolutionary anthropology:

> the institutions of man are as distinctly stratified as the earth on which he lives. They succeed each other in series substantially uniform over the globe, independent of what seem the comparatively superficial differences of race and language, but shaped by similar human nature acting through successively changed conditions in savage, barbaric, and civilized life.[18]

One culture, one progression, one mind. These three assumptions underlie his comparisons of distant cultures, his claims about the standing of each in the scale of cultural evolution, and his understanding of a uniform human psychology.

With these assumptions in place, Tylor was able to deploy the comparative method as a technique for validating ethnographic data. The investigator could minimize the possibility of unreliability by looking for corroborative evidence elsewhere. As Tylor explains, "If two independent visitors to different countries . . . agree in describing some analogous art or rite or myth among the people they have visited, it becomes difficult or impossible to set down such correspondence to accident or willful fraud" (*PC*, 1:9). The quality of data from one part of the world is validated when similar data exists in different parts of the world, because of psychic unity. Reports of unverifiable beliefs or behaviors can then be filtered out, as observational bias or some other form of unreliability. Tylor's comparative method was not a straightforward cross-cultural comparison; because of the universality of social evolution, contemporary societies were comparable to groups from earlier stages of human existence, much as they had been in de Brosses. Nonetheless, for all its flaws, his comparative method began as a serious attempt to correct the crippling subjectivism in ethnography, and it grew logically from his basic assumption about the universality of culture.[19] Later, when that assumption fell, the entire project of evolutionary anthropology went with it.

The largest portion of *Researches* is devoted to problems of language, and this investigation continues in *Primitive Culture*. Tylor was interested in language as a critical element in the study of culture, but he also understood language to be a problem within the methodology of cultural science itself.[20] Peckham points out that "[h]e laid the foundation for the very modern realization that the terms 'culture' and 'meaning' are interchangeable; this was the long-term consequence of sensitivity in the beginning with the problem of language."[21] This interest in the epistemology of cultural signs led to a remarkable subtlety in classifying observed behaviors, but these subtleties also placed new, extraordinary, even impossible demands on ethnographers in the field. Nowhere is this problem more evident than in his system for differentiating the various types of animist belief.

He defined *animism* as broadly as possible as a term, calling it simply "the belief in Spiritual Beings." [22] His concept, he notes, is a modification of Comte's primitive fetishism:

> The President de Brosses, a most original thinker of the last century, struck by the descriptions of the African worship of material and terrestrial objects, introduced the word Fétichisme as a general descriptive term, and since then it has obtained great currency by Comte's use of it to denote a general theory of primitive religion, in which external objects are regarded as animated by a life analogous to man's.[23]

He referenced Comte throughout the study and honored de Brosses with a title-page epigraph. Tylor had much in common with both of these predecessors, and in practice his examples of animism could have served Comte equally well as instances of primitive fetishism. In this respect, his modification of the Positivist vision of early human culture was less original than his treatment of the term *fetishism* itself. For Comte, fetishism was a broadly defined category covering a wide variety of different beliefs in the supernatural qualities of objects. Tylor

reassigned that generic function to animism, while at the same time narrowing
fetishism to a gaunt specter of its former self:

> It seems to me, however, more convenient to use the word Animism for
> the doctrine of spirits in general, and to confine the word Fetishism to
> that subordinate department which it properly belongs to, namely, the
> doctrine of spirits embodied in, or attached to, or conveying influence
> through, certain material objects. (*PC*, 2:144)

This passage can lead to confusion. It mentions "the doctrine of spirits in general," but in Tylor's terms this phrase has a unique meaning, referring to only one
of two types of animistic belief, the *doctrine of souls* and the *doctrine of spirits*. The
first refers to beliefs that a body has an immaterial component, or *soul,* without
which the body will die. By contrast, a *spirit* is a free-floating entity belonging to
no particular body or object; it may take up residence in one, but it is not an
organic part of it. In the first, the object has a given soul, while in the second, the
object is occupied by a spirit with which it has no intrinsic connection. A soul is
an essential element of the object, while a spirit exists apart from it. Thus, when
he subordinates fetishism to "the doctrine of spirits in general," he makes its use
inappropriate for all cases where objects are inhabited by an essential soul, confin-
ing its application to the smaller category of beliefs about objects invested with
life involving an independent spirit.

Both de Brosses and Comte labeled any belief that an object was alive as
fetishism. But for Tylor, fetishism was a particular kind of aliveness, one in which
the animating shade came from outside, rather than inside the object. "Theoretically, we can distinguish the notion of the object acting as it were by the will and
force of its own proper soul or spirit, from the notion of some foreign spirit entering its substance or acting on it from without, and so using it as a body or instrument" (*PC*, 2:153). The first belief is no longer an example of fetishism but
instead illustrates the animistic belief in an *object soul,* Tylor's term for objects that
were seen as alive within the doctrine of the soul rather than the spirit. The
North American Ojibwa "were of the opinion that not only men and beasts have
souls, but inorganic things, such as kettles, &c.," and this illustrates "the doctrine
of object-souls," because the soul is intrinsic to the kettle (*PC*, 1:478). Compare
this to the Brazilian "maraca," which was "no mere rattle, but the receptacle of a
spirit that spoke from it when shaken" and so was an "eminent fetish," because
the spirit had taken up residence in the object (*PC*, 2:154). Both kettle and
maraca were perceived as alive, and in Comte's terms, both were fetishes. But
here, the former is not a fetish but an example of the object soul, an object that
moves through its own power, like a philosophical subject; by contrast, the fetish

is a passive object colonized by an external power. For the same reason, he classified totems—animals inhabited by the shade of a divine ancestor—as a type of
fetish, rather than an object soul.[24] The primitive world still remains one in
which rocks, trees, rivers, and sticks are animated by supernatural life, but we now
have two distinct categories of animation, and Comte's label of *primitive fetishism*
has become too general to suit the more particular world of Tylor's primitive animism and its refined typology of spiritual beliefs.[25]

While the distinction may be clear enough in theory, it is difficult in practice
for an observer to differentiate between the kettle and the maraca. Tylor's revision
requires the investigator to bring a heightened level of attention to the psychological state of the primitive group under question. Observing a case of apparent
tree worship, how should the field worker ascertain whether the tree is a fetish, as
would earlier have been the case, or an animist object soul? Tylor instructs the
observer to look for evidence of the worshipper's subjective state. "To class an
object as a fetish, demands explicit statement that a spirit is considered as embodied in it or acting through it or communicating by it, or at least that the people it
belongs to do habitually think this of such objects" (*PC*, 2:145). In this case, the
worshipper conveniently spells out the nature of the spirit, making classification
relatively easy. Where this is not the case, other evidence must be present: "or it
must be shown that the object is treated as having personal consciousness and
power, is talked with, worshipped, prayed to, sacrificed to, petted or ill-treated
with reference to its past or future behaviour to its votaries" (*PC*, 2:145). In the
second instance, observation is restricted to external behavior, which he describes.
However, here problems arise. These behaviors describe fetish worship, but they
are equally applicable to the worship of object souls. To note that an object is seen
to have "personal consciousness and power" does not differentiate the two types
of animist object worship. As we saw earlier, Tylor points out that the practices of
fetishism and idolatry can appear identical, so that "an image may be, even to two
votaries kneeling side by side before it, two utterly different things" (*PC*, 2:169).
The same logic applies to the worship of the fetish and object soul. The only distinction lies in the mind of the worshipper—the quality attributed to the relationship between material object and immaterial shade. As a consequence, in
ethnographic observation everything depends on ascertaining the unobservable
characteristics of primitive psychology.

Determining that mental state poses a litany of problems. The explicit statement demanded by Tylor's directions requires observers in the field to navigate
the uncertainty of the worshipper's self-representation. Is the speaker sincere or,
for any number of plausible reasons, deliberately misleading the investigator?
Linguistic differences come into play, since the assessment is to be based on
either an observer's translation from the native tongue or on the worshipper's

command of a European tongue. Both are problematic, but the latter case is further complicated by the likelihood that the local speaker has assimilated European beliefs along with the European language, and so is no longer genuinely representative of local culture. These multiple difficulties—by now familiar to every student of anthropology—leave the determination in the field of whether an object is or is not a fetish to float on the murky waters of subjective facts, linguistic confusion, and cultural contamination. To his credit, Tylor recognized all of these problems. Historians describe him as particularly active in advocating more controlled observational techniques and academic training for field workers, so that data gathering might become more professional.[26] But such indeterminacy also placed greater demands on the anthropologist in the study, where the question of interpreting ethnographic data takes on an entirely new importance.

⸺⦾⸺

Tylor's interest in the problems of language served him well in his work as an armchair anthropologist, where the interpretation of documents took precedence over firsthand observation. Because he worked primarily with the written word, analyzing reports and writing up his findings, he was in effect a textual anthropologist.[27] We can graphically conceptualize the central place of textuality in Tylor's science by briefly contrasting his research procedure to that of two ethnographers from two later generations, one at twenty-five years distance, the other at fifty: Mary Kingsley and Bronislaw Malinowski.

Kingsley was a self-taught ethnographer and talented writer whose research in Africa brought her to the attention of professional anthropologists, like James Frazer, and led to an active lecturing career in Britain on African topics.[28] Given her popularity and outsider status, she provides an example of how the ground for anthropology was shifting without regard for the obscure, theoretical debates of the leading ethnologists. In *Travels in West Africa* (1897), she praises Tylor as the "greatest of Ethnologists," describing *Primitive Culture* as a book to be read "until you know it by heart."[29] But she also reflected a new insistence on the importance of fieldwork and the need for anthropology to move out of the study. She traveled with small groups of traders, living largely on local food and sleeping in local huts. This method gave her a more discrete access to villagers, who, while unaccustomed to the large caravans accompanying ethnographic expeditions, were quite used to the traders passing through, and so she was able to talk with villagers in a more relaxed setting. Kingsley wanted to understand how the world appeared to Africans and how they organized their experiences through the magic of fetishism. She called her travels, "Stalking the wild West African idea," and described herself as one "whose fixed desire was to study fetish," which in her hands became a synonym for West African culture (430, 5). The greatest difficulty in this pursuit was the European mind. "Unless you can make it pliant enough to follow the African idea step by step, however much care you may take, you will not bag your game."[30]

Kingsley was writing at the point in time when scientific fieldwork came to dominate professional anthropology. In the 1898 Cambridge Anthropological Expedition to Torres Straits, the distinction between fieldworker and theorist collapsed, as specialists went on their own expedition to gather data, a practice that soon became widespread.[31] Members of the expedition went on to train some of the most prominent anthropologists of the following generation, including Bronislaw Malinowski. In *Argonauts of the West Pacific* (1922), he explained the method of observation that was followed by subsequent generations of anthropologists. Malinowski was a student of one expedition member, Charles Seligman, but his major inspiration was a 1912 article written by another, William H. R. Rivers, on the disturbing effects of anthropologists in the field on the behavior of the people they were trying to observe. Like Kingsley, he sought an "understanding of real native mentality or behaviour," although he studied the "Kula," or tribal trading system in Southern New Guinea, rather than West Africa. Unlike her, he rejected "fetichism" as a "meaningless" term, preferring Tylor's "animism."[32] Malinowski went considerably further with the protocols of direct observation, spelling out more rigorous demands for data collection than Kingsley had been able to practice. "There is all the difference," he argues, "between a sporadic plunging into the company of natives, and being really in contact with them" (7). The ethnographer must "put himself in good conditions of work, that is, in the main, to live without other white men, right among the natives," in order to develop a "natural intercourse" with the villager (6). By this means, "you learn to know him, and you become familiar with his customs and beliefs far better than when he is a paid, and often bored, informant" (7). Participant observation gives the ethnographer access to the small but significant events of daily family life in the village, and it makes possible a new degree of accuracy: "It must be remembered that as the natives saw me constantly every day, they ceased to be interested or alarmed, or made self-conscious by my presence, and I ceased to be a disturbing element in the tribal life which I was to study, altering it by my very approach, as always happens with a new-comer to every savage community" (7–8). Being "in touch with the natives," he argues, is "the preliminary condition of being able to carry on successful field work" (8).

Malinowski in New Guinea was a very long way from Tylor in his Victorian study. The sharpest contrast of all appears in Malinowki's insistence that the ethnographer's sources "are not embodied in fixed, material documents, but in the behaviour and in the memory of living men" (3). While Tylor's method had little in common with Kingsley's or Malinowski's, their objectives were similar; like them, Tylor's goal was to understand the distinct psychology of others. If, unlike Kingsley and Malinowski, he failed to differentiate between cultures, he nonetheless drew critical attention to the serious problem of interpreting ethnographic data, a problem that his successors continued to address. For this, Malinowski praises him: "In Ethnology the early efforts of Bastian, Tylor, Morgan, the German Völkerpsychologen have remoulded the older crude information of travelers, missionaries, etc., and have shown us the importance of applying deeper conceptions and discarding crude and misleading ones" (9).

Because his materials, with few exceptions, were strictly textual, his hunt was qualitatively different from that of Kingsley or Malinowski. Sifting through centuries of ethnographic accounts, he looked for conceptual patterns in the form of analogies that linked details together, and in this his interpretations relied on an innovative hermeneutic method. While not a literary critic in Matthew Arnold's sense, he was nonetheless a critic of writing, and an exceptionally astute and cautious one, at that. His method was deeply flawed—among other problems, it injected subjectivism into the process—but his aim was to devise a consistent, defensible epistemology for making sense of the accumulated mass of ethnographic data. Interpretive method was the *porro unum necessarium* of the new cultural science, even as psychic unity was its foundational assumption.

His technique is spelled out in an extensive section of *Primitive Culture* on the interpretation of mythology.[33] That method is, quite literally, a poetics of mythology. The goal of interpretation is to uncover the hidden poetic meaning in which myth originates. Like Vico, he believes that "[s]avages have been for untold ages, and still are, living in the myth-making stage of the human mind," and their myths are the only "true poetry, and not its quaint affected imitation" (*PC*, 1:283, 1:316). Savagery's characteristic is "the belief in the animation of all nature," and in that "primitive mental state where man recognizes in every detail of his world the operation of personal life and will," the facts of daily experience are readily transfigured into myths of the sun, moon, stars, animals, creation, and other reflections of nature.[34] To the primitive, such myths were not a "mere expressive form of speech, like a modern poet's fanciful metaphor," because primitives lacked the capacity for figurative uses of language, as Comte argued (*PC*, 1:289). To illustrate, he explains, "When the Apache Indian pointed to the sky and asked the white man, 'Do you not believe that God, this Sun (que Dios, este Sol) sees what we do and punishes us when it is evil?' it is impossible to say that the savage was talking in rhetorical simile. There was something in the Homeric contemplation of the living personal Hêlios, that was more and deeper than metaphor" (*PC*, 1:290). Rather than figurative speech, the myths are reifications because they are intended as statements of fact:

> Analogies which are but fancy to us were to men of past ages reality.
> They could see the flame licking its yet undevoured prey with tongues of
> fire, or the serpent gliding along the waving sword from hilt to point. . . .
> Men to whom these were living thoughts had no need of the school-
> master and his rules of composition, his injunctions to use metaphor
> cautiously, and to take continual care to make all similes consistent. The
> similes of the old bards and orators were consistent, because they
> seemed to see and hear and feel them: what we call poetry was to them
> real life . . . . (*PC*, 1:297)

For Tylor, mythology was the way primitives accounted for the chaotic experience of everyday life; it shaped "the familiar facts of daily life into imaginary histories of their own cause and origin, childlike answers to those world-old
questions of whence and why . . ." (*PC*, 1:405). When so understood by the
modern analyst, myth reveals itself as a historical record of the mind, "representing in its extreme abuse that tendency to clothe every thought in a concrete
shape" (*PC*, 1:408). Rather than an individual mind, however, myth represents
the early stage of human psychological evolution. It provides "a means of tracing
the history of laws of mind" generally, because mythology was the realism of the
primitive (*PC*, 1:274).

As culture developed, animism was left behind, and the creativity of myth-
making disappeared. Older myths persisted, but they lost "their first consciousness of origin" as their meaning faded (*PC*, 1:366). Transformed into empty
stories, they "become centres round which floating fancies cluster," and as a
result, "their sense becomes obscure and corrupt" (*PC*, 1:366). Barbarism initiated
the heroic stage of myth, in which the ancient stories were rewritten as allegories
for moral and ethical messages, "the allegorical growth as it were parasitic on an
older trunk of myth without a moral" (*PC*, 1:409). Thus, while myth originated as
poetic realism, it was later corrupted as moral allegory. The anthropologist's task
is therefore a daunting one that bears striking resemblance to the central goal of
nineteenth-century textual criticism: to find a way past later corruptions to
uncover the original "text."[35]

The same assumptions Tylor brought to the problem of myth interpretation
inform his primitive semiotic. Myths are one example of the continuing presence
in advanced culture of *survivals*, remnants from an earlier stage of cultural development. "These are processes, customs, opinions, and so forth, which have been
carried on by force of habit into a new state of society different from that in
which they had their original home, and they thus remain as proofs and examples
of an older condition of culture out of which a newer has been evolved" (*PC*,

1:16). He quotes Comte's assertion that "no conception can be understood except through its history" and then incorporates the principle into the interpretation of survivals (*PC*, 1:19). "Original meaning dies out gradually, each generation leaves fewer and fewer to bear it in mind, till it falls out of popular memory, and in after-days ethnography has to attempt, more of less successfully, to restore it by piecing together lines of isolated or forgotten facts" (*PC*, 2:110–11). Survivals are signifiers that persist out of habit or tradition long after they have lost their signified: an "idea, the meaning of which has perished for ages, may continue to exist simply because it has existed" (*PC*, 1:71). Anthropology's task is to restore that lost meaning to the idea. Traces exist in the quotidian elements of contemporary life: popular phrases, children's games, familiar rhymes, holiday traditions, jokes, baby talk—the ubiquitous features of the everyday.[36] Survivals matter to the anthropologist because they constitute "landmarks in the course of culture. . . . On the strength of these survivals, it becomes possible to declare that the civilization of the people they are observed among must have been derived from an earlier state, in which the proper home and meaning of these things are to be found; and thus collections of such facts are to be worked as mines of historic knowledge" (*PC*, 1:71). But what does it mean to labor in these mines?

First, it means looking for things that do not make sense. Reasoning deductively and making a problematic conceptual leap, Tylor argues that since survivals have lost their original meaning, "[i]t seems scarcely too much to assert, once for all, that meaningless customs must be survivals. . ." (*PC*, 1:94). Drinking one's health, holding the month of May unlucky for weddings, phrases like "he bought a pig in a poke"—all are nonsensical but customary traditions, and that absence of meaning gestures toward their present value as cultural landmarks. Anthropology recognizes in insignificance a lost significance, and so it "has to attempt . . . to restore it by piecing together lines of isolated or forgotten facts. Children's sports, popular sayings, absurd customs, may be practically unimportant, but are not philosophically insignificant . . ." (*PC*, 1:110–11). While studying frivolity, the analyst has "in such inquiries continual reason to be thankful for fools," for in the folly of custom lies the wisdom of the past (*PC*, 1:156). "It is only when men fail to see the line of connexion in events, that they are prone to fall upon the notions of arbitrary impulses, causeless freaks, chance and nonsense and indefinite unaccountability" (*PC*, 1:19). For Tylor, insignificance matters, because it implies a link to the primitive realism of the past, persisting as a signifier that has lost its signified. Through the work of the anthropologist, that original meaning can be rediscovered, and with it will come a better understanding of the mind that saw the world in such unfamiliar terms.

Tylor's interpretive method has an evident similarity to later ideas in Freud's method. Both pursue a hidden level of consciousness in the mind. Both place unusual stress on the significance of insignificance.[37] However, Tylor's psychological model is not that of Freud's dynamic psychology but of its predecessor, the nineteenth-century fascination with a second, independent level of psychological existence—a second mind—such as that inferred from the mesmeric trance, somnambulism, reflexive actions, spiritualism, and dual or multiple personalities.[38] This was not a dynamic model, in which experiences in waking life shape an unconscious that, in turn, influences conscious behaviors. The nineteenth-century model was more unidirectional, positing a second level of consciousness that could influence waking life but was not itself affected by conscious experiences. Perhaps the most unidirectional was the theory of the nervous reflex; Marshall Hall identified it with an evolutionary survival mechanism over which the conscious mind had no control or influence.[39] Hypnotism and mesmerism were more dynamic than this, as the phenomenon of posthypnotic suggestion demonstrated that an action controlled by the hidden mind could manifest in a waking state. Still, until late in the century, connections between the second mind and childhood experiences of the individual were tenuous, and they competed with explanations premised on anti-individualist traits inherited from the distant past, as in degeneration and evolution.

In his theory of survivals, Tylor posits another version of this Victorian story, one closely related to the second mind but that inheres in the psychological register of culture, rather than in the body. Given his assumption of psychic unity, the importance of survivals extends well beyond their connection to any particular lost culture. The mind is constituted by the same natural law in the Australian aborigine, the German peasant, and the English gentleman, so the study of survivals is ultimately an examination of the most basic facts of human psychology. "The thing that has been will be; and we are to study savages and old nations to learn the laws that under new circumstances are working for good or ill in our development" (*PC*, 1:159). Survivals connect modern and savage cultures, so ethnologists are in no way "wasting their hours in the satisfaction of a frivolous curiosity," as antiquarians or folklorists had done (*PC*, 1:159). On the contrary, from the most trifling facts of modern life, the ethnologist "tries to elicit general laws of culture. . ." (*PC*, 1:158). Moving from the logic of myth interpretation to the interpretation of survivals, Tylor describes contemporary life in inverted terms: what seems least significant is therefore the most significant. The details of Victorian culture are so rich with meaning that nothing can be passed over; nothing is accidental or spurious, and everything unintelligible is newly freighted with clues to the most hidden aspects of human nature. Rather than study the psychology of the individual, the evolutionary anthropologist studies the psychology of the species. For Tylor, the interpretation of cultural survivals became the royal road to the primitive mind.

—*w*—

This sketch of Tylor's methodological assumptions allows us to appreciate the significance of later criticism of Tylor and understand how that criticism returns us to the problem of fetishism within Tylor's method itself. His ideas persisted into the early twentieth century, in part due to the enormous popularity of *The Golden Bough*, a late version of evolutionary anthropology, by James Frazer. First issued in 1890 in two volumes, *The Golden Bough* was continuously revised and expanded to twelve volumes in the third edition, 1911–14. The three editions, and a one-volume abridgment published in 1922, sold in the tens of thousands to a broad readership. Among professional anthropologists, Tylor's ideas came under increasing scrutiny during the 1890s. In the discussion that immediately followed his 1889 talk, "On Method," he was challenged by Francis Galton, then President of the Anthropological Institute, who questioned "the degree in which the customs of the tribes and races which are compared together are independent," and not derived instead from a "common source."[40] The need to account first for possible historical contact between cultures was the wave of the future. "Diffusionism," as it was called, began its ascendancy in earnest in 1896, when Franz Boas published his critique of Tylor's method, "The Limitations of the Comparative Method of Anthropology."[41] Directly contradicting the notion of psychic unity, Boas writes,

> the point of view is taken that if an ethnological phenomenon has developed independently in a number of places its development has been the same everywhere . . . [and] the sameness of ethnological phenomena found in diverse regions is proof that the human mind obeys the same laws everywhere. It is obvious that if different historical developments could lead to the same results, that then this generalization would not be tenable.[42]

The two alternatives of independent invention and diffusionism competed for dominance in Britain until about the turn of the twentieth century, when two influential members of the Torres Straits Expedition, Rivers and Alfred Haddon, moved away from evolutionism in favor of interests that were either specifically diffusionist or focused on questions of migration. The debate limped along into the 1920s, until it was finally mooted by the rise of *functionalism*, as articulated by Malinowski and Alfred Radcliffe-Brown. This new method focused on the function served by a behavior or belief within a given society; in examining such functions, questions about how a society historically acquired the trait were largely beside the point.[43] Even more damaging, claims about primitive origins became redefined as misguided and self-serving, and Tylor's reputation suffered accordingly. As Ruth Benedict argued in 1934: "the use of primitive customs to establish origins is speculative. It is possible to build up an argument for any origin that can be desired . . . . Of all the uses of anthropological material, this is the one in which speculation has followed speculation most rapidly, and where in the nature of the case no proof can be given."[44] At this point, Tylor's "science" was seen as an unintended work of prose fiction. His method had been an essentially deductive one, in which the interpretation of culture followed from certain assumptions about primitive psychology, and so it became passé as anthropologists discarded its foundational ideas.

Historians of anthropology have continued to fault the centrality of speculation in Tylor's method and have focused on one point in particular: the assumption that the interpreter's initial classification of a culture was objective.[45] Because cultural signs are polymorphous, they can readily be interpreted in a way that suits the investigator's particular interests. Once a society is conceptually slotted into a given evolutionary stage, then inconsistent beliefs and behaviors can simply be reclassified as survivals. Instead of data shaping the classification, the classification determines the handling of the data. Everything follows from the initial decision, and yet in that crucial area the interpreter's bias has free rein.

Tylor's ethnology is viewed today more as a species of Victorian impressionism than science as such, but this impressionism is precisely why his interpretations are valuable to us. However little they tell us about indigenous cultures, they reveal a great deal about Tylor and about Victorian perceptions of the colonial periphery. Because his claims were about primitive psychology, his impressionism also provides us with an unusually detailed account of how social values were naturalized in Victorian beliefs about the "first" humans. That pattern is most evident in his depiction of the primitive mind. Primitives arrived at the only conclusions possible, given their circumstances and their state of knowledge. This mind ran like a logic machine, progressing through a reasonable sequence of ideas. Passion and irrationality were absent from Tylor's model, as were sexual desires. Although the primitive's basic assumptions were wrong, the chain of logic leading from them to its conclusion was entirely reasonable. Tylor illustrates this process in describing how primitives arrive at the idea of supernatural life:

It seems as though thinking men . . . were deeply impressed by two groups of biological problems. In the first place, what is it that makes the difference between a living body and a dead one . . . ? In the second place, what are those human shapes which appear in dreams and visions? Looking at these two groups of phenomena, the ancient savage philosophers probably made their first step by the obvious inference that every man has two things belonging to him, namely, a life and a phantom. (*PC*, 1:428)

This is certainly how Tylor and his contemporaries would have reacted under similar circumstances, but that is precisely the problem. This logicality looks too much like Tylor himself. He constructs a primitive that conforms to Victorian values of self-restraint and rationality, a point not lost on Tylor's successors. In a late defense of Tylor's legacy, written in the 1930s, Robert Lowie found his primitive man to be unbelievable, complaining that Tylor slighted "the emotional in favor of rational factors."[46] Two decades later, Radin was more blunt. Tylor's primitive "flowed . . . directly from his own personality. Tylor was himself, at times, this simple, hypothetical ancient man."[47] What emerges in twentieth-century studies of Tylor is a new appreciation of the extent to which Tylor's *homo rationalis* was a projection of his own imagination.

It will not surprise anyone that a Victorian intellectual's vision might be colored by the culture that shaped it; it would be remarkable if it were not.[48] But given Tylor's subject matter, this specific form of bias cuts to the heart of his science of culture. In mistaking his self-projection for the primitive as such, his science enacts the same fetishistic psychology that it claims to study. As a science, it reifies the idea of the primitive, even while defining reification as the primitive's essence. If the science of culture was to be the royal road to the primitive mind, as Tylor hoped, then it was a road that ran in a very short circuit indeed, racing around the hamster wheel of the Victorian imagination before appearing, like the ghost of Hamlet's father, as an apparition from beyond.

Nietzche explained the constructed nature of truth by describing a man creating an idea, hiding it behind a bush, as it were, and forgetting it. When he stumbles upon it later, he rediscovers it as an external truth.[49] It is tempting to think that Tylor did something similar, and that his royal road went only far enough for him to mistake self-description for historical description. But there is abundant evidence to the contrary, showing that Tylor never quite suffered that enabling moment of amnesia, instead remaining aware of the self-reflexive element in his vision of the primitive, and we can see it in his description of the gap separating primitive and modern psychology and the speculative thinking it necessitates for the anthropologist.

The psychology of the primitive is most evident in its act of mythmaking, which Tylor explains as follows: "To minds in this mythological stage, the Curse becomes a personal being, hovering in space till it can light upon its victim; Time and Nature arise as real entities; Fate and Fortune become personal arbiters of our lives" (*PC*, 1:300). Tylor is talking about the prelinguistic stage here, with its absolute fetishism. Without language, it is difficult to imagine how concepts like "Time" or "Nature" could exist, but Tylor locates myth's origin in a more fundamental psychological process than even language: he calls it "that great doctrine of analogy, from which we have gained so much of our apprehension of the world around us" (*PC*, 1:296–97). As a mental function, he tells us that analogy precedes language, both historically and psychologically. "Deep as language lies in our mental life, the direct comparison of object with object, and action with action, lies yet deeper"; such comparisons "thrust themselves directly on the mind, without any necessary intervention of words."[50] Thus, in the sequence he lays out, mythology originates as a prelinguistic analogy in the primitive mind, and it begins the process of estrangement from its poetic source at the moment of its entry into language.

The mediation of language affects the content of myth in two, opposite ways, according to Tylor. In the first place, words shape concepts and so make insubstantial ideas seem concrete. Words—here he mentions the pairs *winter* and *summer*, *cold* and *heat*, *war* and *peace*, *vice* and *virtue*—create discrete categories for conditions that lack clear boundaries because they are continuous along a particular axis.[51] Language, "gives the myth-maker the means of imagining these thoughts as personal beings" (*PC*, 1:299). In this first sense, then, language helps to fetishize ideas. However, in a second sense, the exact opposite occurs: language distances people from the immersion in concreteness that characterizes the prelinguistic mind because language inserts a new level of abstraction between mind and object. Tylor summarizes these two contrary effects succinctly:

> Language not only acts in thorough unison with the imagination whose product it expresses, but it goes on producing of itself, and thus, by the side of the mythic conceptions in which language has followed imagination, we have others in which language has led, and imagination has followed in the track. (*PC*, 1:299)

Tylor calls the first type "material myth," because in it language reproduces a prelinguistic primitive realism, and he speculates that the second type, "verbal myth," is a later development. "I am disposed to think . . . that the mythology of the lower races rests especially on a basis of real and sensible analogy, and that the great expansion of verbal metaphor into myth belongs to more advanced periods of civilization" (*PC*, 1:299). Given the distinction between early and modern civilization, Tylor is actually describing three stages in the evolution of mythology: a purely analogical prelinguistic one, an authentic early linguistic one, and an inauthentic later stage of myth "founded on word" and word alone (*PC*, 1:299).

As Tylor points out, Victorians exist in this third stage; they are radically alienated from the concreteness of primitive myth. In modern life, every experience is mediated by abstractions, and so imagining the primitive mind is as impossible for the Victorian as imagining a condition with neither language nor numbers. How, he asks, can the scientist hope to succeed in interpreting the primitive realism of myth? A few people can transcend this barrier, provided they have "the poet's gift of throwing their minds back into the world's older life, like the actor who for a moment can forget himself and become what he pretends to be" (*PC*, 1:305). Poetic imagination and feeling are highly desirable qualities for the scientist in this regard:

> Wordsworth, that "modern ancient," . . . could write of Storm and Winter, or of the naked Sun climbing the sky, as though he were some Vedic poet at the head-spring of the Aryan race, "seeing" with his mind's eye a mythic hymn to Agni or Varuna. Fully to understand an old-world myth needs not evidence and argument alone, but deep poetic feeling. (*PC*, 1:305)

Sadly for science, anthropologists are an unpoetic bunch, as liable to miss the intensity of meaning in myth as to turn it instead into a nonscientific, and very "stupid fiction" (*PC*, 1:305).

Tylor does not advise his prosaic colleagues to embrace the spontaneous overflow of emotion recollected in tranquility, but he does propose a variation of poetic Romanticism. He resolves this problem by incorporating an element of self-reflection into the science of culture. Since primitives were mentally children, then recollections of childhood perceptions could approximate the primitive mind and serve as a route back in evolutionary time. He illustrates this with his own memories of fascination as a young child while staring at the stars. He also advises scientists to recall the "morbid subjectivity of illness," with its perceptual distortions, or to recollect the hallucinations caused by fasting, fatigue, or narcotics (presumably used for medical reasons). By examining the state of mind reflected in such personal experiences, the ethnologist can approximate the poetic condition of the primitive mind within himself (*PC*, 1:307). The unpoetic scientist, in this case, is to interpret mythology through the lens of personal experience. Imperfect as the procedure is, Tylor is explicit:

> In this world one must do what one can, and if the moderns cannot feel myth as their forefathers did, at least they can analyse it. There is a kind of intellectual frontier within which he must be who will sympathise with myth, while he must be without who will investigate it, and it is

our fortune that we live near this frontier-line, and can go in and out. (*PC*, 1:317)

To "sympathise" and "investigate": oscillating between these two contraries, the modern scientist makes a more informed judgment about the meaning of myth than he could using either method by itself. This proposed reciprocal action combines conflicting perspectives in a single evaluation: emotional with rational, subjective with objective. In order to comprehend the "power of myth," the scientist has to cross the "frontier" and see the world through savage eyes, to temporarily adopt the fetishism of the primitive and so see a curse, time, or fate, as material beings, equally substantial to the ground beneath his Wellington boots. At the same time, the scientist must also adopt the position of the analyst, who investigates myth objectively from "without" the frontier, strictly according to the standards of nineteenth-century science.

Because Tylor believed in the continuity of human evolution, he saw evidence of continued animism in modern life, and in a particular sense he used the "primitive within" to flesh out the details of earliest culture that were otherwise irrecoverable. The "threads which connect new thought with old do not always vanish from our sight. It is in large measure possible to follow them as clues leading back to that actual experience of nature and life, which is the ultimate source of human fancy" (*PC*, 1:274). To illustrate his point about the persistence of the past, he quotes from Matthew Arnold's "The Future."

> As is the world on the banks
> So is the mind of the man.
> . . . .
> Only the tract where he sails
> He wots of: only the thoughts,
> Raised by the objects he passes, are his.[52]

The mind of man is continuous, as the banks, but the individual is aware of only a small portion of the whole; however, the rest is still there so that the past remains forever part of the mind and may be accessed, if one tries to enter the frontier.

This ambivalent process of myth interpretation accounts for the echo chamber effect in Tylor's imagined *homo rationalis*: primitive man resembled Tylor because he was a product of Tylor's recollections. He could no more conceive the primitive mind than he could understand the myths it generated without resorting to the subjective experience of Victorian childhood and illness, and *Primitive Culture* is littered with examples of this self-referential procedure. In every instance where Tylor urges us to "place ourselves by an effort in the intellectual position of an uncultured tribe," or to "carry our minds back to the state of knowledge among the lower races," he reinforces the same, fundamentally self-reflexive essence of analysis in evolutionary anthropology (*PC*, 1:477, 2:59). If by now this ambivalence sounds familiar, it is because the two lands on either side of Tylor's mental frontier, civilized anthropologist and primitive animist, restate the two perspectives within the fetish triangle, the critic and the worshipper. What Tylor articulated was the necessity of combining both perspectives within a single, ambivalent subject, arguing that such a fusion is both possible and essential in the practice of cultural science. Without it, mythology could never yield its secrets, and the hope of understanding the primitive mind would be at an end.

—⁓—

"No man ever looks at the world with pristine eyes," writes Ruth Benedict, and this problem is clearly evident in Tylor's work.[53] Peckham calls him "a victim of his own animism," and so he was, but he also recognized and acknowledged the danger of seeing himself reflected in his vision of primitive culture.[54] It is probably less accurate to think of him as a victim of animism than as an experimenter, who used it as a necessary element in his anthropological method. He warns against the danger of self-reflexivity so frequently that it becomes a thematic part of *Primitive Culture*, as he repeatedly faults ethnographers and scientists, present and past, who fall into the trap of confusing their assumptions with external reality. Francis Bacon warns against the problem, Tylor notes, but then points out how Bacon "is seen to be plunging headlong into the very pitfall of which he had so discreetly warned his disciples" (*PC*, 1:277). The allegorical method of Enlightenment mythographers comes in for particular censure. "Any of us may practise this simple art, each according to his fancy. If, for instance, political economy happens for the moment to lie uppermost in our mind, we may with due gravity expound the story of Perseus as an allegory of trade .... To know anything of poetry or of mysticism is to know this reproductive growth of fancy as an admitted and admired intellectual process" (*PC*, 1:278–79). However, more often than not, the myth interpreter's speculation runs amuck, and he finds analogies "wherever it pleases him to seek them" (*PC*, 1:319). Etymology is a particularly guilty practice, with virtually no restraints on the interpreter's hobbyhorse: "His imagination is ever suggesting to him what his judgment would like to find true" (*PC*, 1:202).

Tylor's comparative method responded to precisely these concerns about the debilitating effect of unchecked self-reflexivity. Bias in etymology is to be minimized by comparing word patterns across multiple languages, rather than in isolation (*PC*, 1:325). His eloquent remarks on animistic self-mirroring are perhaps the clearest index of how thoroughly he understood the problem. "Every idea once lodged in the mind of a savage, a barbarian, or an enthusiast, is ready thus to be brought back to him from without" (*PC*, 2:49). With the reference to the savage and the barbarian, Tylor situates the problem of reflection at a safe temporal remove from the present, but his inclusion of the enthusiast in the list removes that distance. In a sarcastic moment, he calls it "a vicious circle; what he believes he therefore sees, and what he sees he therefore believes. Beholding the reflexion of his own mind like a child looking at itself in a glass, he humbly receives the teaching of his second self" (*PC*, 2:49). To different degrees, scientist and savage alike face the problem of the second self, whose teachings are but echoes of the subject's preoccupations.

The litany of warnings suggests that Tylor was aware of the paradox within his scientific method. Animism is the central topic of *Primitive Culture*, which also defines cultural evolution as the psychological transition from animism to positivist objectivity. Primitive realism in mythology and religion, cultural survivals, the primitive mind—all are based on a psychology of animism that forms the beginning point of Tylor's evolutionary narrative. At the same time, his study demonstrates its own version of animism in his representation of the primitive and his interpretation of myth. This self-projection recapitulates the central trait of the animist mind within the very science designed to examine it. There is, in other words, a reciprocity between scientific method and scientific object in *Primitive Culture* that produces an infinite regress, or hall-of-mirrors effect, whereby, in talking about primitives and primitive culture, Tylor is also talking about himself, his civilization, and his science. At this level of analysis, we can say that Tylor collapses the distinction between primitive and civilized, leaving anthropology with itself as the object of study.

In this regard, his engagement with the problem of the primitive resembles that of Comte, Arnold, and Eliot, all three of whom simultaneously critiqued and employed its essential fetishism. For Comte, it was a false but necessary perspective, which could be channeled through the religion of humanity. This pragmatic return to fetishism reappeared in each of the other writers. For Arnold, the fetishized value of free thought was the antidote to Victorian fetishism. For Eliot, the success of her realist critique of fetishism depended on exploiting the fetishism inherent within realism as a literary form. Tylor utilized fetishism similarly. His primitive man, his primitive mythology, his primitive religion—all became real to his contemporaries because they made sense. As products of Tylor's own imagination, these constructs reflected Victorian thinking and values; they seemed believable because they were believable, not because they had scientific value as statements of fact. While classified as nonfiction, *Primitive Culture* is also a form of narrative fiction, similar in its use of profuse details to Eliot's realism, and narrating the plot of mankind's psychological birth, development, and maturity. This kind of plausibility comes with a price. It sounded believable to Victorians because it cast the drama of the primitive with Victorian actors in fancy dress, performing in front of elaborate sets on a stage filled with exotic props. This self-reflexive method invalidates his science as science, but it also invested it with the semblance of truth that struck home with his contemporaries.

To the society that produces it, science is not a given but rather that which is seen as scientific, and in this regard the semblance of truth in *Primitive Culture* was significant. Historically, it led to the establishment of anthropology as an accepted, academic discipline, albeit one that would soon come to disown Tylor's ideas. Compared to that of Arnold, Tylor's deification was relatively short lived, lasting under half a century. Nor did he later reemerge as the household god of anthropology, as Arnold did for literary studies in the second half of the twentieth century. In the conclusion to *Primitive Culture*, Tylor comments on the future, much as Arnold did at the conclusion of "Function of Criticism," and he too criticizes the process of deification:

> It is our happiness to live in one of those eventful periods of intellectual and moral history, when the oft-closed gates of discovery and reform stand open at their widest. . . . But if history is to repeat itself according to precedent, we must look forward to stiffer duller ages of traditionalists and commentators, when the great thinkers of our time will be appealed to as authorities by men who slavishly accept their tenets, yet cannot or dare not follow their methods through better evidence to higher ends. (*PC*, 2:452)

If these words are taken to refer to himself—and in a study loaded with self-reflection, they need to be—then it certainly would have suited his purpose to be superseded, rather than deified, for it suggests his hope that the science of culture might eventually avoid the pitfall of fetishism, even as he puts it to use. He is in essence describing his own undoing, as the ultimate desideratum for the study of culture.

—⁓—

Among later writers to grant Tylor his wish, Ruth Benedict stands out. Her rejection of evolutionary anthropology went beyond its methodological problems to the entire concept of culture, as Tylor defined it, replacing it with a more recognizably modern version. In *Patterns of Culture* (1934), Benedict insists on "the diversity of cultures," as opposed to Tylor's cultural universal.[55] She shifts the focus away from culture in the singular to cultures in the plural. To accomplish this, she remakes individual cultures as significant in their own terms; anthropology is devoted to "the study of cultures as articulated wholes," rather than the study of discrete components across societies, which are understood as synecdoches for the universal whole.[56] Each culture, "like an individual, is a more or less consistent pattern of thought and action," with its own unique "characteristic purposes" (46). These purposes play a constructive role in shaping social behaviors. Identifying them thus becomes a means of explaining each social act. "Taken up by a well-integrated culture, the most ill-assorted acts become characteristic of its peculiar goals," and can be comprehended "only by understanding first the emotional and intellectual mainsprings of that society" (46). Benedict calls this mode of interpretation the "patterning of culture," from which derives the title of her important study (46).

Benedict matters to the question of fetishism in cultural theory because she demonstrates it anew in her concept of culture as a consistent pattern.[57] Describing how cultural purposes act, she explains that a "purpose selects from among the possible traits in the surrounding region those which it can use, and discards those which it cannot."[58] She recognizes that this Darwinian account anthropomorphizes the concept of a "purpose" and explains the problem cogently: "When we describe the process historically, we inevitably use animistic forms of expression as if there were choice and purpose in the growth of this great art-form. But this is due to the difficulty of our language-forms" (47–48). Benedict's argument here is that "animistic" terms in cultural theory are insignificant byproducts of language, and she brackets the possibility of self-reflection by giving us to understand that her use of the term "purpose" is to be silently surrounded by scare quotes. And yet she insists on a term suggestive of a prior intelligence or consciousness for each culture, leaving unanswered the implication that fetishism may be an unavoidable consequence of language, one that can only be bracketed and never entirely eliminated. Whether we accept such a proposition as true or not, Benedict's acknowledgement of it does redefine her relationship to Tylor, whose own reflexivity echoes through the arguments of later anthropologists, even those whose arguments, like Benedict's, explicitly contradict his earlier theory of culture. In this respect, Benedict is once again engaged in the practice of dueling fetishisms, asserting the true value of her culture concept while labeling the other's appraisal as irrational error.

Because of his engagement with self-reflexivity, Tylor has a special claim on our attention in the twenty-first century. After the intellectual transformations of the 1970s and 1980s, his practice of intermittently acknowledging anthropology's self-reflexivity was superseded by a more robust engagement. In 1977, for example, Paul Rabinow characterized anthropology as "the comprehension of the self by the detour of the comprehension of the other," a definition equally well-suited to Tylor's early incarnation of the human science.[59] If Tylor is any guide—and he is certainly one of the better options to choose as a guide—self-referentiality has always been a central problem in anthropology, although its acknowledgment of the difficulty has not always come as readily as it does in his Victorian works. If this is true, then anthropology has, in this one sense, never escaped Tylor's contradictions, for his foundational status can also be seen as a founding statement of the paradox that would bedevil the science of culture long after his own reputation expired.

5

Sexology's Perversion

Two distinct qualities made the primitive fetish readily adaptable to the language of fin-de-siècle psychology. In the first place, it described an entirely psychological phenomenon—a purely speculative one associated with primitives, to be sure, but nonetheless a widely accepted mechanism of mental life, and one that was thought to persist within the modern individual, as we saw in Arnold, Eliot, and Tylor. Second, that mechanism explained how humans invested objects with unusual qualities or extraordinary powers, and so it provided a framework for understanding the psychology of attraction. With the increased professional interest in sexuality at the end of the century, fetishism was a ready-made concept that quickly found a new home.

The association with primitive culture declined over the years, as the sexual meaning grew. Nonetheless, fetishism today still bears a recognizable connection to the fetishism of de Brosses, Comte, and Tylor. How could it not? When erotic fetishism first appeared as a form of sexuality, in the work of the European sexologists in the last quarter of the nineteenth century, it was explicitly described as an adaptation of primitive fetishism. In effect, the sexologists domesticated it, uprooting it from its peripheral locus in the colonies and importing it into the heart of European civilization. It may be tempting to view the rise of interest in sexual fetishism as a reverse colonialism, whereby the European fear of being colonized by its own former subjects was realized in the conceptual transformation of its own sexuality.[1] However, such a view would elide the relational nature of the concept as a product of European encounters with Africa, assuming it to be a fact of African life. Since fetishism was a European interpretation of West African religion, rather than an indigenous practice, it is more useful to think of the rise of sexual fetishism in the late century as the return of a European concept, one that had long sojourned in the imaginary overseas and now relocated to the land of its ancestors. Fetishism was not a foreign concept adapted to European concerns so much as a European concept that finally came home for good.

115

How was this long absent relation greeted on its return? How was it received back into the family of European civilization?

In medical literature, the key element of sexual fetishism appeared as early as 1819, when Jean Étienne Esquirol, French physician of *l'aliénation mentale*, first theorized "Monomania," in the *Dictionnaire des sciences médicales*.[2] As the name suggests, monomania derived from mania, one of the oldest types of madness.[3] The victim of mania suffered a global insanity, one that affected every aspect of his or her existence. In contrast, the monomaniac was mentally healthy in most respects and even functioned normally in everyday life. But he or she was subject to a single pathological preoccupation, and on this one topic the mania rendered the victim insane and sometimes capable of violence, as in *monomanie homicide*. Monomania was a partial insanity caused by a narrow fixation in an otherwise normal mind. In England it was redefined as "Moral Insanity," or "Partial Insanity," in 1835 by James Cowles Prichard, whose *Treatise on Insanity* remained the standard textbook on mental disorders for the next twenty years. Ironically, the same ethnologist who refused to acknowledge de Brosses's *Du culte des dieux fétiches* was also the physician most closely associated in England with the theory of the discrete psychological fixation later reconfigured as fetishism itself.[4]

Esquirol defines a sexual variant of the disorder, erotic monomania, "in which the amorous sentiments are fixed and dominant."[5] He describes it as an "excessive sexual passion; now, for a known object; now, for one unknown," characterized by an "insane tenderness" for either persons or "things inanimate" (335–36). He points out that erotomania differs from other sexual disorders, like nymphomania and satyriasis, which were attributed to damage or injury to the reproductive organs. Erotomania, however, "is a mental affection," rather than a physical one, and so "the sentiment which characterizes it, is in the head" (335). The distinction was crucial: "The nymphomaniac, as well as the victim to satyriasis, is the subject of a physical disorder. The erotomaniac is, on the contrary, the sport of his imagination" (335). Erotomania was thus a fully psychological disorder, unlike the others. Its characteristic attribute was an uncontrolled, narrowly defined sexual fixation, and this quality would reemerge in fetishism, several decades after monomania had passed from the scene of medical psychology.

Erotomania contained one of the key ingredients in sexual fetishism, the discrete fixation, but it lacked any link to a broader theory of sexuality. This connection was made in the second half of the century, in "Inversion du sens génital," the now-famous 1882 paper by the chief physician at the Salpêtrière, Jean-Martin Charcot, and Parisian psychiatrist Valentin Magnan.[6] Although primarily concerned with same-sex attraction, the essay broadens the topic in the second part to take up "autres perversions sexuelles," where they describe sexual interest in objects, such as night bonnets and shoe nails.[7] Obsessions with objects and with people of the same sex, they explain, both involve a similar diversion of the same psychic force out of its "natural" course and into an abnormal one, and thus, whether the passion is for a same-sex lover or a night bonnet, the underlying mechanism is the same.

This was not the first time the word *fetishism* was used for an unusual erotic fixation. That honor goes to the French novelist Nicolas-Edme Rétif de la Bretonne (1734–1806), who compared the sexual power of a woman's shoes to "des fétiches de Guinée," in his posthumous *Histoire des compagnes de Maria* (1811); in 1800, he called spike heels and other items of women's clothing "*fétiches* sacrés."[8] These usages were metaphorical, suggesting the quality of the narrator's fixation. Alfred Binet was the first medical writer to propose *fetishism* as a technical term for an identifiable pathology.[9] Binet was Charcot's pupil, as well as a child psychologist who went on to develop the first system of intelligence testing. In his 1887 article, "Le fétichisme dans l'amour," he described the condition, leading to the widespread adoption of the term for any erotic interest in objects. From Binet it was picked up in 1889 by the Italian Cesare Lombroso and the Austrian Richard von Krafft-Ebing, and in 1905 Freud began to employ it, in *Three Essays on the Theory of Sexuality.*

Binet's essay established the conceptual framework we attribute to fin-de-siècle erotic fetishism. In line with degeneration theory, he credited the pathology to the debilitating effects of an unhealthy social environment.[10] Fetishism was a disease of civilization, he claimed, and one that could be passed on to the next generation as an inherited predisposition. This was a familiar trope in the history of medicine; it appeared in George Cheyne's *The English Malady*, in the mid-eighteenth century, and Thomas Trotter's *Nervous Temperament*, in the early-nineteenth century.[11] According to Binet, each generation becomes increasingly susceptible to the debilitating effects of an over-civilized environment, so that the condition steadily worsens. In time, social evolution comes to a dead halt and then begins to reverse. Each generation travels further back in evolutionary time until humans return to the most primitive state of all; beyond this lies extinction, the ultimate endpoint of degeneration. In the context of this theory, Binet's use of an anthropological term to define a pathological sexual practice was analogically appropriate; it connected the principle psychological characteristic of primitivism with modern degeneration. However, as he points out, degeneration alone does not explain the form fetishism takes in each individual, such as a preference for small feet or large noses. He explains these variations through a theory of psychological association; childhood experiences create particular emotional associations that persist into adulthood, long after the original experience is forgotten. When it manifests as erotic preference in the adult, its origin seems inexplicable. This combination of heredity and personal accident was necessary to explain the emergence of fetishism as infinitely variable while always the same. His explanation had consequences for fin-de-siècle thinking about other sexual pathologies as well. Along with Charcot and Magnan, Binet viewed inversion as one of the many forms of fetishism, one in which childhood experience directs the sexual focus toward a person of the same sex rather than a physical object. Thus fetishism was the underlying mechanism for sexual deviation generally, becoming by 1887 "the model perversion," or the paradigm from which all other perversions derived.[12]

The first book to propose a comprehensive medical taxonomy of sexual perversion was Richard von Krafft-Ebing's *Psychopathia Sexualis*; its author has since been called "the founder of modern scientific sexual pathology."[13] His importance to the field of sexual studies can be judged by the longevity of the labels "sadism" and "masochism," neologisms he established as standard terminology in the literature of perversion.[14] First published in 1886, *Psychopathia Sexualis* is an omnibus account of sexual behavior. It underwent continuous modification until Krafft-Ebing's death in 1902; by then it had been issued in seven languages and twelve editions. This popularity led to professional difficulties for the author. An attempt was made to cancel his membership in the British Medico-Psychological Association—not for writing about sexual perversion, but because he had not "prevented it from being sold indiscriminately."[15] Instead of publishing in Latin, as was customary, he used the vernacular, and nonprofessionals read it, as well as medical practitioners. To guard against this charge, Krafft-Ebing had written particularly explicit phrases in Latin, but this had not proved a deterrent to readers, some of whom found in it a means to understand troubling aspects of their own sexual behavior. *Psychopathia Sexualis* reached an unusually large audience for a medical treatise at the time, and this new readership provided him with additional material. After the first edition, he began receiving letters from readers describing their own cases, which he then incorporated into subsequent editions, usually as part of a growing appendix of case histories.[16]

While the first edition of *Psychopathia Sexualis* included discussions of sadism and masochism, fetishism was absent, since Binet's essay was not published until the following year. When Cesare Lombroso wrote his introduction to the Italian translation of *Psychopathia Sexualis*, published in 1889, he made extensive reference to Binet's new theory, even going so far as to explain its importance to Krafft-Ebing's work. Krafft-Ebing took the hint. He revised his taxonomy to include *pathological fetishism* in the fourth English edition, published in 1889. This edition did not include new case histories of fetishism, as one might expect; instead it reflected a "relabelling of data already collected," reassigning earlier cases to illustrate the new perversion.[17] Certainly there were easier ways to incorporate fetishism into his scheme. As the rearrangement suggests, the new perversion required a reconfiguration of his entire theory; the consequence of this transformation was revealed in later editions, when he added an additional category of fetishism, *physiological fetishism*, to the existing pathological form. By the tenth edition, in 1898, the role of physiological fetishism ballooned into an essential aspect of *all* human sexuality, normal and abnormal alike. It became the missing piece in his taxonomic puzzle, and with its addition, he completed the final revision of the theoretical portion of the work, "Fragments of a System of Psychology of Sexual Life" ("Fragmente einer Psychologie des Sexuallebens"), where he articulated his general theory of sexuality.

He introduces fetishism as an overvaluation of an object and concludes by returning to the familiar primitive fetish and adding a sexual variant:

> The word fetich signifies an object, or parts or attributes of objects, which by virtue of association to sentiment, personality, or absorbing ideas, exert a charm (the Portuguese "fetisso") or at least produce a peculiar individual impression which is in no wise connected with the external appearance of the sign, symbol or fetich.
>
> The individual valuation of the fetich extending even to unreasoning enthusiasm is called fetichism. . . . It is most commonly found in *religious* and *erotic* spheres.[18]

While he suggests that the two are closely related, he is quick to point out that they are not synonymous. Indeed, in his mind they possess completely different epistemologies. The older form, religious fetishism, stems from the:

> delusion that its object . . . is not a mere symbol, but possesses divine attributes, and ascribes to it peculiar wonder-working (relics) or protective (amulets) virtues. (*PS*, 18)

This is a straightforward description of the primitive fetish. It recapitulates the fetishistic triangle by having the critic (here, Krafft-Ebing) interpret the local's worship of the object as "delusion." However, when he turns to the newer form, its erotic twin, the triangular relationship falls apart:

> *Erotic* fetichism makes an idol of physical or mental qualities of a person or even merely of objects used by that person, etc., because they awaken mighty associations with the beloved person, thus originating strong emotions of sexual pleasure. (*PS*, 18)

The difference between these two definitions resides in the opposite status the objects possess as forms of representation. The religious fetish is anicomic because it "possesses divine attributes," and so is believed to be meaningful in and of itself. The erotic fetish *is* a representational object because it stands for the beloved through a conscious association.

We can better appreciate the consequences of this difference by comparing Krafft-Ebing's erotic fetish to that of Binet. Like him, Krafft-Ebing uses association to explain the special attraction of the fetish, but instead of connecting it to a forgotten event in childhood, he ties it to the present-day beloved. This difference points to a diminished role for psychological factors in his account of fetishism because it replaces the assumption of a forgotten-but-persistent source of attraction with a conscious association. But where does the lover's attraction to the beloved originate? Fetishism is "physiological" because it is built into the body's structure as an inherited system of sexual attraction—a biological eroticism. From evolutionary adaptation "springs the particular choice for slender or plump forms, for blondes or brunettes . . ." (*PS*, 19). Certain body parts lend themselves to this preferentiality more regularly than others: "the HAIR, the HAND, the FOOT of woman, or the expression of the EYE," are all mentioned, as well as the "odour of the hair or body (even artificial perfume)" and the sound of the voice (*PS*, 21, 19). The ability to procreate supplies an important survival advantage, a fact that provides an anthropological justification for heterosexuality: one of the refinements of evolution is the fact that love "can only exist between persons of different sex capable of sexual intercourse" (*PS*, 13). Evolution is hard at work on the opposite side of the attraction equation as well, with bodies developing desirable attributes to gain admirers: "The germ of sexual love is probably to be found in the individual charm (fetich) with which persons of opposite sex sway each other" (*PS*, 18). While this might logically lead to biological libertinism, monogamy fortunately flows, too, from the evolutionary past: "adaptation" accounts for "the fact of fascination by one person of the opposite sex with indifference towards all others" (*PS*, 17). Through this deductive logic, Krafft-Ebing naturalizes monogamous heterosexuality, which then becomes the speculative norm against which perversion is to be defined.

While the concept of an innate sexual attraction might be culturally acceptable for male bodies, it appeared to contradict nineteenth-century gender assumptions about the absence of sexual feelings in women.[19] But Krafft-Ebing finds a way to have his cake and eat it too, agreeing that the female in advanced civilization "has but little sensual desire" (*PS*, 14). He accomplishes this disappearing act by arguing that physiological fetishism is indeed part of the female body; in her, "the physical as well as the mental qualities of man assume the form of the female fetich" (*PS*, 23). But this erotic attraction is sublimated; she experiences it without any "conscious sensuality," so while subject to the principle of sexual attraction, she remains unaware of it as sexual, and thus her virtue remains unimpeachable (*PS*, 23). In his doctrine, the particular qualities in men that elicit such sublimated responses are "physical strength, courage, nobility of mind, chivalry, self-confidence, even self-assertion, insolence, bravado, and a conscious show of mastery over the weaker sex" (*PS*, 23). Woman prefer to be dominated because the male's strength is advantageous to survival, so her preference for submission is, once again, a product of evolution. Ultimately, he concludes, "The fetichism of body and mind is of importance in progeneration; it favours the selection of the fittest and the transmission of physical and mental virtues" (*PS*, 23).

This normality of physiological fetishism explains why it departed from the ethnographic form. In Krafft-Ebing's hands, the fetishistic triangle of early anthropology collapses because he leaves no room for an outsider. As the essence of all sexuality, fetishism is practiced by everybody, so there is no "outside" for the critic to occupy as the skeptical observer. In cases of physiological fetishism, the physician can only issue a diagnosis of normality. While not experiencing the same emotional association with the object, the interpreter is, by definition, also subject to physiological fetishism. In consequence, both critical interpreter and fetishist accept the value of the fetish object as normative. In the anthropological paradigm, such an agreement negated the entire concept of fetishism.

The physiological fetish also differed from the primitive fetish because of its newly acquired status as a representation. Even for Binet, the fetishist did not know why the fetish was erotic; having forgotten the childhood association, the fetishist imagined the object as if it were meaningful in and of itself. But when Krafft-Ebing switched the time of association to the present, that amnesia disappeared, and the fetish became what it could never be: an acknowledged form of representation. It reminded the fetishist of the beloved, whom it signified, and its value came from that association rather than any quality within the object. In essence, the physiological form recapitulated the "icon" of Comte and Tylor's evolutionary anthropology, rather than the primitive fetish.

Krafft-Ebing pointed to the object's status as representation in differentiating physiological fetishism from the religious form. He used the same standard to distinguish between physiological and pathological fetishism. "[T]he fetich may exercise its power so long as its leading qualities represent the integral parts, and so long as the love engendered by it comprises the entire mental and physical personality" (*PS*, 20). As he emphasizes, "the term real love (so often misused) can only apply where the entire person of the beloved becomes the physical and mental object of veneration" (*PS*, 20). Whether a lock of hair or a handkerchief, the physiological fetish is a synecdoche, in which hair or cloth is a fragment that stands for the whole of the beloved, rather than becoming significant as an object in itself.

Ultimately, physiological fetishism combined two incompatible elements to make its whole: a theory of naturalized preferences and an insistence on association. Together, they created a circular logic in his explanation of sexual attraction. Where do these preferences come from? On the one hand, individual preferences are products of evolutionary heredity, long preceding the discovery of the particular beloved. On the other, the beloved is an object of desire in her or his entirety; the beloved's attributes only assume a heightened erotic quality because they represent the whole person. This creates a chicken-and-egg predicament: the lover's interest in a particular person depends on a pre-existing preference for the type, such as brown eyes, but an erotic affinity for brown eyes can only follow from an association with someone already beloved. What remains is a half-anthropological, half-psychological structure in which individual love begins as a nonrepresentational, hereditary attraction and ends as a representational attraction based on conscious association.

While physiological fetishism broke with the older primitive fetish, Krafft-Ebing's second form of fetishism, the pathological, embraced it wholesale. Rather than an essential element of healthy sexuality, pathological fetishism was a disease.[20] In describing the difference between the two forms, he again emphasizes their opposite relationships to representation:

> In the ecstatic love of a man mentally normal, a handkerchief or shoe, a glove or letter, the flower "she gave," or a lock of hair, etc., may become the object of worship, but only because they represent a mnemonic symbol of the beloved person—absent or dead—whose whole personality is reproduced by them. The pathological fetichist has no such relations. The fetich constitutes the entire content of his idea. When he becomes aware of its presence, sexual excitement occurs, and the fetich makes itself felt. (*PS*, 221)

Like the two religious worshippers in Tylor's example, Krafft-Ebing's two lovers appear outwardly identical, but the psychological significance of their worship is completely different. The normal lover sees the object as a representation, but the pathological fetishist sees it as significant in itself. While physiological fetishism transforms the object into a symbol, pathological fetishism makes it intrinsically erotic.

What were the causes and consequences of pathological fetishism? Krafft-Ebing's explanation focuses on three broad issues: impotence, heredity, and association. Of the first, he remarks that "pathological fetishism is not infrequently a cause of *psychical impotence*. Since the object upon which the sexual interest of the fetichist is concentrated stands, in itself, in no *immediate* relation to the normal sexual act, it often happens that the fetichist diminishes his excitability to normal stimuli by his perversion . . ." (*PS*, 223). The foot fetishist, for example, has a diminished interest in coitus. In this regard, the fetichist is distinct from the sadist or masochist: either has too much sexual energy and is regarded as a "*monstrum per excessum*" (*PS*, 220). The fetichist, by contrast, is a "*monstrum per defectum.*" As he notes, "Here the abnormality consists only in the fact that the whole sexual interest is concentrated on the impression made by a part of the person of the opposite sex, so that all other impressions fade and become more or less indifferent" (*PS*, 219–20). The pathology lies not in being stimulated by the part, but rather in the absence of any connection between it and the rest of the beloved. In this sense, the fetichist's sexual interests are diminished because they are narrowed to the fragment, and so the pathology is characterized by "what does not affect him,—the limitation of sexual interest that has taken place in him" (*PS*, 220).

Paradoxically, this diminution of interest leads to both impotence and excessive sexual energy, called "hyperaesthesia." Like the force generated by a broad river channeled into a narrow valley, the fetichist's *vita sexualis* develops "a correspondingly greater and abnormal intensity," because it is confined "within its narrower limits" (*PS*, 220). This focused intensity becomes the diagnostic criterion of pathological fetishism:

> The concentration of the sexual interest on a certain portion of the body that has no direct relation to sex (as have the mammae and external genitals)—a peculiarity to be emphasized—often leads body-fetichists to such a condition that they do not regard coitus as the real means of sexual gratification, but rather some form of manipulation of that portion of the body that is effectual as a fetich. (*PS*, 220)

Thus the disease gives itself away by a patient's sexual interest in nongenital areas (for the "body-fetichist"), or inanimate objects (for the "object-fetichist"). The finding is then confirmed by discovering impotence in the absence of the fetish. The diagnostic importance of hyperaesthesia, in part, explains why "only cases of pathological fetishism in men have thus far been observed" (*PS*, 224). While women are subject to physiological fetishism, their sublimated sexuality is, presumably, incompatible with an identifiable object.[21]

Some fetishes—a lock of hair, a handkerchief—entail little if any possibility for physical stimulation of the genitals and thus are inadequate for complete sexual gratification. For that purpose, he argues, the fetichist relies on self-stimulation, and so fetishism creates "conditions favouring psychical and physical onanism, which again reacts deleteriously on the constitution and sexual power."[22] While the practice further endangers the physical state of the body, that danger originates in a predisposition that was already there: "pathological fetichism seems to arise only on the basis of a psychopathic constitution that is for the most part hereditary" (*PS*, 221). Hence fetishism is both a product of and a contributor to the problem of degeneration. It is inherited, as are sadism and masochism; however, "if fetichism also rests upon a congenital general psychopathic disposition, yet this perversion is not, like those previously considered, essentially of an original nature; it is not congenitally perfect . . ." (*PS*, 221). Like Binet, Krafft-Ebing must account for both the general perversion and its specific form, and while heredity alone explains sadism or masochism, it does not explain the fetishist's preference for one object over another: "there must be a particular reason in every individual affected" (*PS*, 222). Although he rejected childhood associationism when theorizing physiological fetishism, he accepts it in the case of the pathology, and even paraphrases: "*Binet's* conclusion that *in the life of every fetichist there may be assumed to have been some event which determined the association of lustful feeling with the single impression*" (*PS*, 222). That event occurs in childhood "with the first awakening of the *vita sexualis*"; it becomes "associated with some partial sexual impression . . . and stamps it for life as the principal object of sexual interest" (*PS*, 222). Again the passage of time obscures the original event: "The circumstances under which the association arises are usually forgotten; the result of the association alone is retained" (*PS*, 222).

This amnesia, we have seen, differentiates pathological from physiological fetishism. It also redefines the physician's relationship to the fetishist. When a patient is stimulated by his lover's brown hair because it symbolizes all of the beloved's qualities, then patient and analyst agree on the sexual value of the object. Once that referentiality is "forgotten," fetishist and physician no longer agree. To the fetishist, brown hair is intrinsically erotic, and he cannot comprehend why everyone else does not feel the same. But to the physician, the hair is falsely valued, and here the fetishistic triangle reemerges. Rather than a European interpreting West African religious worship, we have the physician interpreting his patient's sexual practice, but in both cases the fetishist sees the object as attractive in and of itself, while the critic sees that attraction as evidence of delusion. That delusion—the essence of pathological fetishism—is linked with primitivism in two further senses. First, through the logic of degeneration, the inherited predisposition of the fetishist represents a reversion to a more primitive stage of development in the species. Second, through the logic of early childhood association, the fetishist's condition becomes meaningful in relation to an earlier stage of individual development, and so it represents a psychological primitivism within the individual.

Krafft-Ebing's pathological fetishism was an adaptation of the ethnological mechanism of primitive fetishism to describe the psychological mechanism of the modern individual. In *Psychopathia Sexualis*, fetishism still indicates an early stage of development, but it has migrated from the geographical space of primitive culture to that of the psychological subject in modern society. Krafft-Ebing created two distinct forms of fetishism, a pathological one that left its primitive associations intact, and a normal one that modified its structure and became the theoretical basis for human sexual attraction. In both cases, fetishism has successfully made the discursive shift from "savage" to "civilized," and in adapting it to the new science, sexologists successfully domesticated the primitive fetish, bringing it back, from its long colonial residency, to the heart of Europe's cultural framework.

A similar duality between two forms of fetishism exists in Freud's writing. He and the older Krafft-Ebing historically have been considered antagonists; among other differences, they took opposite stances on evolutionary biology, which Freud rejected. Nonetheless, Krafft-Ebing occupied a prominent place in Freud's early work: in *Three Essays on the Theory of Sexuality* (1905), his is the first name in the first note to the first essay.[23] *Three Essays* also contains Freud's earliest discussion of fetishism, and his approach to it demonstrates more affinity with, than antagonism toward Krafft-Ebing. In the first edition, the fetishistic triangle remains intact, much as it did in Krafft-Ebing's fourth edition, sixteen years earlier. It did not stay that way for long, and in Freud's later writing that triangle undergoes significant modifications, out of which will emerge the concept of *fetishistic disavowal*, the ambivalent characteristic that defined fetishism after Freud.[24]

Freud's engagement with the topic began inauspiciously; fetishism was a relatively minor concern in *Three Essays*, occupying less than three pages in the first essay, "The Sexual Aberrations." Like Krafft-Ebing, he viewed the disorder in relation to the full spectrum of sexual perversions and not as an isolated pathology. But Freud's explanation for deviance differed radically from that of the older sexologist. Where Krafft-Ebing pointed to anthropological inheritance, Freud rejected the degenerationist model and saw the perversions as outcroppings from a single, universal sexual instinct.[25] Without degeneration to explain their existence, he could not attribute them to the patient's physical constitution; instead, he argued that their origin lay in "something innate in *everyone*" that was variously shaped by individual childhood experiences (*SE*, 7:171). As in Krafft-Ebing, normal sexuality was narrowly defined, consisting of brief erotic play that culminated in heterosexual copulation. But Freud used the narrow definition in a different way, suggesting that fewer people wholly conformed to it than was generally believed, so that "we have quite remarkably increased the number of people who might be regarded as perverts" (*SE*, 7:171). This diminished range of normal sexuality was further reduced by the neuroses. Normal sexuality for Freud existed at the center of a continuum, and on either side were opposite degrees of success at repressing the sexual instinct. Excessive repression led to the neuroses; unable to find an outlet, the sexual instinct flowed into conversion symptoms. In the opposite case, too little repression led to the perversions, by allowing the sexual instinct to express itself in its rawest form. Thus, where Krafft-Ebing defined the sexual fetishist as a *monstrum per defectum*, Freud reclassified him as a *monstrum per excessum*. He summarized the inverse relationship between the two ends of the sexual continuum by emphasizing that *"neuroses are, so to say, the negative of perversions"* (*SE*, 7:165). Squeezed in the middle, normal sexuality became the remaining range of behaviors, bounded by the excessive expression or repression of a single sexual instinct. As manifestations of the sexual instinct in uninhibited form, the perversions thus afforded a unique opportunity to study the raw material of normal sexuality.

In Freud's explanation of specific perversions, fetishism, while a comparatively minor topic, receives a unique treatment. He classifies the perversions within two broad categories, depending on whether they deviate in the sexual *object* ("the person from whom sexual attraction proceeds") or *aim* ("the act toward which the instinct tends") (*SE*, 7:125–36). To use a grammatical analogy, the object and aim are respectively the noun and verb in the syntax of sexuality. In normal sexuality, noun and verb are both appropriate to heterosexual copulation. In the perversions, one or both are inappropriate. Inverts, pedophiles, and zoophiles represent deviations of sexual object; their disorders are like sentences in which the noun does not match the verb. Deviations of aim involve a misuse of the sexual verb, as in the case of oral, anal, or other nongenital sexual acts.

He terms fetishism a "highly interesting group of aberrations of the sexual instinct among the deviations in respect of the sexual *object*" (*SE*, 7:153). In explaining the practice, Freud refers back to the primitive fetish, as Binet and Krafft-Ebing had done: "Such substitutes are with some justice likened to the fetishes in which savages believe that their gods are embodied" (*SE*, 7:153). His simile likens the patient to the savage, but it also implies that the therapist is like the European trader, who labels the assessment of the object as overvalued. This aspect of the therapeutic role is consistent with his explanation of the key ingredient of fetishism, "sexual overvaluation," so that, once again, we are trading in competing definitions of value (*SE*, 7:150). Overvaluation, he points out, is commonplace: while the normal aim is theoretically restricted to "union of the actual genitals," only in "the rarest of instances" is interest confined to the genitals alone

(*SE*, 7:150–51). The "psychical valuation that is set on the sexual object" can extend to the lips and even the whole body, for example (*SE*, 7:151). While such extensions switch the sexual noun, they can also produce a secondary shift in the sexual verb: "it helps to turn activities connected with other parts of the body into sexual aims" (*SE*, 7:151). In fetishism:

> What is substituted for the sexual object is some part of the body (such as the foot or hair) which is in general very inappropriate for sexual purposes, or some inanimate object which bears an assignable relation to the person whom it replaces and preferably to that person's sexuality (e.g. a piece of clothing or underlinen). (*SE*, 7:153)

As a result of the substitution, fetishism involves an actual "abandonment of the sexual aim," along with the substitute object; along with voyeurism/exhibitionism and sadism/masochism, it is one of the perversions that entails both a substitute object and a substitute aim. Instead of normal sexual gratification, "the longing for the fetish . . . actually *takes the place* of the normal aim" (*SE*, 7:154). At this point, he leaves aside the problem of how this process of psychic overvaluation can produce a "longing" that, by itself, becomes the new sexual aim, but what he does describe is an object whose sole sexual function is that of being desired, and in that respect, Freud defines the fetish as self-justifying.

Because sexuality exists on a continuum, he needs to articulate the dividing line between "what is physiological from pathological symptoms" (*SE*, 7:161). These are the same two terms that Krafft-Ebing used, of course, and like him, Freud agrees that a "certain degree of fetishism is thus habitually present in normal love" (*SE*, 7:154). In addition to retaining Krafft-Ebing's terms, he also centers the question of difference on whether or not the object has the status of a representation. Fetishism becomes "pathological . . . when the fetish becomes detached from a particular individual and becomes the sole sexual object" (*SE*, 7:154). In the normal version of fetishism, the object is a synecdoche for the whole person and assists in accomplishing the normal aim; thus the sexual syntax remains intact. In the pathological version, however, the object loses its connection to the whole person and becomes meaningful in itself; divorced from representation, it transubstantiates, taking on an apparently intrinsic erotic quality. Therefore the distinguishing feature of pathological fetishism is the transformation of the object into a thing of overvalued meaning. He uses the same distinction, more broadly, to theorize the relationship between the perversions generally and normal sexuality. Behaviors that are otherwise perverse can emerge as components within normal sexuality, without contradicting it, so long as they appear as part of the normal sexual aim and object. But if the perversion "ousts them completely and takes their place in *all* circumstances—if, in short, a perversion has the characteristics of exclusiveness and fixation," then it crosses the border-line into the terrain of the pathological (*SE*, 7:161). At this stage of his thinking, Freud's fetishism still resembled Krafft-Ebing's, even in making the key distinction between the normal, representational form and the pathological, non-representational variant.

—⁓—

Freud regularly revisited the topic until his death, in 1939. He began to modify his initial views soon after the first edition of *Three Essays*, and the changes show up in the footnotes he added in 1910, 1915, and 1920.[26] He summarized and consolidated these diffuse notes in "Fetishism," a short paper published in 1927 that introduced the major elements of his revised theory.[27] Several vital points were taken up in more detail in two later works, "The Splitting of the Ego in the Process of Defense" (1938) and chapter 8 of *An Outline of Psychoanalysis* (1940).[28] Taken together, these three pieces outline the architecture of his final theory of fetishism. The modifications occurred along two parallel conceptual tracks, both of which need further discussion: the interpretation of the fetish as psychologically symbolic and the theory of the split ego. The first has an immediate bearing on the concept of fetishism, while the second is a redefinition of human psychology, in which fetishism serves as the primary example.

He first touched on the symbolic nature of the fetish in the first edition of *Three Essays*. Explaining the fetishist's choice of object, he asserts cryptically that "the replacement of the object by a fetish is determined by a symbolic connection of thought, of which the person concerned is usually not conscious" (*SE*, 7:155). Like Krafft-Ebing, he uses Binet's logic of forgotten, early associations and points out that, because the fetishist cannot explain the attraction, the analyst may be unaware of its underlying symbolic logic. The first hint of what he will make of that symbolism appears in a note on foot fetishism, added in 1910, where he connects the interest in feet to early childhood sexuality, claiming, "the foot represents a woman's penis, the absence of which is deeply felt" (*SE*, 7:155n2). In "Fetishism," this association with the imaginary female penis becomes the general rule rather than a particular case. There, he tells us that the symbolic "meaning and purpose of the fetish" is always the same: "The fetish is a substitute for the woman's (the mother's) penis that the little boy once believed in and—for reasons familiar to us—does not want to give up" (*SE*, 21:152–53). Freud's mythic little boy fears being punished by the father, with whom he competes for the mother's affections. According to this *bildungsroman*, his first glimpse of the mother's genitals seems to show him what that punishment will entail; since he naively imagines that her genitals are like his own, he concludes that she has been castrated and that the same lies in store for him. In normal sexual development, he finally accepts this "fact" and submits to the father's will by giving up his narcissistic fantasies about the mother, but in fetishism the boy's response takes a different turn. He fixates on something that symbolizes the mother's penis to him, and this object emotionally reassures him that the father's threat is not real. Thus fetishism serves as a defense mechanism, alleviating his fear by creating a substitute for the absent penis. It also impairs the process of his psychological maturation. Fetishism allows him to continue denying the reality of those external forces that exist outside the narcissistic world of early childhood.[29]

Freud leaves unexplained the question of why "the fright of castration at the sight of a female genital" leads to fetishism in some but not in others (*SE*, 21:154). The question is critical. Because he rejects the theory of degeneration, he must find an alternate account for the uneven occurrence of fetishism in the population. Furthermore, while some react to the fear of castration through fetishism, and most "surmount it" to develop normal adult heterosexuality, still others become homosexual; the causes for these different outcomes are unclear (*SE*, 21:154). Although he does not solve the problem at this point, he does reconfigure the relationship between homosexuality and fetishism. Charcot, Magnan, and Binet all defined homosexuality as a form of fetishism; Krafft-Ebing disagreed on this point, arguing that homosexuality also had a strong congenital component created by degeneration.[30] Freud argues that the two are antithetical; most fetishists are heterosexual, he claims, and from this hypothesizes that fetishism "saves the fetishist from becoming a homosexual, by endowing women with the characteristic which makes them tolerable as sexual objects" (*SE*, 21:154).

The reasoning behind the specific choice of fetish object also remains enigmatic. While all fetishes function "as substitutes for the absent female penis," not all physically resemble a penis (*SE*, 21:155). Referencing Binet, he asserts that it is not always possible for the analyst to discover how the choice of fetish is determined; however, he goes further to speculate that the object choice resembles "the stopping of memory in traumatic amnesia," in which the last thing the subject remembers is overvalued (*SE*, 21:155). In this theory of temporal metonymy, the last object glimpsed before the infant is traumatized by the discovery of castration becomes "retained as a fetish" (*SE*, 21:155). A toddler's position beneath the standing mother explains the frequency of a foot or shoe fetish; fur and velvet are particularly difficult to reconcile with phallic symbolism, yet they resemble the pubic hair seen immediately prior to recognizing the traumatic absence; undergarments "crystallize the moment of undressing, the last moment in which the woman could still be regarded as phallic" (*SE*, 21:155). Through accidents of temporal proximity, any object can become a phallic symbol.

Whatever object is chosen, its symbolic significance as a substitute for the female phallus is necessarily ambivalent, and Freud explains this complication by focusing on the interrelationship of its two contrary facets. The fetish is both "a token of triumph over the threat of castration and a protection against it" (*SE*, 21:154). Mannoni explains the ambivalence clearly: "The fetish represents the indelible stigma, the memorial to the discovery of feminine castration and, at the same time, to the conservation of a contrary and hidden belief," and thus embodies the "possibility of simultaneously embracing two contrary beliefs, one official and one secret, secret even from the subject. . . ."[31] Simultaneously, the fetish obviates the fear of castration and reaffirms its reality. The substitute is only meaningful because the phallus it represents is in fact absent. It comforts and reassures, but it is also a product of the traumatic discovery, becoming the objective proof of the discovery it symbolically elides. In Freud's narrative, the child "has retained" the belief in the woman's phallus, "but he has also given it up" (*SE*, 21:154). He describes a two-sided object, in that "both the disavowal and the affirmation of the castration have found their way into the construction of the fetish itself" (*SE*, 21:156). As an example of how it comes to stand for two opposite things simultaneously, he mentions the Chinese practice of foot binding: the mutilation symbolically affirms castration, while the club-like foot also substitutes for the mother's penis. Fetishistic ambivalence is thus the distinguishing feature of Freud's fetish.[32]

The ambivalence theorized in "Fetishism" is further examined in its sequel, "The Splitting of the Ego in the Process of Defence" (*SE*, 23:273–78). A sketchy, unfinished paper, it presents the case history of a three- or four-year-old boy; he was caught masturbating by his "energetic nurse and was threatened with castration, the carrying out of which was, as usual, ascribed to his father" (*SE*, 23:276). Given this threat, he must choose between his pleasure in masturbation and his fear of punishment. Freud views this situation as a conflict between the internal demand of the sexual instinct and the external demand of the real world, which prohibits infantile sexuality. In Freud's analysis, the boy chooses both options. On the one hand, he finds a way to rationalize his continued masturbation by consciously disavowing the reality of the threat. On the other, he develops a phobia of having his little toes touched, which Freud interprets as evidence that he has displaced his castration fear onto a phallic substitute. The result is that the boy forms two contradictory psychical attitudes that then coexist indefinitely.

Fetishism became the particular pathology through which Freud constructed his late theory of the split ego. In the posthumously published *An Outline of Psycho-Analysis* (1940), he consolidates his theory and describes the split ego as the simultaneous holding of two contrary attitudes: "one, the normal one, which takes account of reality, and another which under the influence of the instincts detaches the ego from reality" (*SE*, 23:202). Fetishism proves to be "a particularly favourable subject for studying the question," and he produces his final, definitive description of the psychological process through which the fetish is constructed:

> This abnormality . . . is, as is well known, based on the patient (who is almost always male) not recognizing the fact that females have no penis—a fact which is extremely undesirable to him since it is a proof of the possibility of his being castrated himself. He therefore disavows his own sense-perception which showed him that the female genitals lack a penis and holds fast to the contrary conviction. The disavowed perception does not, however, remain entirely without influence, for, in spite of everything, he has not the courage to assert that he actually saw a penis. He takes hold of something else instead—a part of the body or some other object—and assigns it the role of the penis which he cannot do without. It is usually something that he in fact saw at the moment at which he saw the female genitals, or it is something that can suitably serve as a symbolic substitute for the penis. (*SE*, 23:202–3)

Fetishists characteristically maintain the contradictory attitudes "side by side throughout their lives without influencing each other," both avoiding the fear of castration and accepting it, and this "may rightly be called a splitting of the ego" (*SE*, 23:203). Because the split ego is not specific to fetishists so much as an attribute of human psychology, in the final analysis, pathological fetishism seems little different from its normal, physiological twin. As a perversion, it sits on the border with normal sexuality because it is "so often only partially developed" (*SE*, 23:203). As he explains, "In fetishists, therefore, the detachment of the ego from the reality of the external world has never succeeded completely" (*SE*, 23:203). This imperfect state of affairs leads him to redefine pathological fetishism as the residual trace of a perversion that "does not govern the choice of object exclusively but leaves room for a greater or lesser amount of normal sexual behaviour; sometimes, indeed, it retires into playing a modest part or is limited to a mere hint" (*SE*, 23:203). In effect, Freud inflates the categorical boundary of the pathology to include behaviors previously defined as physiological.

The consequence of this more expansive view can readily be seen in the diminution of fetishism's effects. The new fetishist presents symptoms far less debilitating than those of the earlier generation. Krafft-Ebing's perverts are tortured by their condition, and many of their case histories are a litany of despair:

> Case 96. Mr. V., thirty years, civil servant; parents neuropathic. Since his seventh year he had for a playmate a lame girl of the same

age. . . . Always heterosexual but abnormally sensual he sought early relations with the opposite sex, but was absolutely impotent with women who were not lame. . . . As, in consequence of his fetishism the opportunities for coitus occurred but seldom, he resorted to masturbation, but found it a disgusting and miserable substitute. His sexual anomaly rendered him very unhappy, and he was often near committing suicide, but regard for his parents prevented him. (*PS*, 236–37)

Case 122. Mr. Z., an American, thirty-three years of age, manufacturer, for eight years enjoying a happy married life, blessed with offspring; consulted me for a peculiar troublesome glove-fetishism. He despised himself on account of it, and said it brought him well nigh to the verge of despair and even insanity. (*PS*, 277)

These early fetishists regularly suffer "*taedium vitae*," following from the self-loathing caused by the condition and the behaviors to which it drives them. The end result is usually the same: "His present existence was one of untold misery" (*PS*, 236). In stark contrast, Freud's new fetishists are untroubled by their perversion. "Usually they are quite satisfied with it, or even praise the way in which it eases their erotic life. As a rule, therefore, the fetish made its appearance in analysis as a subsidiary finding" (*SE*, 21:152). While the early fetishist has an urgent need for the physician to treat the disability, the new one feels little need of therapy on this account, appearing to be a comparatively happy subject who rarely seeks help for the condition. Thus Freud's fetishism was both more widespread and less devastating than the pathology his predecessor described.[33]

In consequence, the relationship between patient and therapist changes; however much the therapist believes the patient to need treatment, the patient no longer sees a need for the therapist, and in that sense, the therapist is newly relegated to the sidelines. This diminished role reflects a fundamental transformation that takes place in the structure of fetishism, once the conflict between disavowal and affirmation is introduced. In terms of the fetishistic triangle, the critic is no longer entirely distinct from the worshipper. The outsider's position resides within the subject as the affirmative aspect of the split ego. Recovered patients have taught Freud, "that at the time in some corner of their mind (as they put it) there was a normal person hidden, who, like a detached spectator, watched the hubbub of illness go past him" (*SE*, 23:202). As this anecdote suggests, while Freud retains the opposition between critic and worshipper, he also combines them within a single psychological subject, who both accepts and rejects the belief in the fetish, maintaining two contradictory positions simultaneously. In ethnological terms, this fetishist is part worshipper and part outsider, primitive savage and civilized colonizer combined. This new fetishism inevitably demotes the importance of the analyst, who now duplicates the critical perspective already located within the subjectivity of the new fetishist. Thus, while retaining the basic triangular structure of fetishism, Freud imagines a psychological subject who independently embodies the dynamic of primitive fetishism.

—⁂—

The critic within: fetishism as such originates here, in the internal assessment of the object as erotically overvalued and thus a fetish. Unlike the colonial encounter, both the critic and fetish worshipper now coexist in the same psychological subject, where they take the form of ongoing debate. This instability appears as "an uneasy mixture of credulity and disbelief."[34] The most well-known "formula of fetishistic disavowal" is the expression, "I know very well, but still . . . ," illustrating a subject who both believes and disbelieves at the same time.[35] This can only happen when the critic, previously associated with the external physician or analyst, is incorporated into the theoretical model of the patient's psychology. Implicit in this formulation is an act of self-reflexivity. Freud imagines the mind of the patient and sees himself staring back at him in the shape of the patient's affirming aspect, that inner person who stands apart and watches "the hubbub of illness go past him." This "detached spectator" looks more than a little like the physician observing the patient—after all, it plays the same role as the physician within the inner theatrics of fetishistic ambivalence. In much the same manner that Tylor saw himself in his primitive man, Freud looks into his patient and discovers an alienated version of himself, here redefined as the principle of fetishistic affirmation.

That fetishism should form a necessary part of Freud's act of writing about it is, of course, a problem that, having seen it in Arnold, Eliot, and Tylor, by now we readily expect. Other scholars have already discussed the fetishism within his theory of fetishism and linked it to the construction of the primal scene. Freud grounded the pathology on the family narrative of the boy who is traumatized by the absence of the penis in the mother, and he used this scene to establish what he calls "the unwelcome fact of women's castration" (*SE*, 21:156). Resisting this fact leads to the production of the fetish as the object of disavowal. But, as Bernheimer has discussed, her castration never was a "fact."[36] She was only castrated in Freud's hypothetical reconstruction of a generic boy's imaginary logic, where, the argument goes, castration *ought* to be seen as fact, even though it is not a fact. As the building block for the climactic acceptance of the reality principle, the reverse logic of the primal scene is less than ideal. It makes the acceptance of the real contingent on accepting a delusion. While this might have some logical force as a means to assert the primacy of psychological reality over objective fact, it proves wholly illogical as the basic precondition to a theory of fetishism. By most definitions, the belief that something false is true is magical thinking. In this instance, Freud describes how the mother's body takes on the false value of mutilation and becomes symbolically inhabited by the evil spirit of the boy's male ancestor, intent on doing him harm. If this were a colonial encounter, the critic would label the boy's perception an example of fetishism. Freud insists on the psychological necessity of the unconditional belief in the mother's penis, consciously giving himself over to this "reality," and fully experiencing the horror of the loss that did not happen. There is a compulsory, paradoxical fetishism at work in this narrative because the acceptance of reality can only be accomplished through the acceptance of a fantasy, and one that Freud identifies as a delusion. While the basic principle he asserts with this narrative is the child's need to give over his primary narcissism, the means he posits to achieve this goal requires a deeper immersion in the child's narcissism, becoming a subject wholly centered on his penis and its universality. Such a perspective makes it impossible for the boy to see the physical reality of the female anatomy displayed in front of him. Bernheimer defines the delusion of the normal boy as the actual fetishism: "The fetishist is characterized not by his incapacity to accept woman's lack but rather by his incapacity not to see woman as lacking" (81). McClintock makes a related claim, arguing that Freud's fin-de-siècle cultural values led him to define the male body as universal and the female body as its mutilation, and this creates problems in his valuation of the penis: "the logic by which Freud privileges the penis in the scenario of fetishism is itself fetishistic."[37] Both commentaries thus point out the circular grounding of Freud's theorization of fetishism in fetishism, arguing that he reproduces the logic of fetishism in the act of its description. At this point in the study of Freud's work, identifying him or his theories as fetishistic is a familiar trope, thanks to the work of these and other critics. Indeed, one need only consider the volume of articles written on his use of cigars alone to get a sense of how well-worn a theme Freud's fetishism has become.[38] However, by considering his version of fetishism in relation to its Victorian predecessor, we can also see that this self-reflexive pattern was not unique to him, nor was he any more or less guilty of it than the Victorians.

Ultimately, fetishism must be divorced from the primal scene and its linchpin of castration.[39] Anthropological fetishism certainly enjoyed a life apart from the primal scene, but this was not, as we have seen, a "better" or less self-contradicting ideology so much as a different manifestation of the same problem. The primitive fetish was rooted in an alternate fantasy, that of the European encounter with a culture whose existence was no more real than Freud's suppositious female penis. Replacing the primal scene with a "primitive" one merely substitutes one set of problems for a second, closely related set. The real value of considering the two different theories of fetishism in tandem is that it allows us to see their commonality, apart from an erotic or anthropological context. Fetishism needs to be stripped down to this core, as a commentary on relationships and an example of positionality. It is premised on neither specifically colonial nor therapeutic relationships but on the underlying ability to define someone else as guilty of overvaluation. Corollary to that is the inevitability of having your own values labeled as fetishes. This essential dialogue is adaptable to many situations, of course, and this protean quality gives it a broad utility, as its lengthy history suggests. Once we accept that basic premise, we are finally able to consider the specificity of fetishism in the nineteenth century and the very different uses to which fetishism was put by psychoanalysis, in the twentieth. Fetishism is a dialogue premised on the logic of the fetish triangle, with which we began, in which one's claim of fetishism entails contamination by the thing it voices. To understand fetishism in this stripped-down form is to understand why its future promises to be every bit as long, drawn out, ideologically charged, and contentious as its past. That prospect explains why the analysis of fetishism will long remain a necessary part of scholarly discourse.

Conclusion

The nineteenth-century debate over culture proved to be a generative argument. It led to questions about both the value of art and the logic of social bodies. At the same time, it defined their opposites: the concept of artifacts sans aesthetic value and the irrationality of particular social bodies. Writers on culture positioned fetishism as its antithesis. To the extent that they could convincingly define the imaginary state of cultural absence, they succeeded in constructing culture as a real and definite system of values in high art and as a tangible object of ethnographic description. It was thus incumbent upon Arnold, Eliot, and Tylor to dwell on the details of a life with too little culture in order to shape their concepts of culture through high relief.

Despite their differences—Arnold's rhetorical ambiguity, Eliot's detailed realism, Tylor's scientific methodology—these writers of the 1860s and 1870s drew on primitive fetishism as the fundamental trope for defining the lack of culture. In this assumption, they were guilty of projection. Working with the limited evidence available, they colored in the outline of unculture in terms that made sense to them, as if this imaginary being were an extension of themselves. These projections were taken as factual because they accounted for the evidence and they fit with mid-Victorian beliefs. Ironically, these writers accused the uncultured of anthropomorphizing the world, while unaware that they, too, were engaging in the practice. In the case of unculture, this was defined as a dangerously subjective perspective with a distinct resemblance to solipsism. This imaginary primitive was in part a metaphorical embodiment of that central Victorian fear, in which the individual's subjectivity is all-in-all, leaving no room for the shared experience of a common, external world. "I will not shut me from my kind," famously declares the speaker of *In Memoriam*: "What find I in the highest place, / But mine own phantom chanting hymns?"[1] He rejects these self-reflections, and so we can begin to recognize how frequently the fear of self-projection appears in Victorian literature and how closely that fear relates to the reaction against the earlier, positive perspective on the imagination in Romantic literature.[2] And so to explain culture in terms of fetishism was a less surprising move at the time than it would seem today, when the idea of primitives and primitive fetishism are historical relics, when "primitive" and "modern" are not considered the antipodes of an evolutionary continuum, and when fetishism is associated with sexuality or economics rather than the generic condition of unculture.

Fetishism stood in opposition to culture, and, for related reasons, it also stood in opposition to representation, including language. Now as then, the concept of fetishism points to an extralinguistic space. Paradoxically, it represents representation's limit, insisting on the presence of something incapable of being represented in language. It was not the only limit case filling the generic role of the extralinguistic sphere. Classifying emotion as occupying that same, great beyond is far more familiar to us, as when Arnold writes: "And long we try in vain to speak and act / Our hidden self, and what we say and do / Is eloquent, is well—but 'tis not true!"[3] This well-known passage is self-contradicting, in that Arnold defines the idea of something outside language in language. This is more than a case of being tongue-tied. The poem illustrates that this "hidden self" is not so hidden, after all, but rather something made visible in writing. If you did not have a visibly hidden self before reading this poem, you certainly would after reading it, because the poem creates the condition it pretends to describe. "The Buried Life" is one example among many of how language is used to create the concept of something outside it. Though less understood today, the interest in fetishism is another example, and so the parallel with Arnold's not-so-hidden self is heuristic. Fetishism was not ultimately independent of representation, any more than Arnold's hidden self. More particularly, the fetish concept is the byproduct of representation's construction of an outside; its status as truth depends upon representation's insistence on a space that cannot be represented. While fetishism is positioned as the antonym of representation, it is also representation's creature. The impetus of language to create its own outside helps to explain the relationship between culture and primitive fetishism. The representation of fetishism as outside culture is itself a cultural product. In the same way that Arnold's language represents the space of the so-called extralinguistic, so culture represents the space of unculture. In nineteenth-century Britain, that space was characterized as primitive fetishism.

By the early twentieth century, the relationship between fetishism and culture had undergone a sea change, as both *fetishism* and *culture* separately took on new meanings. When fetishism became sexualized, it ceased to serve as a term of opposition to culture. Erotic fetishism was a disease of civilization; as such, it was a condition produced by the excesses of modern culture rather than its insufficiency, so that fetishism and culture were no longer mutually exclusive. The anthropological fetish might have continued to serve that oppositional function if anyone still accepted it, but once the concept of social evolution developing in uniform stages collapsed, the binary opposition between the two extremes of that continuum, primitive fetishism and advanced civilization, fell apart. When anthropology shifted from the singular *culture* to the all-encompassing notion of *cultures*, fetishism (in the newer form of *animism*) returned to something more like the circumscribed position it had held prior to the Enlightenment, as a purely localized practice.[4] Primitive fetishism as the stereotype of unculture did not disappear entirely, of course; it remained a staple of popular adventure stories for boys, such as those written in the mold of William H. G. Kingston, and it seems to have enjoyed a long afterlife in cinematic treatments of "savages" and "lost worlds."[5]

The problems fetishism posed to the writers discussed in this book were products of assumptions that flowered—if one can call it that—during the second half of the nineteenth century. This was a specifically Victorian fetishism, one that had its day and has since been forgotten. Similarly, the fetishistic triangle and its dialectic were historically-bound patterns and not generic problems of truth and falsity in epistemology. The fetish triangle was one kind of misunderstanding, with several defining traits. As a perception of overvaluation, it was necessarily tied to the world of concrete objects, rather than abstractions; thus an error in formulating a mathematical equation or logical argument would not qualify as a form of fetishism. But not all abstractions were excluded. Fetishism was a statement about perceptions of material reality, rather than material reality as such. As Tylor demonstrated, ideas can take on the mantle of objects through the process of reification, and in those cases, abstractions could and did take on the qualities of primitive fetishes.[6] Unlike all forms of misapprehension, fetishism applied only to errors of projection; the fetishist was a genuine worshipper, lacking an awareness that he or she was anthropomorphizing the object; thus intentional falsification was not fetishism. Finally, while the Victorian fetish was an object, fetishism itself was a triangulated relationship between the object and two people with competing standards of value. It was ultimately an assessment by one of the other's belief in the supernatural qualities of the object, but instead of a straightforward relativism—a disagreement between equals—fetishism had a distinct hierarchical register, in which the worshipper is posited as socially inferior to the more advanced critic. Without this last attribute, it would never have been possible to deploy fetishism as a rhetorical tool of social critique.

Significant differences exist between the idea of fetishism, then and now, and they need mention in order to draw attention to the strangeness of the concept to our modern sensibilities. While it used to imply supernaturalism, it now implies eroticism, and these implications resonate differently. While the concepts of the spiritual and sexual have much in common, their metaphorical uses are in many ways complete opposites. As Tylor and his contemporaries understood it, the fetish had spiritual and religious associations; it was a thing promising health or sickness, fortune or impoverishment, protection against one's enemies or vulnerability. As a metaphor, it could be used by social conservatives to describe a tradition of reverence and obedience to an external power, as Carlyle did; progressives could use the same associations to describe superstition and ignorance, as Arnold and Eliot showed us. Perhaps most importantly, fetishism then bore the full weight of social meaning as a sign of inferior status, whether used to denigrate Africans, women, provincials, or servants.[7] With its translation from the domain of cultural evolution to Freudian psychology, it lost that explicit connection to the social, entering instead the ahistorical domain of psychological universalism. Freud further limited its usefulness as an indirect term of social commentary (one in which the stages of psychological development might be coded as social development): while it was a sign of psychological immaturity, it was one of the weakest because it was a marginal instance, situated on the border with normality. Instead of the polar opposite of normal sexuality, fetishism was its closest relation.[8] Fetishism can be adapted to social critique, but in the main, Freudianism stripped it of its overt social meaning, and that deracination is one of the most noticeable differences between twentieth-century fetishism and its long-lived predecessor.[9]

Victorian fetishism is largely unfamiliar today, and doubtless we are better off without it. But that historical distance matters. The fetish dialectic implicates all acts of writing about fetishism, including this one, and from the moment I began working on this topic, I considered how it must implicate my own critique. And yet, in the end, I believe the case is no more or less difficult than that of writing on any other topic in cultural history. The historical specificity that gave rise to the belief in primitive fetishism is long gone; the urgency it possessed for them does not hold for us. With the intervention of a century and more, the context for writing is changed, and that makes it possible to approach this topic in a different way from that of the Victorians because I have had to reconstruct a debate whose terms have been lost. That makes it easier to attempt as objective an analysis of the older paradigm as possible. Others will argue whether or not the present work achieves that goal, but, for me, the difficulty posed by the self-reflexive nature of Victorian fetishism pales in comparison to the importance of establishing the paradigm's prominence in Victorian culture. Whether or not I succeed in making the case for fetishism's significance will ultimately be the only ground on which my act of writing about fetishism, and about the problems it posed to Victorian writers, can rest.

Notes

Introduction

1. The current debate concerns several different theories of culture, rather than one, though we still refer to it as "the" culture debate. On the varieties of current definitions and the arguments about them, see William H. Sewell, Jr., "The Concept(s) of Culture," *Beyond the Cultural Turn*, ed. Victoria E. Bonnell and Lynn Hunt, New Directions in the Study of Society and Culture (Berkeley: University of California Press, 1999). On the earlier genealogy of cultural studies through the 1980s, see Stuart Hall, "Cultural Studies: Two Paradigms," *Culture / Power / History: A Reader in Contemporary Social Theory*, ed. Nicholas B. Dirks, Geoff Eley, and Sherry B. Ortner (Princeton: Princeton University Press, 1994).

2. Brad Evans, *Before Cultures: The Ethnographic Imagination in American Literature, 1865–1920* (Chicago: University of Chicago Press, 2005), 190. Evans views the lack of definition favorably. For other essays in this vein, see Andrew Ross, "Giving Culture Hell: A Response to Catherine Gallagher," *Social Text 30* 10, no. 1 (1992); and Cary Nelson, Paula Treichler, and Lawrence Grossberg, "Cultural Studies: An Introduction," *Cultural Studies*, ed. Lawrence Grossberg, Cary Nelson, and Paula Treichler (New York: Routledge, 1992). Complaints about definitional failure can be found in Christopher Herbert, *Culture and Anomie: Ethnographic Imagination in the Nineteenth Century* (Chicago: University of Chicago Press, 1991); Catherine Gallagher, "Raymond Williams and Cultural Studies," *Social Text 30* 10, no. 1 (1992); Geoffrey H. Hartman, *The Fateful Question of Culture*, The Wellek Library Lecture Series at the University of California, Irvine (New York: Columbia University Press, 1997); and Terry Eagleton, *The Idea of Culture*,

Chapman's Quarterly Series (Oxford: Blackwell, 2000). Bonnell and Hunt adopt a nonjudgmental, historical stance in the important essay introducing their anthology; see Victoria E. Bonnell and Lynn Hunt, introduction to *Beyond the Cultural Turn: New Directions in the Study of Society and Culture* (Berkeley: University of California Press, 1999).

3. Most discussions of the history of the culture concept in literary studies refer back to Raymond Williams, *Culture and Society: 1780–1950* (New York: Columbia University Press, 1958). His focus on the history of ideas is convincingly critiqued in Herbert, *Culture*. Another important account is Eagleton, *Idea of Culture*, chapter 1.

4. E. P. Thompson, "The Long Revolution (Part 1)," *New Left Review* 1, no. 9 (1961): 33.

5. Gallagher, "Raymond Williams," 80.

6. Tylor's definition of culture begins, "Culture or civilization . . . is that complex whole," and he wavered between using the accepted term, *civilization,* or adapting the German word *Cultur* for an English audience. See A. L. Kroeber and Clyde Kluckhohn, *Culture: A Critical Review of Concepts and Definitions*, Papers of the Peabody Museum of American Archaeology and Ethnology, Vol. 47, No. 1 (Cambridge, MA: Peabody Museum, 1952), 9. The importance of his dual usage is discussed in George W. Stocking, "Matthew Arnold, E. B. Tylor, and the Uses of Invention," *American Anthropologist* 65 (1963).

7. See Henri J. M. Claessen, "Evolution and Evolutionism," *Encyclopedia of Social and Cultural Anthropology*, ed. Alan Barnard and Jonathan Spencer (New York: Routledge, 1996).

8. Tylor argued that there is no scientific evidence to document a state of life without culture; while theoretically possible, such a condition was wholly unavailable to us except as sheer speculation. For Tylor, primitives were at the first stage of cultural development, rather than entirely without culture. See Edward B. Tylor, *Primitive Culture: Researches into the Development of Mythology, Philosophy, Religion, Language, Art, and Custom*, 2nd ed., 2 vols. (London: John Murray, 1873), chapter 2.

9. E. D. Hirsch, Jr., *Cultural Literacy: What Every American Needs to Know* (New York: Vintage, 1988). In Hirsch, breadth becomes the result of exposure to the "best" ideas.

10. On the relationship between Arnold and Tylor's theories of culture, see Marc Demarest, "Arnold and Tylor: The Codification and Appropriation of Culture," *Bucknell Review* 34, no. 2 (1990); and Stocking, "Matthew Arnold."

11. Matthew Arnold, *The Complete Prose Works of Matthew Arnold*, ed. R. H. Super, 11 vols. (Ann Arbor: University of Michigan Press, 1960), 5:218,

5:235. Further references are abbreviated *CP* and cited in the text. As I discuss in chapter 4, Tylor took issue with Comte's overly broad definition of *fetishism*, substituting the term *animism* for the same condition and redefining *fetishism* in a more restricted sense.

12. Friedrich Nietzsche, "On Truth and Lying in a Non-Moral Sense," *The Birth of Tragedy and Other Writings*, ed. Raymond Geuss and Ronald Speirs, trans. Ronald Speirs, Cambridge Texts in the History of Philosophy (Cambridge: Cambridge University Press, 1999), 146.

13. Harriet Martineau published the first English translation of *Cours* in 1853, but the French text was available in Britain as early as 1837. See chapter 1.

14. George W. Stocking, *Victorian Anthropology* (New York: Free Press, 1987), 1–6.

15. See Yvonne ffrench, *The Great Exhibition: 1851* (London: Harvill, 1950), 211–36.

16. Ibid., 130–31.

17. Flora lived to the age of twenty-two, dying in 1864. She and Martinas are examples from a long history of the carnivalesque display of "savages" in Europe and America, a history that neither began nor ended with the Crystal Palace. See Roslyn Poignant, *Professional Savages: Captive Lives and Western Spectacle* (New Haven: Yale University Press, 2004), 189–201. Poignant's work is a detailed history of two groups of Australian aborigines who were paraded around the world in the late nineteenth century, and it places them within the broader context of similar human displays.

18. Pierre Bourdieu, *Distinction: A Social Critique of the Judgement of Taste*, trans. Richard Nice (Cambridge: Harvard University Press, 1984), 7.

19. Henrika Kuklick, *The Savage Within: The Social History of British Anthropology, 1885–1945* (Cambridge: Cambridge University Press, 1991), 21. I am indebted to Kuklick for her comments on chapter 5.

20. Sally Shuttleworth, introduction to *The Mill on the Floss*, by George Eliot (London: Routledge, 1991). Eliot is by no means alone in this usage; primitive fetishism is used by writers as diverse as Samuel Taylor Coleridge, Thomas Carlyle, Coventry Patmore, Ouida, and H. Rider Haggard. The conservative Patmore dismisses the "stupid and debasing idolatry" of Catholic religious art, asserting, "Such things were made fetish" (while simultaneously insisting on the "moral and spiritual power" inherent in the image of a face containing "the highest moral qualities of man"). Coventry Patmore, "The Ethics of Art," *British Quarterly Review* 10 (1849): 457. Ouida, on the other hand, uses the term to express attachment to an object of fashion: "A cashmere is a Parisian's soul, idol, and fetish." Ouida, *Under Two Flags: A Story of the Household and the Desert*, 3 vols. (London: Chapman

and Hall, 1867; Literature Online, 2000), 136, http://gateway.proquest. com/. Haggard refers generically to "a savage fetish dance." H. Rider Haggard, *She: A History of Adventure* (London: Longman, 1887), 218. On Coleridge and the use of fetishism in Romantic writing, see David Simpson, *Fetishism and Imagination: Dickens, Melville, and Conrad* (Baltimore: Johns Hopkins University Press, 1982).

21. This information is scattered throughout her diaries and letters. For the Müller reference, see *The George Eliot Letters*, ed. Gordon S. Haight, 9 vols. (New Haven: Yale University Press, 1954–78), 4:7. For Lubbock, see her diary entry for 6 March 1868, in *The Journals of George Eliot*, ed. Margaret Harris and Judith Johnston (Cambridge: Cambridge University Press, 1998), 132. Further references are cited in the text as *Journals*. For the Tylor reference, see entry 306 in *A Writer's Notebook, 1854–1879, and Uncollected Writings*, ed. Joseph Wiesenfarth (Charlottesville: University Press of Virginia, 1981), 133.

22. See entry 306n4 in Eliot, *Writer's Notebook*, 218.

23. Alfred Binet, "Le fétichisme dans l'amour," *Revue Philosophique* 12, no. 2 (1887).

24. See *Encyclopedia Britannica*, 11th ed., s.v. "fetishism."

25. The demise of evolutionary anthropology was a gradual process in Britain. Stocking views the period 1888 to 1922 as an interregnum between the two classical moments of British anthropology: social evolutionism and structural functionalism. George W. Stocking, *After Tylor: British Social Anthropology, 1888–1951* (Madison: University of Wisconsin Press, 1995), 14. In the United States, the situation was quite different, and 1896 is a sharper demarcation, since it was the year that Franz Boas published his important challenge to evolutionary anthropology, "The Limitations of the Comparative Method of Anthropology," *Science* 4 (1896). See Stocking, *After Tylor*, 124–25. I use 1900 to approximate the end of the Victorian belief in the primitive fetish because the 1890s marked the convergence of three relevant events: Boas's article, the end of Tylor's productive career in 1896, and the establishment of fetishism as the central trope of sexology's perversions.

26. See Stocking, *After Tylor*, 12–14.

27. Alfred Burdon Ellis, *The Land of Fetish* (London: Chapman, 1883); Mary H. Kingsley, *Travels in West Africa: Congo Français, Corisco, and Cameroons* (1897; London: Cass, 1965), 5.

28. Stocking, *After Tylor*, 388.

29. Geoffrey Parrinder, *West African Religion: A Study of the Beliefs and Practices of Akan, Ewe, Yoruba, Ibo, and Kindred Peoples* (New York: Barnes and Noble, 1969), 9.

30. In a closely related borrowing of the archived anthropological sense, fetishism resurfaced in art museums in the twentieth-century displays of "primitive" objects. See Shelly Errington, *The Death of Authentic Primitive Art and Other Tales of Progress* (Berkeley: University of California Press, 1998); and James Clifford, *The Predicament of Culture: Twentieth-Century Ethnography, Literature, and Art* (Cambridge: Harvard University Press, 1988), 189–214.

31. Arnold's vagueness is deliberate, as has been noted elsewhere; see Gerald Graff, "Arnold, Reason, and Common Culture," *Culture and Anarchy*, by Matthew Arnold, ed. Samuel Lipman, Rethinking the Western Tradition (New Haven: Yale University Press, 1994), 189; and Herbert, *Culture*, 55–56.

32. William Pietz, "The Problem of the Fetish, I," *Res* 9 (1985): 5. There is a strong body of literature on the history and theory of fetishism. Fundamental is the account of the ethnographic origins of the fetish in this and the two other articles by Pietz. See William Pietz, "The Problem of the Fetish, II: The Origin of the Fetish," *Res* 13 (1987); William Pietz, "The Problem of the Fetish, IIIa: Bosman's Guinea and the Enlightenment Theory of Fetishism," *Res* 16 (1988); and the collection by Emily Apter and William Pietz, eds., *Fetishism as Cultural Discourse* (Ithaca: Cornell University Press, 1993).

33. On the history of the earliest Portuguese traders in West Africa, see Pietz, "Fetish II," 36–39.

34. Slavoj Žižek, *The Plague of Fantasies* (London: Verso, 1997), 98.

35. Pietz, "Fetish I," 14.

36. "The term 'contact zone' . . . refer[s] to the space of colonial encounters, the space in which peoples geographically and historically separated come into contact with each other and establish ongoing relations, usually involving conditions of coercion, radical inequality, and intractable conflict." Mary Louise Pratt, *Imperial Eyes: Travel Writing and Transculturation* (New York: Routledge, 1992), 6.

37. Pietz, "Fetish I," 10–11.

38. My use of the terms "value" and "evaluation" throughout this work is informed by Barbara Herrnstein Smith, *Contingencies of Value: Alternative Perspectives for Critical Theory* (Cambridge, MA: Harvard University Press, 1988).

39. See Pietz, "Fetish I," 16–17.

40. See Žižek, *Plague*, 97. While the fetishist and subject are typically distinct in the ethnographic version of fetishism, Freud combines the two within a single split subject; see chapter 5.

41. Auguste Comte, *The Positive Philosophy of Auguste Comte*, trans. Harriet Martineau (New York: Calvin Blanchard, 1855; repr., New York: AMS

Press, 1974), 558. Further references are abbreviated *PP* and cited in the text. I rely on the Martineau translation because it was the edition of Comte's philosophy that was the most familiar to Victorian readers.

42. Giancarlo Carabelli, *In the Image of Priapus* (London: Duckworth, 1996), 49. As early as 1897, ethnographers began to challenge this point as a fact of West African religion; see Robert Hamill Nassau, *Fetichism in West Africa: Forty Years' Observation of Native Customs and Superstitions* (New York: Young People's Missionary Movement, 1904); and Kingsley, *Travels*, ch. 19.

43. Pietz, "Fetish I," 15.

44. Karl Marx, *Capital: A Critique of Political Economy*, trans. Ben Fowkes, vol. 1 (New York: Vintage, 1977), 165.

45. Tylor, *PC*, 2:152. The original story appears in Darwin's *Journal of Researches* (1845), in the entry for 3 April 1836. See Charles Darwin, *Journal of Researches into the Natural History and Geology of the Countries Visited during the Voyage of H.M.S. Beagle round the World, under the Command of Capt. Fitz Roy, R.N.*, 2nd. ed. (New York: Harper, 1846): 2:250.

46. Žižek discusses this life and death oscillation beautifully; see Žižek, *Plague*, 86–90.

47. I use *form* here in Jameson's sense of the "poetics of social form" and its "cultural logic." See Fredric Jameson, "The Cultural Logic of Late Capitalism," *Postmodernism, or The Cultural Logic of Late Capitalism* (Durham, NC: Duke University Press, 1991). Ten years earlier, he theorized the related concept of a *subtext*, or social ideology as an integral part of a text; such concerns had previously been relegated to the extra-textual domain of *context*. See Fredric Jameson, *The Political Unconscious: Narrative as a Socially Symbolic Act* (Ithaca: Cornell University Press, 1981). *Form* has two conflicting meanings: (1) outward attributes, as distinct from the inner meaning; (2) Platonic essence. See Raymond Williams, *Keywords: A Vocabulary of Culture and Society* (New York: Oxford University Press, 1983), 137–40.

48. Terry Eagleton, *Literary Theory: An Introduction*, 2nd ed. (1983; Minneapolis, MN: University of Minnesota Press, 1996), 42.

49. The fetishism of *Pinocchio* is briefly discussed in chapter 3.

50. See chapter 3 for the discussion of realism as fetishism. The basic reference for social construction (the way ideas shape the perception of the material world) is Michel Foucault, *The Order of Things: An Archaeology of the Human Sciences* (London: Routledge, 2001).

51. This conflict between the representation of fetishism and the fetishism of representation is not unique, but to a greater or lesser extent informs all attempts to keep representation separate from the real it represents and constructs. The problem is merely more insistent in fetishism because it brings

the implicit interplay between representation and the real closer to the conceptual surface. See the discussion of "The Reality of Representation and the Representation of Reality" in the conclusion to Bourdieu, *Distinction*, 482–84.

52. Freud's fetishism was a specifically male perversion because he could not make his model of castration fully functional for the female. See chapter 5.

53. Herbert, *Culture*, 302.

54. In a thorough examination of Marx's use of *fetishism*, Pietz documents his refinement of the concept, beginning with earliest articles and concluding with *Capital*. See William Pietz, "Fetishism and Materialism: The Limits of Theory in Marx," in Apter and Pietz, *Fetishism*.

1. Primitive Fetishism from Antiquity to 1860

1. American Psychiatric Association, *Diagnostic and Statistical Manual of Mental Disorders: DSM-IV-TR* (Washington, DC: American Psychiatric Association, 2000), s.v. "Fetishism." See also "302.3 Transvestic Fetishism," which is distinct from fetishism proper in that sexual arousal does not stem from the female attire a heterosexual male wears but from the thought or image he gets of being female.

2. See especially Emily Apter, *Feminizing the Fetish: Psychoanalysis and Narrative Obsession in Turn-of-the-Century France* (Ithaca: Cornell University Press, 1991). As I discuss in chapter 5, the relationship between fetishism and gender is particularly significant in psychoanalytic theory because of the theoretical impossibility of female fetishism within an Oedipal sexual economy.

3. Marx, *Capital*, 165–77. On commodity fetishism, see Terry Eagleton, *Ideology: An Introduction* (London: Verso, 1991), 84–88. Pietz discusses Marx's earliest uses of the term *fetish*, long before *Capital*. Pietz, "Fetishism and Materialism."

4. For the basic analysis of this usage of *fetish*, see Jean Baudrillard, *For a Critique of the Political Economy of the Sign*, trans. Levin Charles (St. Louis, MO: Telos, 1981), 88–101. This topic is critically summarized in Pietz, "Fetishism and Materialism," 120–29.

5. Jud Stacer, "Horrific Hat Fad Takes Over Athens," *Redandblack.com*, 27 October 2003; Gerald Graff, "Assessment Changes Everything," *MLA Newsletter* (Spring 2008): 3.

6. For the history of fetishism in the seventeenth and eighteenth centuries, see Pietz, "Fetish I," "Fetish II," and "Fetish IIIa."

7. Norman Davis, et al., *A Chaucer Glossary* (Oxford: Clarendon, 1979), s.v. "fetis."

8. Geoffrey Chaucer, *The Works of Geoffrey Chaucer*, ed. F. N. Robinson, 2nd ed. (Boston: Houghton Mifflin, 1957), fragment A, lines 776, 532. Although distrustful of most claims by etymologists, Tylor knew the etymology of *fetish* well enough to cite Chaucer's usage. See Tylor, *PC*, 143–44.

9. This duality is familiar in Victorian literature, where it shows up both in Walter Pater's theory of aestheticism in *The Renaissance* and in the poet Gerard Manley Hopkins's concept of "inscape."

10. See *Inferno* (10.13–15). Jones tells the story of the reception of Epicurus's ideas, from ancient Greece to the eighteenth century, with intelligence and lucidity. Howard Jones, *The Epicurean Tradition* (London: Routledge, 1989). Konstan has written an excellent summary. David Konstan, "Epicureanism," *The Blackwell Guide to Ancient Philosophy*, ed. Christopher Shields, Blackwell Philosophical Guides (Madden, MA: Blackwell, 2003). For the textual history for Epicurus's writings, see Brad Inwood and Lloyd P. Gerson, eds., *Hellenistic Philosophy: Introductory Readings*, 2nd ed. (Indianapolis, IN: Hackett, 1997). The broader context of ideas about primitivism in classical antiquity is documented in Arthur O. Lovejoy and George Boas, *Primitivism and Related Ideas in Antiquity*, Contributions to the History of Primitivism (1935; New York: Octagon, 1965).

11. Fifteenth- and sixteenth-century writers favorably discussing Epicurus include: Desiderius Erasmus, "Epicureus," in *Opera Omnia Desiderii Erasmi Roterodami*; Lorenzo Valla, in *De voluptate* (On Pleasure); Giordana Bruno, in *Degli eroici furori*; and Michel de Montaigne, "Of Experience," in *Essays*. See Eugene O'Connor's introduction to *The Essential Epicurus: Letters, Principal Doctrines, Vatican Sayings, and Fragments* trans. Eugene O'Connor, Great Books in Philosophy (Amherst, NY: Prometheus, 1993).

12. James H. Nichols, Jr., *Epicurean Political Philosophy: The "De Rerum Natura" of Lucretius* (Ithaca: Cornell University Press, 1976), 181–82.

13. *Essential Epicurus*, 62. These passages are taken from the Letter to Menoeceus. Further references are cited in the text.

14. Lucretius restated Epicurean philosophy at length in *De Rerum Natura*, written in the first century BCE. Because Epicurus's own writings survived only in fragments, *De Rerum Natura* later became the essential account of Epicureanism. In the third century CE, Diogenes Laertius helped to keep the knowledge of Epicureanism alive by discussing the poem in book 10 of *The Lives of Eminent Philosophers*.

15. Lucretius, *The Way Things Are: The "De Rerum Natura" of Titus Lucretius Carus*, trans. Rolfe Humphries (Bloomington: Indiana University Press,

1968), 187. Further references are cited in the text.

16. Konstan, "Epicureanism," 247.

17. Lucretius, *De Rerum*, 117, 110. Similarly, Epicurus wrote, "death is nothing to us," in his Letter to Menoeceus. Epicurus, *Essential Epicurus*, 63.

18. For more on primitivism in Europe during the middle ages, see George Boas, *Essays on Primitivism and Related Ideas in the Middle Ages*, Contributions to the History of Primitivism (New York: Octagon, 1966).

19. Frank E. Manuel, *The Eighteenth Century Confronts the Gods* (Cambridge, MA: Harvard University Press, 1959), 190.

20. Seventeenth-century allegorists are treated favorably in Walter Pater's *The Renaissance*, when Pico della Mirandola's eclectic method of myth interpretation is described in similar terms. Pater explicitly prefers it to the post-Comtian view of religion as having continuous historical development. Walter Pater, *The Renaissance* (New York: Oxford University Press), 22–23.

21. Manuel, *Eighteenth Century*, 31.

22. Because David Hume lived in the more secular Britain, he had less need to mask his unorthodox ideas; see Ibid., 188.

23. Several of Fontanelle's works were translated into English by Aphra Behn, including his rewrite of Anthony Van Dale's *De Oraculis Ethnicorum*, as *The History of Oracles and the Cheats of the Pagan Priests* (London, 1688), and his *The Theory or System of Several New Inhabited Worlds Lately Discover'd, and Pleasantly Describ'd* (London: L. Briscoe, 1700).

24. Manuel terms this group the "historico-psychological mythographers of the eighteenth century." Manuel, *Eighteenth Century*, 132.

25. In their environmental determinism, the Enlightenment mythographers were repeating ideas from Lucretius; see *De Rerum*, book 5.

26. Giambattista Vico, *New Science: Principles of the New Science Concerning the Common Nature of Nations*, trans. David Marsh, 3rd ed. (New York: Penguin, 1999), 140. Vico's giants also resemble those of Hobbes.

27. This triad of stages was already conventional when Vico used it; see Manuel, *Eighteenth Century*, 151.

28. Vico, *New Science*, 174.

29. Manuel argues that Vico was more well known in his own day than most scholars allow. Manuel, *Eighteenth Century*, 149–50. See also Andrew Von Hendy, *The Modern Construction of Myth* (Bloomington: Indiana University Press, 2002), 8–15. Throughout these remarks, I am indebted to Anthony Grafton's summary of Vico's life and work. See his introduction to *New Science: Principles of the New Science Concerning the Common Nature of Nations*, by Giambattista Vico, trans. David Marsh, 3rd ed. (New York: Penguin, 1999).

30. David Hume, *The Natural History of Religion*, ed. H. E. Root, A Library of Modern Religious Thought (1777; Stanford, CA: Stanford University Press, 1956), 32. Hume discusses many writers from classical antiquity, including Epicurus and Lucretius. Hume, *Natural History*, 36–39.

31. The connection with Marx is mentioned in Manuel, *Eighteenth Century*, 186. Comte's awareness of *Dieux fétiches* is discussed below.

32. On Bosman, see Pietz, "Fetish IIIa."

33. I rely here on the analysis of de Brosses in Manuel, *Eighteenth Century*, 203–7.

34. See Christine Clarke-Evans, "Charles de Brosses and Diderot: Eighteenth-Century Arguments concerning Primitive Language, Particular Natural Languages and a National Language," *History of European Ideas* 16 (1993).

35. Manuel, *Eighteenth Century*, 186. Hodgen claims that de Brosses's doctrine was widely disseminated; while this is ultimately correct, it is more accurate to note that his theory of primitive fetishism was not circulated until later, at the turn of the century, and even then it was done through the agency of other writers who frequently neglected to acknowledge him. Margaret T. Hodgen, *Early Anthropology in the Sixteenth and Seventeenth Centuries* (Philadelphia: University of Pennsylvania Press, 1964), 491.

36. See Pietz, "Fetishism and Materialism," 131. Pietz cites Christoph Meiners, *Allgemeine kritische Geschichte der Religionen*, 2 vols. (Hannover: Im Verlage der Helwingischen Hof-Buchhandlung, 1806); Philipp Christian Reinhard, *Abriss einer Geschichte der Entstehung und Aubbildung der religiösen Ideen* (Jena: 1794); Jacques Antoine Dulaure, *The Gods of Generation: A History of Phallic Cults among Ancients and Moderns* (1805; New York: Panurge, 1933); and Charles François Dupuis, *The Origin of All Religious Worship* (1794; New Orleans: 1872).

37. For more on this point, and on Prichard's relation to the philosophes, see George W. Stocking, introduction to *Researches into the Physical History of Man*, by James Cowles Prichard (Chicago: University of Chicago Press, 1973), ix–cx.

38. Stocking, *Victorian Anthropology*, xliv.

39. Ibid., 29.

40. Roy Ellen, "Fetishism," *Man* N.S. 23, no. 2 (1988): 214. Ellen also notes that Tylor "rejected Comte's use" of fetishism, by "restricting" it to a more narrow usage. Ellen, "Fetishism," 214. See my discussion of this topic in chapter 4.

41. Mary Pickering, *Auguste Comte: An Intellectual Biography*, vol. 1 (New York: Cambridge University Press, 1993), 203. I am indebted to Pickering's discussion of the law of three stages. See Ibid., 199–203.

42. Before revising it for 1824, Comte first published the fundamental opuscule

in 1822, under the slightly different title *Prospectus des travaux nécessaires pour réorganiser la société*. It had appeared under the name of Saint-Simon rather than Comte, a fact that contributed to the ending of their collaboration. See Ibid., 224–26.

43. G. H. Lewes, *Comte's Philosophy of the Sciences: Being an Exposition of the Principles of the "Cours de Philosophie Positive" of Auguste Comte* (London: Bohn, 1853), 26.

44. On Comte's method, see Larry Lauden, "Towards a Reassessment of Comte's 'Méthode Positive'," *Philosophy of Science* 38, no. 1 (1971).

45. Auguste Comte, *Cours de philosophie positive*, ed. Michel Serres, et al., 2 vols. (Paris: Hermann, 1975), 1:71, quoted in Pickering, *Auguste Comte*, 576.

46. Pickering, *Auguste Comte*, 568. Comte's emphasis on the role of imagination in science reappears in George Eliot's fiction; see Peter Melville Logan, "Conceiving the Body: Realism and Medicine in *Middlemarch*," *History of the Human Sciences* 4 (1991).

47. See Pickering, *Auguste Comte*, 563.

48. See Ibid., 46. In *Des l'esprit de lois* (1748), Montesquieu insisted on the existence of an intelligible order behind social phenomena and tried to discover the laws that might account for the evident diversity of societies in the world. To do so, he established a basic, three-fold classification of societies, although his determining factor was not the state of science but of government: despotism was the least advanced, followed by monarchism and finally republicanism.

49. Ibid., 48. Pickering also points out that Comte later decided that Montesquieu was a more significant thinker than Condorcet; see Pickering, *Auguste Comte*, 215. Condorcet's theory of limitless progress was influential in William Godwin's philosophy, particularly in his appendix to *Enquiry Concerning Political Justice* (1793). At the same time, Thomas Malthus used Condorcet as his philosophical sparring partner, in *An Essay on the Principle of Population* (1798).

50. See Pickering, *Auguste Comte*, 51.

51. Comte's theory of milieu was later adopted by the French historian Hippolyte Taine, who used it in his *History of English Literature*, to argue that literature is the product of "race, surroundings, and epoch." Hippolyte Taine, *History of English literature*, trans. Henri Van Laun, 4 vols. (1883; New York: Ungar, 1965), 1:17.

52. Lewes, *Comte's Philosophy*, 275.

53. William Paley, *Natural Theology: Or, Evidences of the Existence and Attributes of the Deity, Collected from the Appearances of Nature*, 6th ed. (London: R. Faulder, 1803), 3–4.

54. On the importance of ambivalence in pre-Freudian theories of fetishism, see chapter 5.

55. Pickering, *Auguste Comte*, 108.

56. Walter M. Simon, *European Positivism in the Nineteenth Century: An Essay in Intellectual History* (Ithaca: Cornell University Press, 1963), 6.

57. Pickering, *Auguste Comte*, 698.

58. Auguste Comte, *System of Positive Polity*, trans. John Henry Bridges, et al., 4 vols. (1851–1854; London: Longman, 1875), 4:39, quoted in James McLaverty, "Comtean Fetishism in *Silas Marner*," *Nineteenth-Century Fiction* 36, no. 3 (1981): 322.

59. Simon, *European Positivism*, 6.

60. See Pickering, *Auguste Comte*, 698–99. On the appeal Comte's Religion of Humanity held for George Eliot, see chapter 3.

61. On the reception of *Cours* in France, see Simon, *European Positivism*, 73–79, 83–89, 90–93.

62. See Pickering, *Auguste Comte*, 586.

63. The story of positivism's diffusion in England and Scotland has received a good deal of historical attention. Cashdollar offers a fascinating analysis that focuses on the clerical reception but tells the larger story particularly well. Charles D. Cashdollar, *The Transformation of Theology, 1830–1890: Positivism and Protestant Thought in Britain and America* (Princeton, NJ: Princeton University Press, 1989). Simon covers a larger geographical range but has additional details on J. S. Mill, G. H. Lewes, George Eliot, and the full cast of English positivists. Simon, *European Positivism*. Wernick is an important source on the reception of Comte's later theory of positivist religion; he is also helpful in discussing the revitalized role Comte gave to fetishism in the new religion. Andrew Wernick, *Auguste Comte and the Religion of Humanity: The Post-Theistic Program of French Social Theory* (Cambridge: Cambridge University Press, 2001). McGee is a basic but dated source of factual information, told from the perspective of a true believer. John Edwin McGee, *A Crusade for Humanity: The History of Organized Positivism in England* (London: Watts, 1931).

64. The relationship between Mill and Comte is discussed in Simon, *European Positivism*, 172–95.

65. Gustave d'Eichthal broke with Comte and converted to Saint-Simonianism in 1828. Pickering, *Auguste Comte*, 415–16. See also Cashdollar, *Transformation*, 23–24.

66. Auguste Comte, *Auguste Comte: Correspondance générale et confessions*, ed. de Berrêdo Carneiro, et al., 8 vols. (Paris: Ecole des Hautes Etudes en Sciences Sociales, 1973–90), 2:346, quoted in Pickering, *Auguste Comte*, 514.

67. John Stuart Mill, *Autobiography of John Stuart Mill*, ed. John Jacob Coss (1924; New York: Columbia University Press, 1960), 174n1.

68. Pickering, *Auguste Comte*, 518.

69. Wheatstone long claimed that these were the first copies of *Cours* in England, but this has since been questioned. See Cashdollar, *Transformation*, 24.

70. [David Brewster], review of *Cours de philosophie positive*, by Auguste Comte, *Edinburgh Review* 67 (1838). On Brewster, see Cashdollar, *Transformation*, 24–28.

71. Comte, *Correspondance*, 2:358, quoted in Pickering, *Auguste Comte*, 534.

72. Pickering, *Auguste Comte*, 536.

73. Mill's *Logic* demonstrated an "almost complete adherence" to Comte's doctrine. Ibid., 538. John Morely, the publisher who initially rejected *Logic*, noted in a retrospective article that Mill's book "did more than any other to prepare the minds of the English philosophic public" for positivism. *Macmillan's Magazine* 36 (May 1877): 53.

74. Mill, *Autobiography*, 194.

75. Anna Theresa Kitchel, *George Lewes and George Eliot: A Review of Records* (New York: John Day, 1933), 41.

76. Lewes to Comte, 10 July 1846, London Positivist Society Papers, British Library of Political and Economic Science, London School of Economics, quoted in Cashdollar, *Transformation*, 38.

77. See Rosemary Ashton, *George Eliot: A Life* (London: Hamish Hamilton, 1996), 105.

78. Lewes, *Comte's Philosophy*, iv.

79. See Cashdollar, *Transformation*, 47. He mentions the young liberals at Oxford in the early 1850s, including Richard Congreve, as keeping their own counsel on positivism, 32–33. See also his discussion of Alexander Bain, 36.

80. Ibid., 55–56.

81. Harriet Martineau, preface to *The Positive Philosophy of Auguste Comte*, by Auguste Comte (New York: Calvin Blanchard, 1855; repr., New York: AMS Press, 1974), 4.

82. Cashdollar, *Transformation*, 62. On Martineau and Comte, see Simon, *European Positivism*, 213–17.

83. See Cashdollar, *Transformation*, 63.

84. See Wernick, *Auguste Comte*.

85. Cashdollar, *Transformation*, 72, 89. It is impossible here to do justice to the wealth of information and insightful analysis in chapters 1 and 2 of Cashdollar's work, to which I am indebted throughout this discussion.

86. John Stuart Mill, *On Liberty*, ed. Gertrude Himmelfarb (1859; New York: Penguin, 1974), 73.

87. G. H. Lewes, "Auguste Comte," *Fortnightly Review* 3 (1866), quoted in Simon, *European Positivism*, 200.
88. Pickering, *Auguste Comte*, 274n175, 274.
89. Ibid., 273–75. Although de Brosses is more often cited as the source of Comte's neologism, Pickering argues persuasively that it was Constant.
90. Ibid., 274.
91. Thomas Masterman Winterbottom, *An Account of the Native Africans in the Neighbourhood of Sierra Leone: To Which is Added, An Account of the Present State of Medicine among Them*, 2 vols. (London: John Hatchard and J. Mawman., 1803), 1:123.
92. Maria Edgeworth, "The Grateful Negro," *Tales and Novels*, vol. 5 (London: Baldwin and Cradock, 1832), 256–57. Edgeworth cites ethnographic works to validate the details of her representation.
93. Samuel Taylor Coleridge, *The Friend*, ed. Barbara E. Rooke, 16 vols., vol. 4 (2 vols.), Bollingen series 75 (London: Routledge, 1969), 432.
94. Immanuel Kant, whom both Coleridge and Carlyle read, discussed fetishism and religious faith; see Immanuel Kant, *Religion within the Limits of Reason Alone*, trans. Theodore M. Greene and Hoyt H. Hudson (Chicago: Open Court, 1934), 165–68, 181–90. Carlyle's interest in and use of German philosophy, including Kant, is discussed in Ruth apRoberts, *The Ancient Dialect: Thomas Carlyle and Comparative Religion* (Berkeley: University of California Press, 1988), chapters 1 and 2.
95. Ralph Waldo Emerson, "The American Scholar: An Oration Delivered before the Phi Beta Kappa Society at Cambridge, August 31, 1837," *Nature, Addresses, and Lectures* (London: Routledge, 1849; Chadwyck-Healey, 1999), 102.
96. Thomas Carlyle, *Sartor Resartus* (London: Dent, 1908; New York: Chelsea House, 1983), 120.
97. Thomas Carlyle, *On Heroes, Hero-Worship, and the Heroic in History* (New York: D. Appleton, 1841), 140–41.
98. On Carlyle and universalism, see apRoberts, *Ancient Dialect*.
99. On the issue of usage in the early nineteenth century, particularly within Romanticism, see Simpson, *Fetishism and Imagination*, 20.
100. I used the third edition, available at the University of Toronto Electronic Library, to arrive at this number. Matthew Arnold, *Culture and Anarchy*, 3rd ed. (New York: Macmillan, 1882; Toronto: University of Toronto English Library, 1998), http://www.library.utoronto.ca/utel/. Fetishism in *Culture and Anarchy* is discussed at length in chapter 2.
101. *Poole's Index to Periodical Literature, 1802–1907*, in *C19: The Nineteenth Century Index* (ProQuest Information and Learning), http://collections.chadwyck.com (search: keywords fetish* fetich*; accessed 28 April 2007).

102. *Wellesley Index to Victorian Periodicals, 1824–1900*, in *C19: The Nineteenth Century Index* (ProQuest Information and Learning), http://collections. chadwyck.com (search: keywords fetish* fetich*; accessed 28 April 2007).

103. *Periodicals Index Online*, in *C19: The Nineteenth Century Index* (ProQuest Information and Learning), http://collections.chadwyck.com (search: keywords fetish* fetich*; accessed 28 April 2007).

104. For missionary and popular science journals, see *British Periodicals*, in *C19: The Nineteenth Century Index* (ProQuest Information and Learning), http://collections.chadwyck.com (search: keywords fetish* fetich*; accessed 29 April 2007).

105. *The Nineteenth-Century Fiction Database*, ed. Danny Karlin and Tom Keymer, in *Chadwyck-Healey Literature Collections* (ProQuest Information and Learning), http://collections.chadwyck.com (search: keywords fetish* fetich*; accessed 28 April 2007). The 1849 work, not surprisingly, is James Anthony Froude, *The Nemesis of Faith* (London: Chapman, 1849).

106. *English Poetry*, 2nd ed., in *Chadwyck-Healey Literature Collections* (ProQuest Information and Learning), http://collections.chadwyck.com (search: keywords fetish* fetich* fetisch*; accessed 28 April 2007). The database searched 91,607 poems written in the British Isles, Australia, and New Zealand by writers active between 1800 and 1899. The two poems from the 1820s were: Josiah Conder, "The Star in the East," *The Star in the East* (1824); and Louisa Stuart Costello, "Lament of an Ashantee Warrior, Condemned to Death as a Sacrifice to their Gods," *Songs of a Stranger* (1825).

2. Matthew Arnold's Culture

1. Oscar Wilde later made a virtue of this ability, playing with Arnold's phrase in exactly the same way, in "The Critic as Artist, Part 1." Oscar Wilde, *The Major Works*, ed. Isobel Murray (Oxford: Oxford University Press, 1989), 264.

2. Matthew Arnold, "Empedocles on Etna," *The Poems of Matthew Arnold*, ed. Kenneth Allott, 2nd ed. (London: Longman, 1965), 1.2.272–76. Further references are cited in the text.

3. Arnold, *CP*, 1:32–34.

4. See Matthew Arnold, *Matthew Arnold*, ed. Miriam Allott and Robert H. Super (Oxford: Oxford University Press, 1986), 520n76.

5. See Park Honan, *Matthew Arnold: A Life* (Cambridge, MA: Harvard University Press, 1983), 88, 127.

6. Several earlier examples of his dislike of provincialism are discussed following, but for a late example, see "Equality." On the importance of provincialism in Arnold's thought, a thorough source is David J. DeLaura, *Hebrew and Hellene in Victorian England* (Austin: University of Texas Press, 1969), 40–49 and passim. Stefan Collini shows that the intensity of Arnold's opposition to provincialism and his insistence on the need for a central authority was a product of his experience as a School Inspector; see *Arnold* (Oxford: Oxford University Press, 1988), 80.

7. On Arnold's entry into criticism, see Honan, *Matthew Arnold*, 309.

8. As Venuti points out, Newman's translation has merits that Arnold failed to recognize. See his important discussion of Newman's often overlooked position in the controversy. Lawrence Venuti, *The Translator's Invisibility: A History of Translation* (New York: Routledge, 1995), 118–47.

9. The essay was first published in the *Cornhill Magazine* for August 1864 and is included in *Essays in Criticism*, published six months later, in February 1865.

10. Arnold, *CP*, 3:245, italics original. Arac points out that Arnold explored the same issue in his religious writings, where the "note" becomes redefined as "tact," meaning a discriminative reading process. Jonathan Arac, *Critical Genealogies: Historical Situations for Postmodern Literary Studies* (New York: Columbia University Press, 1987), 123.

11. On Arnold's relationship with the thought of John H. Newman, see DeLaura, *Hebrew*, 39–61.

12. Quoted in Ibid., 48.

13. In *Culture and Anarchy*, "Hebraism" refers to the social qualities of strictness, obedience, and practicality, while "Hellenism" refers to artistry, an openness to new ideas, and innovation.

14. In addition to *Culture and Anarchy*, Arnold's major comments on convention and innovation are found in the earlier essays, "The Literary Influence of Academies" and "The Function of Criticism at the Present Time," and in the later essays, "Wordsworth" and "The Study of Poetry."

15. As DeLaura points out, this optimistic tone was not long-lived in Arnold; by 1870, he believed the two would be forever in conflict. DeLaura, *Hebrew*, 73.

16. Arnold, *CP*, 5:96. Arnold's preference for content over form is a consistent feature of his literary criticism; it appears as the major issue in his first extended comment on poetry, the 1853 preface to *Poems*.

17. Arnold believed that his historical narrative was the most intellectually significant part of his book; see Super's explanatory note: Ibid., 5:415.

18. For a concurring opinion, see Simpson, *Fetishism and Imagination*, 20.

19. Mill's relationship to Comte is discussed in the previous chapter. Henry Thomas Buckle published his *History of Civilization in England* in 1857–61; while not a Comtist, he quoted Comte's theory of history favorably at the beginning; see Simon, *European Positivism*, 219–21.

20. Machann and Vogeler have both noted Harrison's prominence in Arnold's writing. See Clinton Machann, preface to *The Essential Matthew Arnold: An Annotated Bibliography of Major Modern Studies* (New York: G. K. Hall, 1993), 95; and Martha Salmon Vogeler, "Matthew Arnold and Frederic Harrison: The Prophet of Culture and the Prophet of Positivism," *SEL: Studies in English Literature, 1500–1900* 2 (1962): 441.

21. "Anarchy and Authority," *Cornhill* 17 (January 1868): 31–32. The excised response to Harrison is reproduced in Arnold, *CP*, 5:504–6. See also Vogeler, "Matthew Arnold," 453.

22. While my remarks are limited to Comte's description of primitive fetishism, Vogeler explains the major similarities between Comte's full philosophy and Arnold's *Culture and Anarchy* in her discussion of Harrison. Vogeler, "Matthew Arnold," 454–58.

23. Carl Dawson and John Pfordresher, eds., *Matthew Arnold: Prose Writings*, Critical Heritage (London: Routledge, 1979), 237.

24. Frederic Harrison, *Tennyson, Ruskin, Mill, and Other Literary Estimates* (London: Macmillan, 1900), 132. In retrospect, the comment seems diplomatic. Arnold continued to describe Harrison in unflattering terms in his last years. In 1885, he wrote that Harrison "in the exuberance of youthful energy weighted himself for the race of life by taking up a grotesque old French pedant upon his shoulders." Arnold, *CP*, 10:207. The remark was originally published in "A Word More about America," *Nineteenth Century* 17 (February 1885): 219–36.

25. On commodity fetishism, see Marx, *Capital*, 163–77. See the introduction for further discussion of this passage.

26. Anthony Howe, *Free Trade and Liberal England, 1846–1946* (Oxford: Clarendon, 1997), 198.

27. Ibid. As Howe notes, the reference to the "free trade fetish" appeared in the *Final Report of the Royal Commission on the Depression in Trade and Industry* (1886), which was dominated by the opposing "fair traders." Howe, *Free Trade*, 191–229.

28. Williams, *Culture*, 117.

29. Herbert also notes Arnold's double use of *freedom*. Herbert, *Culture*, 45–46. The problems in the idea of "free thought," and the position resulting for cultural intellectuals, are discussed in John Frow, *Cultural Studies and*

Cultural Value (Oxford: Clarendon, 1995), chapter 4. See also James Clifford, "Introduction: Partial Truths," *Writing Culture: The Poetics and Politics of Ethnography*, ed. James Clifford and George E. Marcus (Berkeley: University of California, 1986).

30. Honan, *Matthew Arnold*, 346.

31. Goh argues that "Arnold's discourse invests even freedom with mechanical qualities," and thus undermines the possibility of an independent human subject, that is, one who is not defined by the mode of production. Robbie B. H. Goh, "Unwritten Fetishes and Rhetorical Strategies in Matthew Arnold's Criticism," *The Silent Word: Textual Meaning and the Unwritten*, ed. Robert Young, Robbie B. H. Goh, and Kan Choon Ban (Singapore: Singapore University Press, National University of Singapore, World Scientific, 1998), 142. I am indebted to Goh for his helpful comments on an early draft of this material.

32. Collini, *Arnold*, 6.

33. Williams, *Culture*, 117.

34. See J. G. A. Pocock, *The Machiavellian Moment: Florentine Political Thought and the Atlantic Republican Tradition* (Princeton, NJ: Princeton University Press, 1975), 110–13, 22–23. See also my earlier discussion of commercial ideology and medicine. Peter Melville Logan, *Nerves and Narratives: A Cultural History of Hysteria in Nineteenth-Century British Prose* (Berkeley: University of California Press, 1997), 30–36.

35. Collini, *Arnold*, 78.

36. Ivan Waddington, *The Medical Profession in the Industrial Revolution* (Dublin, Ire.: Gill, 1984), 1–28.

37. Bill Bell, "Beyond the Death of the Author: Matthew Arnold's Two Audiences, 1888–1930," *Book History* 3 (2000): 158.

38. On value and evaluation, see Herrnstein Smith, *Contingencies*.

39. This summary of Adam Smith's philosophy draws on Robert L. Heilbroner, *The Worldly Philosophers: The Lives, Times, and Ideas of the Great Economic Thinkers* (New York: Simon and Schuster, 1986), 42–74.

40. Adam Smith, *An Inquiry into the Nature and Causes of the Wealth of Nations*, ed. Edwin Cannan (New York: Modern Library, 1937), 55.

41. Ibid., 59. Adam Smith is only concerned with overvaluation, since the undervaluation of products, he argues, can never sustain itself for long.

42. Hartman, *Fateful Question*, 35.

43. Arnold put his own spin on the term *disinterest*, meaning detached neutrality. This was different from the Romantic sense of the term, when it meant the ability to imagine other selves. See David Bromwich, "The Genealogy of Disinterestedness," *Raritan* 1 (1982): 64–66.

44. In this symbolic function, we can also see how Arnold "spoke against" the middle class, as Arac notes, while remaining a product of it. Arac, *Critical Genealogies*, 136.

45. As a School Inspector, Arnold was intimately aware of the widespread problems facing impoverished families in Victorian Britain. "He was to talk to more working-class children than any other poet who has ever lived." Honan, *Matthew Arnold*, 218–19.

46. Williams, *Culture*, 126.

47. Initially published as the general introduction to Humphry Ward's four-volume anthology, *The English Poets* (London: Macmillan, 1880), "The Study of Poetry" reappeared as the opening essay in *Essays in Criticism: Second Series* (1888).

48. Bromwich, "Genealogy," 64; for a succinct and important discussion of the contradictions within Arnold's theory of culture, see 64–75.

49. Arnold's reputation since his death and his iconic status in the culture wars are usefully discussed in Collini, *Arnold*, 110–19. However, as a corrective to Collini's standard assumptions about the reception of Arnold's poetry, see Bell, "Beyond."

50. Bromwich, "Genealogy," 64. Obviously I would argue with Bromwich's implication in this passage that Arnold is fundamentally canonical and that any other uses are "awkward."

51. Bell, "Beyond," 163. Bell's argument focuses on the contrast between the critical assumption that Arnold's poetry appealed only to an elite few and the publication history, showing that the opposite was in fact the case.

52. David J. DeLaura, "What, Then, Does Matthew Arnold Mean?" *Modern Philology* 66 (1969): 345.

53. For a short tour of the complications in Arnold's reception, see Machann, preface, vii–x.

54. Lionel Trilling, *Matthew Arnold* (New York: Harcourt, 1977), 410. Trilling's comment, which came despite his own discomfort with Arnold's ideas, dates back to 1939.

55. On this paradox, see also Goh's suggestive conclusion that Arnold's discourse creates the same fetishistic quality it critiques: "Unwritten Fetishes," 143.

56. Collini, *Arnold*, 115.

57. William J. Bennett, "'To Reclaim a Legacy': Text of Report on Humanities in Education," *Chronicle of Higher Education* 28 (1984): A17.

58. Ibid., A19. Bennett's arguments are silently paraphrased by John M. Ellis, a prominent conservative voice because of his position for many years as the theorist for and Secretary Treasurer of the Association of Literary Scholars and Critics. See his *Literature Lost: Social Agendas and the Corruption of the*

Humanities (New Haven: Yale University Press, 1997), 204–30. Since its founding, the Association has received most of its grant funding from the Lynde and Harry Bradley Foundation, on which William Bennett served as a member of the Board of Directors.

59. Bennett proposes thirty-nine core canonical texts that "virtually define the development of the Western mind," and in it two female authors and one racial minority make the cut: Jane Austen, George Eliot, and Martin Luther King. Bennett, "Reclaim," A18.

60. Gerald Graff, *Professing Literature: An Institutional History* (Chicago: University of Chicago Press, 1987), 5.

61. T. S. Eliot, "The Perfect Critic," *The Sacred Wood: Essays on Poetry and Criticism* (London: Methuen, 1948), 1. Eliot's ambivalent attitude toward Arnold is characterized by a combination of extensive borrowings from Arnold and an apparent need to deprecate him; see Thomas Marion Hoctor, introduction to *Matthew Arnold's Essays in Criticism: First Series* (Chicago: University of Chicago Press, 1968), xxxiii–xliii.

62. William K. Wimsatt and Cleanth Brooks, *Literary Criticism: A Short History* (New York: Knopf, 1957), 444.

63. Ibid., 448. Wimsatt and Brooks argue that the year 1930 "announced the end of a didactic critical movement which, adequately defined in Arnold's terms of 1880, had in the humanism of his successors moved no nearer to a distinct concern for literature," because it had yet to free itself from Arnold's concern for the social (451).

64. Arac, *Critical Genealogies*, 121.

65. Collini, *Arnold*, 3.

66. Interpellation, or the process of recognizing one's identity through another's address, is explained in Louis Althusser, "Ideology and Ideological State Apparatuses (Notes towards an Investigation)," *Lenin and Philosophy and Other Essays*, ed. Ben Brewster (New York: Monthly Review Press, 1971).

67. The first prophecy appears in "The Function of Criticism in the Present Day," when he tells of the great literary epoch to come. The second, from *Culture and Anarchy* and repeated in "The Study of Poetry," predicts that culture will one day serve the function of religion.

3. George Eliot's Realism

1. On the Ilfracombe celebration, see Ashton, *George Eliot*, 158.

2. George Eliot, *The George Eliot Letters*, ed. Gordon S. Haight, 9 vols. (New Haven: Yale University Press, 1954–78), 2:248. Further references are cited

in the text as *Letters*. On the relationship between her letters and fiction, see Rosemarie Bodenheimer, *The Real Life of Mary Ann Evans: George Eliot, Her Letters and Fiction* (Ithaca: Cornell University Press, 1994), 1–22.

3. Eliot, *Journals*, 60.

4. George Eliot, "The Natural History of German Life," *Westminster Review* 66 (1856).

5. In the interest of clarity, subsequent references to Marian Evans generally use her penname, Eliot. There are more precise options, but all require prior familiarity with her biography to be readily intelligible. Her given name was Mary Anne Evans. As a teenager, she trimmed the decorative "e" of the middle name, reducing it to Ann. Upon moving to London, in 1851, she fused her two first names into the more urbane Marian. After her unrecognized marriage to George H. Lewes, she became Marian Evans Lewes. Late in life, she married John Cross, changed her surname, and also returned to her childhood name, becoming Mary Ann Cross. This is the name found on her tombstone today.

6. Eliot, *Writer's Notebook*, 97, 133.

7. Quoted in Ibid., 97, 218.

8. U. C. Knoepflmacher, *George Eliot's Early Novels: The Limits of Realism* (Berkeley: University of California Press, 1968), 1.

9. Eliot, *Letters*, 4:300. Her letter to Harrison is dated 15 August 1866. Eliot did not entirely succeed in avoiding the temptation to polemicize in her fiction; the most egregious example is "Address to Working Men, by Felix Holt," originally published in *Blackwood's Edinburgh Magazine,* January 1868; see George Eliot, *Essays of George Eliot*, ed. Thomas Pinney (New York: Columbia University Press, 1963), 415–30. Further references are cited in the text as *Essays*.

10. The date of Eliot's "discovery" of Comte has been a matter of dispute. Citing Sydney Eisen's 1957 dissertation, Simon suggests her understanding of Comte began in 1851, when she first came in contact with the editors of the *Leader,* most notably Lewes. Sydney Eisen, "Frederic Harrison: The Life and Thought of an English Positivist" (Ph.D. diss., Johns Hopkins University, 1957). Simon argues that a more serious interest began in 1859, after her friendship with the Congreves was established. Simon, *European Positivism*, 207.

11. See Eliot, *Letters*, 1:310. On Mill's role in introducing positivism in England, see chapter 1.

12. Nancy L. Paxton, *George Eliot and Herbert Spencer: Feminism, Evolutionism, and the Reconstruction of Gender* (Princeton, NJ: Princeton University Press, 1991), 18. On Spencer and Comte, see also Simon, *European Positivism*, 217–19.

13. Eliot, *Journals*, 97. Since Congreve's description of *Spanish Gypsy* as "a mass of Positivism" in 1869, the poem has regularly been discussed as a positivist text, though opinions differ. See Simon, *European Positivism*, 209–11; and Martha Salmon Vogeler, "George Eliot and the Positivists," in "George Eliot: 1880–1980," *Nineteenth-Century Fiction* 35, no. 3 (1980): 414–15.

14. See Simon, *European Positivism*, 208; and Gordon S. Haight, *George Eliot: A Biography* (New York: Oxford University Press, 1968), 390. Haight pegs the contribution at £5 annually contributed to Congreve's group and the same amount to Harrison's group, after the rupture between the two leaders in 1878. Haight, *George Eliot*, 460.

15. See Eliot, *Journals*, 133, 141. Eliot returned to *Système de politique positive* in 1880; see Eliot, *Journals*, 212. The volume of Comte's letters was: Auguste Comte and Pierre Laffitte, *Lettres d'Auguste Comte á M. Valat, 1815–1844* (Paris: Dunod, 1870).

16. Francis Wrigley Hirst, *Early Life and Letters of John Morley*, 2 vols. (London: Macmillan, 1927), 1:178, quoted in Simon, *European Positivism*, 207. Morely, who followed Lewes in the editorship of *Fortnightly Review*, is discussed in Simon, *European Positivism*, 202–7.

17. The subject of Eliot's enthusiasm for positivism has been contentious. In his 1968 biography, Haight insists, "The extent of Eliot's concern with positivism has been greatly exaggerated." He cites Simon, "who has made the most thorough study of the subject," and finds "only a handful of brief passages that will bear any sort of Positivist interpretation." Haight, *George Eliot*, 301–2. Simon's study is certainly thorough in most regards, but his survey of Eliot's writings is superficial; he restricts it to one novel, *Daniel Deronda,* and her poetry, including *Spanish Gypsy.* Simon, *European Positivism*, 210n32, 296. McLaverty appears to be the first to have pointed out the discrepancy between Haight's comprehensive claim and Simon's selectivity. McLaverty, "Comtean Fetishism," 310–20. For an example of the polarities in the debate, compare Haight's claim, "There is certainly little sign of positivism in *The Mill on the Floss*," with McLaverty's argument, "The contrast at the heart of *Silas Marner* . . . draws its fullest significance from Comte's theory of fetishism," and with Shuttleworth's more recent observation, "the religion and social practices of Maggie's surrounding family had scarcely advanced beyond the conditions of primitive fetishism." Haight, *George Eliot*, 302; McLaverty, "Comtean Fetishism," 318; and Shuttleworth, introduction, xiv. The case for Eliot's "attenuated" positivism is made by Vogeler, who examines how she was perceived by the principle English positivists, Congreve, Harrison, and Edward Spencer Beesly (with passing remarks on John Henry Bridges). Vogeler's review of criticism on Eliot and positivism up to 1980 remains use-

ful today. Vogeler, "George Eliot," 407–8. The case for a connection between Eliot's positivism and early feminism is taken up in Nancy L. Paxton, "Feminism and Positivism in George Eliot's *Romola,*" *Nineteenth-Century Women Writers of the English-Speaking World,* ed. Rhoda B. Nathan, Contributions in Women's Studies (New York: Greenwood, 1986).

18. Quoted in Vogeler, "George Eliot," 423. The comment is reported by the publisher Charles Kegan Paul.

19. On Mill and Lewes in relation to Comte, see the discussion in chapter 1.

20. Frederic Harrison, "The Life of George Eliot," review of *George Eliot's Life, as Related in Her Letters and Journals,* by John Cross, *Fortnightly Review* 37 n.s. (1885): 320.

21. See Vogeler, "George Eliot," 423.

22. On the conflict over art, see discussion below about her relationship with Harrison. Semmel's analysis of Eliot's relationship to Comtianism, while generally fair, is unduly critical of Harrison; see Bernard Semmel, *George Eliot and the Politics of National Inheritance* (New York: Oxford University Press, 1994), 10.

23. Pinney identifies this as her earliest reference to Comte. Eliot, *Essays,* 28.

24. See Haight, *George Eliot,* 80.

25. Eliot, *Essays,* 37. Eliot's essays and reviews are collected in different volumes, each with their own strengths and weaknesses. For the purposes of preference in citation, I have turned first to *Essays of George Eliot,* edited by Pinney, cited in the text as *Essays;* then to *Selected Critical Writings,* ed. Rosemary Ashton (Oxford: Oxford University Press, 1992); and third to *Selected Essays, Poems, and Other Writings,* ed. A. S. Byatt and Nicholas Warren (New York: Penguin, 1990).

26. Tylor, *PC,* 1:94. On Tylor, see chapter 4.

27. I do not mean to overstate the relationship between the two philosophers; in *The German Ideology,* Marx ruthlessly criticizes Feuerbach for his insufficient materialism.

28. Ludwig Feuerbach, *The Essence of Christianity,* trans. George Eliot, Great Books in Philosophy (New York: Prometheus, 1989), xiv.

29. Gillian Beer, *George Eliot* (Bloomington: Indiana University Press, 1986), 75.

30. Feuerbach, *Essence,* xix.

31. Simpson, *Fetishism and Imagination,* xiii.

32. See the discussion of *Du culte des dieux fétiches* and its reception in chapter 1.

33. On Lucretius, see chapter 1.

34. Feuerbach, *Essence,* 52.

35. She began writing "Worldliness and Other Worldliness" on 22 April 1856, but set it aside to write "The Natural History of German Life," "Silly Novels

by Lady Novelists," and "Amos Barton," which she finished on 5 November 1856. Then she returned to the article on Young, completing it on 4 December 1856.

36. George Eliot, *Selected Essays*, 287, 288.

37. George Eliot, *The Mill on the Floss*, ed. Gordon S. Haight (Oxford: Clarendon, 1980), 176.

38. Žižek, *Plague*, 89, 88.

39. Eliot, *Mill*, 24.

40. Ibid., 25. West African art does include fetish dolls heavily studded with nails, but the narrator of *The Mill on the Floss* attributes the image instead to a Biblical story.

41. This was the same book that led to Eliot's break with religion and caused the crisis in her relationship with her father.

42. Eliot agreed to take over the translation in January 1844. Rufa Brabant's father was a physician and a German scholar who seems to have introduced his patient Samuel Taylor Coleridge to German philosophy.

43. Ashton's discussion of the Brabant incident argues that Eliot's after-the-fact claim that she laughed at him in her sleeve is "half-truth." Ashton, *George Eliot*, 61.

44. See introduction.

45. McKeon has examined the consequences of this philosophic shift in the epistemology of the novel in detail. Michael McKeon, *The Origins of the English Novel, 1600–1740* (Baltimore: Johns Hopkins University Press, 1987). See also Levine's analysis of the shift and its implications for nineteenth-century realism. George Levine, *The Realistic Imagination: English Fiction from Frankenstein to Lady Chatterley* (Chicago: University of Chicago Press, 1981), 3–22. Schor discusses particularity in the history of philosophy. Naomi Schor, *Reading in Detail: Aesthetics and the Feminine* (New York: Methuen, 1987), 1–22.

46. Ian Watt, *The Rise of the Novel: Studies in Defoe, Richardson, and Fielding* (Berkeley: University of California Press, 1957), 30, 29.

47. Barbara Hardy, *The Appropriate Form: An Essay on the Novel* (London: Athlone, 1964), 5.

48. Arnold Kettle, *An Introduction to the English Novel*, 2nd ed., 2 vols. (London: Hutchinson, 1967), 1:13.

49. William John Harvey, *Character and the Novel* (London: Chatto, 1965), 28, 30.

50. Henry James, *The Art of Criticism: Henry James on the Theory and the Practice of Fiction*, ed. William Veeder and Susan M. Griffin (Chicago: University of Chicago Press, 1986), 174.

51. Eliot, *Selected Critical Writings*, 248.

52. John Ruskin, *Modern Painters: Of Many Things*, vol. 3 (Boston: Estes, 1873), 65. Further references are cited in the text.

53. On Binet, see chapter 5. Krafft-Ebing, for example, defines fetishism as "the pronounced preference for a certain portion of the body," instead of an attraction to the whole person. Richard von Krafft-Ebing, *Psychopathia Sexualis, with Especial Reference to the Antipathetic Sexual Instinct: A Medico-Forensic Study*, trans. F. J. Rebman, 12th ed. (New York: Physicians and Surgeons, 1922; repr., 1935), 187. Further references are abbreviated *PS* and cited in the text. On Binet, see Apter, *Feminizing*, 18–30. On the fetishism of the detail, Apter's remarkable study is essential, as is Schor, *Reading*.

54. Ruskin, *Modern Painters*, 60.

55. For a poetic statement on this aspect of realism, see Elizabeth Barrett Browning, *Aurora Leigh*, book 5.

56. Ruskin, *Modern Painters*, 67–68.

57. This is a common strand in writings by other Victorian realists, most notably Elizabeth Barrett Browning, Robert Browning, and Arthur Hugh Clough.

58. Eliot, *Selected Critical Writings*, 15.

59. For De Quincey's two types of literature, see "Letters to a Young Man Whose Education Has Been Neglected," *The Collected Writings of Thomas De Quincey*, ed. David Masson, 14 vols., vol. 10 (Edinburgh: Adam and Charles Black, 1889–90).

60. Eliot, *Selected Critical Writings*, 240, 241.

61. Robert Browning, "Fra Lippo Lippi," line 330, 329. Stephen Greenblatt describes a similar historical incident from the Renaissance, the defacement of devils in Paolo Uccello's *Profanation of the Host*. Catherine Gallagher and Stephen Greenblatt, *Practicing New Historicism* (Chicago: University of Chicago Press, 2000), 95–96.

62. In the theory of novel, this reformist power has occasionally been used as the definitive quality of the genre as a whole, rather than something specific to the Victorian realist novel. As Robert writes, "For if reality is permanently beyond [the novel's] reach, nevertheless it has access to it at one crucial point and that is in its endeavor to transform it." Marthe Robert, "Origins of the Novel," *Theory of the Novel: A Historical Approach*, ed. Michael McKeon (Baltimore: Johns Hopkins University Press, 2000), 66–67.

63. Richard Stang, *The Theory of the Novel in England: 1850–70* (London: Routledge, 1959), 45.

64. Žižek touches on the ambivalence expressed in the phrase "as if." Slavoj Žižek, *The Sublime Object of Ideology* (London: Verso, 1989), 18.

65. John Ruskin, *Sesame and Lilies*, ed. Harold Bloom, Prophets of Sensibility: Precursors of Modern Cultural Thought (New York: Chelsea House, 1983), 86.
66. Eliot, *Letters*, 4:300.
67. Feuerbach, *Essence*, 80.

4. Edward Tylor's Science

1. Stocking suggests that Tylor actively engaged in a conceptual dialogue with Arnold; see George W. Stocking, "Matthew Arnold, E. B. Tylor, and the Uses of Invention," *American Anthropologist* 65 (1963).
2. Tylor, *PC*, 1:1. In 1952, Kroeber and Kluckhohn credited Tylor with the "birth of the scientific concept," and thus the creation of anthropology, in this substantive definition. Kroeber and Kluckhohn, *Culture*, 147. A decade later, Stocking called this claim a creation myth; "Matthew Arnold," 783. He reiterated this 1963 thesis thirty years later, in "Edward Burnett Tylor and the Mission of Primitive Man," introduction to *The Collected Works of Edward Burnett Tylor*, by Edward B. Tylor, 8 vols., vol. 1 (London: Routledge/Thoemmes, 1994). Herbert has written an important analysis of the paradox in Tylor's formulation of culture as a "complex whole"; see Herbert, *Culture*, 1–21.
3. For an overview of the relationship between *culture* and *civilization* from the late-eighteenth to mid-twentieth century, see Herbert, *Culture*, 204–24. See also Stocking's discussion of Tylor's use of *civilization* as a synonym for *culture*, in "Matthew Arnold," 784, 792–93.
4. In his extensive discussion of primitive religion, for example, Tylor argues that morality emerges in recognizable form only in the transition from savagery to barbarism; see *PC*, 1:427. He does allow for a pragmatic "lower ethics" in primitive culture but differentiates it from morality as such; see *PC*, 2:89–90. Stocking argues that Tylor's idea was closer to the contemporary humanist theory of culture than generally thought, while Arnold's version more nearly represents the anthropological; see "Matthew Arnold."
5. On the distinction between fieldworker and armchair anthropologist, see Kuklick, *Savage Within*, 89–94. As a stereotype, the "armchair anthropologist" label oversimplifies a complex situation. Tylor did some of his own fieldwork, as did Morgan. But both relied extensively on existing accounts by missionaries, travelers, traders, and others, and it is this practice that the label more successfully captures.

6. For example, see Benedict's comments on evolutionary anthropologists, in Ruth Benedict, *Patterns of Culture* (1934; Boston: Houghton Mifflin, 1959), 18–19, 48–49.

7. The economic status and backgrounds of Victorian anthropologists and archeologists differed widely. Some, like Thomas Huxley, had to work for a living, while Francis Galton and others were independently wealthy. Galton (grandson of Erasmus Darwin) inherited a fortune from his banker-father. Augustus Lane Fox Pitt Rivers was a lieutenant-general in the army and the son of an army officer; he became wealthy when he inherited the estate of a cousin. John Lubbock was a banker who took over as head of his father's bank. Huxley grew up on the edge of poverty; his father was a mathematics teacher at an unsuccessful school, and Huxley became a science teacher. William Crooke's father was a physician. E. Sidney Hartland was a lawyer and the son of a Congregational minister. Among those with manufacturing backgrounds were William Flower, whose father was a brewer, and Arthur Evans, the son of a paper manufacturer. See Kuklick, *Savage Within*, appendix 2.

8. For details of Tylor's life and work, see Andrew Lang, "Edward Burnett Tylor," in Tylor, *Collected Works*; R. R. Marett, *Tylor* (New York: J. Wiley, 1936); Robert H. Lowie, "Edward B. Tylor," *American Anthropologist* 19 (1917); Joan Leopold, *Culture in Comparative and Evolutionary Perspective: E. B. Tylor and the Making of Primitive Culture* (1980); and Stocking, *Victorian Anthropology*, 156–64. See also Chris Holdsworth's biography, in *Oxford Dictionary of National Biography*, s.v. "Tylor, Sir Edward Burnett (1832–1917)."

9. Lang, "E. B. Tylor," 15.

10. Stocking, *Victorian Anthropology*, 299–301. The position at Oxford was created at the insistence of Pitt Rivers, as the condition of a bequest to their collection.

11. Edward B. Tylor, *Anthropology: An Introduction to the Study of Man and Civilization* (New York: D. Appleton, 1898), v.

12. Tylor's emphasis was reflected in nineteenth-century museum exhibits, which displayed clothing separately from pottery, weapons, and so forth. In 1887, Franz Boas criticized the practice in a famous dispute with the curator at the Smithsonian and argued that displays needed to reflect specific cultures. See Susan Hegeman, *Patterns for America: Modernism and the Concept of Culture* (Princeton: Princeton University Press, 1999), 37–47; and Franz Boas, *A Franz Boas Reader: The Shaping of American Anthropology, 1883–1911*, ed. George W. Stocking (Chicago: University of Chicago Press, 1982), 61–67.

13. On the paradox of relativism in anthropology, see Herbert, *Culture*, 7–8.

14. See George W. Stocking, "Franz Boas and the Culture Concept in Historical Perspective," *Race, Culture, and Evolution: Essays in the History of Anthropology* (New York: Free Press, 1968). As Stocking points out, Boas was the first anthropologist to use the plural form, *cultures.*

15. Although *savage* is now used only as an abusive, disrespectful term, at the time it had the more positive meaning of living free of all social constraints, and Tylor used it in this older, less judgmental sense. He used *primitive* interchangeably with *savage* as terms for the earliest stage of culture. Thus the title of his book, *Primitive Culture,* was synonymous with "savage culture." This suggests how wrong the idea is that evolutionary anthropology viewed the "idea of savagery" as "*outside* the reach or below the line of Culture altogether," as Buzard claims. James Buzard, *Disorienting Fiction: The Autoethnographic Work of Nineteenth-Century British Novels* (Princeton, NJ: Princeton University Press, 2005), 6. On the history of the words, *savage, barbarian,* and *civilized,* see Frederick J. Teggart, *Theory and Processes of History* (Berkeley: University of California Press, 1977), 77–98. Tylor defines his three stages in *Anthropology,* 23–25. He occasionally employed Comte's terms, as well; see *PC,* 1:104, 2:109. While Tylor's savage stage was consistent with Comte's theological stage, Tylor's version of barbarism lacked the characteristic ambivalence that Comte attributed to its parallel, the metaphysical stage.

16. Edward B. Tylor, *Researches into the Early History of Mankind and the Development of Civilization,* ed. Paul Bohannan (Chicago: University of Chicago Press, 1964), 236.

17. See Stocking, "Matthew Arnold." Stocking goes on to argue that this shift of emphasis in evolutionary causation directly affected Tylor's definition of culture. Catherine Gallagher notes a related shift, though with a different emphasis; she argues that his early work was preoccupied with the production side of the Malthusian equation, while the later work was more concerned with the consumption side; see *The Body Economic: Life, Death, and Sensation in Political Economy and the Victorian Novel* (Princeton, NJ: Princeton University Press, 2005), 166–68. David Bidney is the dissenting vote, arguing that Tylor's emphasis was consistent throughout; see *Theoretical Anthropology* (New York: Schocken, 1967), 200.

18. Edward B. Tylor, "On a Method of Investigating the Development of Institutions, Applied to Laws of Marriage and Descent," *Journal of the Anthropological Institute of Great Britain and Ireland* 18 (1889): 269. See Stocking's analysis of this essay and its importance within the history of social anthropology; *After Tylor,* 3–14. On evolutionary anthropology's assumptions, see Kuklick, *Savage Within,* 75–118.

19. Problems in the comparative method are discussed in Ruth Mace and Mark Pagel, "The Comparative Method in Anthropology," *Current Anthropology* 35, no. 5 (1994); A. R. Radcliffe-Brown, "The Comparative Method in Social Anthropology," *Journal of the Royal Anthropological Institute of Great Britain and Ireland* 51, no. 1/2 (1951); and I. Schapera and Milton Singer, "Wenner-Gren Foundation Supper Conference: Comparative Method in Social Anthropology," *American Anthropologist* N.S. 55, no. 3 (1953).

20. On Tylor and language, see Morse Peckham, *Victorian Revolutionaries: Speculations on Some Heroes of a Culture Crisis* (New York: George Braziller, 1970), 197. See also the discussion of symbolism in Herbert, *Culture*, 260–62.

21. Peckham, *Victorian Revolutionaries*, 200–1.

22. Tylor, *PC*, 1:424. Tylor's new terminology persists in the twenty-first century. In 2005, the *New York Times* explained, of the Moken sea gypsies of Southeast Asia: "They are animists who believe that the sea, their island and all objects have spirits, and the Moken use totem poles to communicate with them." Abby Goodnough, "Survivors of Tsunami Live on Close Terms with Sea," *New York Times*, 23 January 2005. In general, *animism* today applies to the religious beliefs of tribal or indigenous groups, but particularly those in Southeast Asia.

23. Tylor, *PC*, 2:144. On Tylor's intellectual borrowing from and revisions of Comte, see Teggart, *Theory and Processes*, 110–27. See also Bidney, *Theoretical*, 183–214.

24. On totems, see Tylor, *PC*, 2:234–35. Totemism was only a minor topic in *Primitive Culture*. Tylor's contemporary John McLennan introduced the concept into anthropology in 1869, in "The Worship of Animals and Plants, Part 1," *Fortnightly Review* (n.s.) 6: 407–27. But it was not until James Frazer wrote about it twenty years later, for the ninth edition of the *Encyclopedia Britannica*, that it became a significant topic of discussion. See Stocking, *Victorian Anthropology*, 297.

25. Peckham also notes that Tylor identified his theory of animism with "Comte's notion of fetishism." *Victorian Revolutionaries*, 194.

26. See George W. Stocking, "The Ethnographer's Magic: Fieldwork in British Anthropology from Tylor to Malinowski," *History of Anthropology*, ed. George W. Stocking, vol. 1 (Madison: University of Wisconsin Press, 1983). The implications of Tylor's redefinition of field work were not lost on Lowie; see his "Edward B. Tylor," *The History of Ethnological Theory* (New York: Holt, Rinehart and Winston, 1937).

27. For an assessment of Tylor's reputation, see Stocking, *After Tylor*, 15–17. In the 1930s, Lowie insisted that "Tylor was not technically a field worker, yet

he was the very opposite of an armchair anthropologist," because of his early forays into Mexico, his work at the Deaf Institute, and his observations of metropolitan London life. "E. B. Tylor," 69. This was one of several elements in an argument stressing the specific attributes of Tylor's life and writings that coincided with the practices of Lowie's contemporaries. He also emphasized Tylor's early diffusionism, arguing that if Tylor was not an extreme diffusionist, neither was he a strict believer in independent invention. The one theory that Lowie rejects entirely is Tylor's "inadmissibly vague phrase 'psychic unity.'" "E. B. Tylor," 79.

28. For Kingsley, see Dea Birkett, *Mary Kingsley: Imperial Adventuress* (Basingstoke: Macmillan, 1992). Kingsley's first lecture, delivered to the Scottish Geographical Society, was read by a male fellow while she sat on the platform. See Birkett's article, *Oxford Dictionary of National Biography*, s.v. "Kingsley, Mary Henrietta (1862–1900)."

29. Kingsley, *Travels*, 435. Kingsley visited the missionary-ethnographer Robert Nassau while in West Africa and made extensive use of his observations on fetishism in her study. She also encouraged him to publish his observations, which were based on a lifetime spent living there. When he did so in *Fetichism*, his views were largely consonant with those contained in Kingsley's work.

30. Kingsley, *Travels*, 434. One of the specific difficulties she cites is the erroneous belief (which Tylor advocated) that primitives were analogous to children; instead, she argues that ". . . Africans have often a remarkable mental acuteness and a large share of common sense; . . . there is nothing really 'child-like' in their form of mind at all." *Travels*, 439.

31. A more comprehensive historical account would include the field study of Baldwin Spencer and F. J. Gillen in Central Australia in 1896–97. I am grateful to Henrika Kuklick for sharing an early copy of her article on the history of anthropology with me and correcting several of my mistakes. Henrika Kuklick, "The British Tradition," *A New History of Anthropology*, ed. Henrika Kuklick (Oxford: Blackwell, 2007).

32. Bronislaw Malinowski, *Argonauts of the Western Pacific: An Account of Native Enterprise and Adventure in the Archipelagoes of Melanesian New Guinea* (London: Routledge, 1922), 9.

33. Tylor's treatment of mythology is usefully discussed in relation to Comte in Von Hendy, *The Modern Construction of Myth*, 83–88. Margot K. Louis, in a useful survey of mythography in the nineteenth century, explores the changing treatment it received in British poetry. However, in viewing the treatment of mythic gods as "little more than ceremonial puppets" in James Frazer's work, Louis misrepresents the centrality of myth to evolutionary

anthropology, as it was spelled out by Tylor. Margot K. Louis, "Gods and Mysteries: The Revival of Paganism and the Remaking of Mythography through the Nineteenth Century," *Victorian Studies* 47, no. 3 (2005): 352.

34. Tylor, *PC*, 1:285. In yet another illustration of the principle of fetishism, Tylor supplied an example parallel to the one used by Arnold in *Empedocles* (see chapter 2). Quoting Grote, Tylor notes, "even an intelligent man may be impelled in a moment of agonizing pain to kick or beat the lifeless object from which he has suffered." *PC*, 1:286.

35. The German philologist Karl Lachmann (1793–1851) spelled out the dominant nineteenth-century theory of classical textual criticism, which relied on the comparison of textual errors to establish the origin of a manuscript. For an introduction to Lachmann, see Jerome J. McGann, *A Critique of Modern Textual Criticism* (Charlottesville: University Press of Virginia, 1992).

36. Herbert has an important analysis of symbolic systems in Victorian anthropology, with reference to Tylor. See his *Culture*, 260–65.

37. In Freud's theory of displacement, spelled out in *Interpretation of Dreams*, the dream elements that seem least significant are to be regarded as, potentially, the most significant.

38. See Henri F. Ellenberger, *The Discovery of the Unconscious: The History and Evolution of Dynamic Psychiatry* (New York: Basic, 1970), chapters 2 and 3.

39. On Hall, see Logan, *Nerves*, 166–68.

40. Tylor, "On Method," 270.

41. For an introduction to the contribution of Boas, see the selections from his work in *A Franz Boas Reader: The Shaping of American Anthropology, 1883–1911*, ed. George W. Stocking (Chicago: University of Chicago Press, 1982).

42. Boas, "Limitations," 903.

43. Hegeman complicates the conventional assumption of a clean break between Tylor's Victorian and modernist anthropology. See "Franz Boas and Professional Anthropology: On Mapping the Borders of the 'Modern'," *Victorian Studies* 41, no. 3 (1998). On diffusionism and functionalism, see Kuklick, *Savage Within*, 119–81, 264–76; and see Stocking, *After Tylor*, 11–14.

44. Benedict, *Patterns*, 19.

45. Kuklick, *Savage Within*, 78–89.

46. Lowie, "E. B. Tylor," 84.

47. Paul Radin, introduction to *Religion in Primitive Culture*, by Edward B. Tylor (New York: Harper, 1958), xiii.

48. The problem of reflexivity is a long-standing issue in anthropology. Lowie discussed it in 1937, for example, in "E. B. Tylor," 84.

49. Nietzsche, "Truth."

50. Tylor, *PC*, 1:298. I fully recognize that there are serious theoretical problems associated with the concept of pre- or extralinguistic thinking.

51. Tylor's approach to taxonomy functioned in much the same way that cataloging does in Bourdieu's theory, where it becomes a means of reifying abstractions; see *Distinction*, 466–84.

52. Quoted in Tylor, *PC*, 1:274. Tylor's elision.

53. Benedict, *Patterns*, 2.

54. Peckham, *Victorian Revolutionaries*, 201.

55. Benedict, *Patterns*, 21.

56. Ibid., 48. Benedict retained some of Tylor's evolutionary assumptions, nonetheless. The value of studying primitive cultures, she explains, is what they can teach about "our own cultural processes." *Patterns*, 56. While "our" culture is too complex to comprehend directly, primitive cultures are "simpler" and more "transparent," because they are "less complicated."

57. Herbert first drew my attention to this problem in Benedict's work. See his *Culture*, 9.

58. Benedict, *Patterns*, 47.

59. Paul Rabinow, *Reflections on Fieldwork in Morocco* (Berkeley: University of California Press, 1977), 161–62. Rabinow paraphrases Paul Ricoeur in this passage. For an introduction to self-reflexivity in recent anthropology, see James Clifford and George E. Marcus, eds., *Writing Culture: The Poetics and Politics of Ethnography* (Berkeley: University of California Press, 1986); and see Judith Okely and Helen Callaway, eds., *Anthropology and Autobiography* (New York: Routledge, 1992).

5. Sexology's Perversion

1. On reverse colonialism, see Pratt, *Imperial Eyes*, 16.

2. Esquirol's paper on monomania was edited and incorporated into his well-known *Des maladies mentales* (1838), which was published in English translation by the American physician E. K. Hunt in 1845. The translation used here is Hunt's. On Esquirol and monomania, see Jan Goldstein, *Console and Classify: The French Psychiatric Profession in the Nineteenth Century* (Cambridge: Cambridge University Press, 1987), 152–78.

3. On the concept of madness that Esquirol inherited, see Roy Porter, *Mind-Forg'd Manacles: A History of Madness in England from the Restoration to the Regency* (Cambridge, MA: Harvard University Press, 1987), 1–32. On the place of Esquirol's monomania in the history of obsession, see German E. Berrios, "Obsessional Disorders during the Nineteenth Century: Termino-

logical and Classificatory Issues," *The Anatomy of Madness: Essays in the History of Psychiatry*, ed. W. F. Bynum, Roy Porter, and Michael Shepherd, 3 vols., vol. 1 (London: Tavistock, 1985).

4. Prichard's theory of Moral Insanity is also available in two excellent anthologies of medical texts on mental conditions, Richard Hunter and Ida Macalpine, *Three Hundred Years of Psychiatry, 1535–1860: A History Presented in Selected English Texts* (London: Oxford University Press, 1963), 836–42; and Jenny Bourne Taylor and Sally Shuttleworth, eds., *Embodied Selves: An Anthology of Psychological Texts: 1830–1890* (Oxford: Clarendon, 1998), 251–56.

5. Jean Étienne Esquirol, *Mental Maladies: A Treatise on Insanity*, trans. E. K. Hunt (Philadelphia: Lea and Blanchard, 1845), 335.

6. Jean-Martin Charcot and Valentin Magnan, "Inversion du sens génital," *Archives de neurologie* 3–4 (1882). My comments on this essay summarize elements of Robert Nye's splendid essay, "The Medical Origins of Sexual Fetishism," in Apter and Pietz, *Fetishism*. Charcot and Magnan did not produce the earliest accounts of same-sex desire. German psychiatrist Wilhelm Greisinger defined it as a nervous disease in 1868; his successor, Carl von Westphal, published a study of *conträre Sexualempfindung* (contrary sexual feeling) in 1869. See Harry Oosterhuis, *Stepchildren of Nature: Krafft-Ebing, Psychiatry, and the Making of Sexual Identity*, Chicago Series on Sexuality, History, and Society (Chicago: University of Chicago Press, 2000), 43.

7. Charcot and Magnan, "Inversion," 4:296. See also Nye, "Medical Origins," 21.

8. Quoted from Amy S. Wyngaard, "The Fetish in/as Text: Rétif de la Bretonne and the Development of Modern Sexual Science and French Literary Studies, 1887–1934," *PMLA* 121 (2006): 672. Rétif was later referenced by French sexologists seeking a pedigree for fetishism, according to Wyngaard, who cites Jean Avalon, "Restif de la Bretonne fétichiste," *Aesculape* (1912); Louis Barras, *Le Fétichisme: Restif de la Bretonne, fut-il fétichiste?* (Paris: Maloine, 1913); Louis Charpentier, *Restif de la Bretonne, son fétichisme* (Bordeaux: Destout, 1912); and Dr. Louis, "Un Romancier fétichiste: Restif de la Bretonne," *La Chronique médicale* 1 (1904). See also Amy S. Wyngaard, "New Perspectives on Rétif de la Bretonne: Introduction," *Symposium (Washington, D.C.)* 60, no. 3 (2006): 133n3.

9. Binet cites Rousseau's *Confessions* as an early example of fetishism. See Apter, *Feminizing*, 18–23. On Binet, see also Jann Matlock, "Masquerading Women, Pathologized Men: Cross-Dressing, Fetishism, and the Theory of Perversion, 1882–1935," in Apter and Pietz, *Fetishism*.

10. On degeneration, see William Greenslade, *Culture, Degeneration, and the Novel* (Cambridge: Cambridge University Press, 1994).

11. On Cheyne and Trotter, see Logan, *Nerves*, 15–42.

12. Michel Foucault, *The History of Sexuality: An Introduction*, trans. Robert Hurley, vol. 1 (New York: Vintage, 1990), 154.

13. Ellenberger, *Discovery*, 297. Recent scholarship on Krafft-Ebing has challenged the prevalent view of his work as unsympathetic to the needs of his patients and correspondents; see Oosterhuis, *Stepchildren*.

14. Although often thought to be original to Krafft-Ebing, the terms *sadism* and *masochism* were suggested to him by others. See Renate Hauser, "Krafft-Ebing's Psychological Understanding of Sexual Behaviour," *Sexual Knowledge, Sexual Science: The History of Attitudes to Sexuality*, ed. Roy Porter and Mikulás Teich (Cambridge: Cambridge University Press, 1994), 213–14.

15. Ellenberger, *Discovery*, 299.

16. Freud's readers also wrote to him, and their comments contributed to his revisions of psychoanalytic theory; see John C. Burnham, "The 'New Freud Studies': A Historiographical Shift," *Journal of the Historical Society* 6, no. 2 (2006): 227.

17. Hauser, "Krafft-Ebing," 221.

18. Krafft-Ebing, *PS*, 17–18.

19. The most familiar reference for this aspect of beliefs about female sexuality is William Acton's statement, in 1857, that "the majority of women . . . are not very much troubled with sexual feeling of any kind." William Surgeon Acton, *The Functions and Disorders of the Reproductive Organs in Youth, in Adult Age, and in Advanced Life*, 4th ed. (London: John Churchill, 1865), 112–13.

20. Krafft-Ebing was careful to differentiate disease from moral vice; while physical disease causes "perversion," moral vice leads instead to "perversity." Krafft-Ebing, *PS*, 79.

21. Krafft-Ebing did not deny the possibility of pathological fetishism in women, as Freud later did. He suggested that the absence of female doctors, "medical women," retarded the scientific study of the subject. Ibid., 23. Though he viewed evidence of female fetishism as lacking, Binet and other contemporaries described many cases; see Matlock, "Masquerading Women."

22. Krafft-Ebing, *PS*, 224. For the basic history of masturbation, see Thomas W. Laqueur, *Solitary Sex: A Cultural History of Masturbation* (New York: Zone Books, 2003); and see E. H. Hare, "Masturbatory Insanity: The History of an Idea," *Journal of Mental Science* 108 (1962). See also Cohen's discussion of the Victorian history of masturbation, in relation to Charles Dickens's novels: William A. Cohen, *Sex Scandal: The Private Parts of Victorian Fiction* (Durham, NC: Duke University Press, 1996), 26–45.

23. Sigmund Freud, *The Standard Edition of the Complete Psychological Works of Sigmund Freud*, trans. James Strachey, 24 vols. (London: Hogarth, 1953–), 7:135n1. Further references are abbreviated *SE* and cited in the text. Freud expresses indebtedness to Krafft-Ebing and other sexologists in his head note. Some recent scholars emphasize Freud's dependence on Krafft-Ebing's conceptual work. See Hauser, "Krafft-Ebing," 210.

24. As Freud used it, *disavowal* was one of two aspects of fetishism, the denial of external reality; the other aspect, *affirmation*, referred to its acknowledgment. In current usage, the combination of the two aspects is also referred to as "fetishistic disavowal." For the sake of consistency, the remainder of this chapter uses *disavowal* to refer to the denial of reality. The combination of disavowal and affirmation is referred to as *fetishistic ambivalence, Freud's fetish*, or simply *fetishism* (where the reference is clearly to Freud's idea).

25. At this stage, Freud bears a closer resemblance to Edward Tylor than to Krafft-Ebing. Tylor also rejected degenerationism and turned instead to a universal model—his "psychic unity"—to explain the behaviors of primitive culture.

26. His footnotes on fetishism reflect the development of his thinking on the topic; see Freud, *SE*, 7:154n2, 155n1, 155n2. For a comprehensive summary of Freud's published writing on the topic, see the headnote to "Fetishism," in Freud, *SE*, 21:149–51.

27. Freud, *SE*, 21:152–57. "Fetishism" was earlier published in German as "Fetishismus," *Almanach 1928* (1927): 17–24.

28. The two pieces are found in Freud, *SE*, 23:273–78, 23:144–207.

29. The gendered consequence that follows from this formulation, of course, is that fetishism is a specifically male perversion. That Freud was biased in his interpretation is a given, in my view. Thus my analysis of Freud's narrative posits it as a wholly imaginary story, without basis in fact. While he positions the fetish as a defense against the little boy's fear, more recently critics working toward revisions of the psychoanalytic narrative have substituted other, gender-neutral sites for the lack the child fears, so that the narrative becomes operational for both male and female psychology. See in particular: Elisabeth Bronfen, *The Knotted Subject: Hysteria and its Discontents* (Princeton: Princeton University Press, 1998). The topic of female fetishism has itself become an important part of psychoanalytic gender theory. See Marcia Ian, *Remembering the Phallic Mother: Psychoanalysis, Modernism, and the Fetish* (Ithaca: Cornell University Press, 1993); Teresa De Lauretis, *The Practice of Love: Lesbian Sexuality and Perverse Desire* (Bloomington: Indiana University Press, 1994); and Elizabeth Grosz, "Lesbian Fetishism?," in Apter and Pietz, *Fetishism*.

30. See Krafft-Ebing, *PS*, 341–42.
31. Octave Mannoni, *Freud: The Theory of the Unconscious*, trans. Renaud Bruce (London: Verso, 1983), 151.
32. While it functions as a means of unconscious denial, disavowal is distinguished from repression in Freud's later writing. As his editor notes, "'repression' applies to defence against internal instinctual demands and 'disavowal' to defence against the claims of external reality." Freud, *SE*, 21:153n4.
33. Krafft-Ebing thought fetishism was normally impossible to cure and held out little hope to the clients in his case histories.
34. Apter, *Feminizing*, 13.
35. Žižek, *Sublime Object*, 18. See the discussion of word usage at note 24 above.
36. For his discussion of this topic, see Charles Bernheimer, "Fetishism and Decadence: Salome's Severed Heads," in Apter and Pietz, *Fetishism*, 80–83.
37. Anne McClintock, *Imperial Leather: Race, Gender, and Sexuality in the Colonial Contest* (New York: Routledge, 1995), 190.
38. Burnham has produced a remarkable study of recent developments in scholarship on Freud, to which I am indebted; see his "New Freud Studies."
39. In arguing the need to divorce fetishism from castration, I endorse a point made previously by a chorus of others. See, for example: McClintock, *Imperial Leather*, 202–3; Bernheimer, "Fetishism and Decadence," 83; and Matlock, "Masquerading Women," 61.

Conclusion

1. Alfred Tennyson, *In Memoriam*, section 108, lines 1, 9–10.
2. On the reaction in Victorian poetry against the subjectivism of the Romantics, see Carol T. Christ, *Victorian and Modern Poetics* (Chicago: University of Chicago Press, 1984). David Simpson takes the opposite view and examines the persistence of Romantic tropes in Victorian fiction. See *Fetishism and Imagination*.
3. Matthew Arnold, "The Buried Life," lines 64–66.
4. The intertwining of the two tendrils is not entirely undone. "There is surely a danger of allowing Culture also to become a fetish," wrote Williams fifty years ago, speaking of Arnold's theory. Williams, *Culture*, 126. A. R. Radcliffe-Brown made a similar point about anthropology when he complained that culture was a "fantastic reification of abstractions." A. R. Radcliffe-Brown, "On Social Structure," *Journal of the Royal Anthropological Institute* 70 (1940): 10, quoted in Herbert, *Culture*, 21. By articulating the "superstitions of culture," Herbert situates the concept squarely in the realm of magic and

supernaturalism, nudging it that much closer to the magical thinking against which it was once defined. Herbert, *Culture*, 1.

5. Between 1851 and his death, popular English novelist William H. G. Kingston (1814–1880) produced over 130 tales of adventure for boys. For an example of his treatment of fetishism, see his *The Two Supercargoes: Adventures in Savage Africa* (1878).

6. For an example of the difference between an abstract idea and a reification, consider Christopher Ricks's pithy comment, in his review of a book by Harold Bloom: "Bloom had an idea; now the idea has him." Christopher Ricks, "Poetry and Repression," *New York Times Book Review*, 14 March 1976.

7. Tylor did not use fetishism in overtly racial terms. He excluded race as a category from his study, arguing that it was "both possible and desirable to eliminate considerations of hereditary varieties or races of man, and to treat mankind as homogeneous in nature, though placed in different grades of civilization," and thus he was able to claim that there was "scarce a hand's breadth distance between an English ploughman and a negro of Central Africa." Tylor, *PC*, 1:7.

8. Female fetishism, certainly, presented a clear case of social differentiation, but as a rhetorical element of social critique, its usage is unclear; the social inferiority of women is being equated with the absence of fetishism, rather than its presence, because Freud's term of difference between the sexes was the symbolic value of the penis, not the presence or absence of fetishism itself.

9. For examples of how erotic fetishism can successfully be adapted to social critique, see McClintock, *Imperial Leather*, chapter 4; and see Apter and Pietz, *Fetishism*.

Bibliography

Acton, William Surgeon. *The Functions and Disorders of the Reproductive Organs in Youth, in Adult Age, and in Advanced Life*. 4th ed. London: John Churchill, 1865.

Althusser, Louis. "Ideology and Ideological State Apparatuses (Notes towards an Investigation)." In *Lenin and Philosophy and Other Essays*, edited by Ben Brewster, 136–70. New York: Monthly Review Press, 1971.

American Psychiatric Association. *Diagnostic and Statistical Manual of Mental Disorders: DSM-IV-TR*. Washington, DC: American Psychiatric Association, 2000.

apRoberts, Ruth. *The Ancient Dialect: Thomas Carlyle and Comparative Religion*. Berkeley: University of California Press, 1988.

Apter, Emily. *Feminizing the Fetish: Psychoanalysis and Narrative Obsession in Turn-of-the-Century France*. Ithaca: Cornell University Press, 1991.

Apter, Emily, and William Pietz, eds. *Fetishism as Cultural Discourse*. Ithaca: Cornell University Press, 1993.

Arac, Jonathan. *Critical Genealogies: Historical Situations for Postmodern Literary Studies*. New York: Columbia University Press, 1987.

Arnold, Matthew. *The Complete Prose Works of Matthew Arnold*. Edited by R. H. Super. 11 vols. Ann Arbor: University of Michigan Press, 1960.

———. *Culture and Anarchy*. 3rd ed. New York: Macmillan, 1882. Toronto: University of Toronto English Library, 1998. http://www.library.utoronto.ca/utel/.

———. *The Poems of Matthew Arnold*. Edited by Kenneth Allott. 2nd ed. London: Longman, 1965.

———. *Matthew Arnold*. Edited by Miriam Allott and Robert H. Super. Oxford: Oxford University Press, 1986.

———. *Unpublished Letters of Matthew Arnold*. Edited by Arnold Whitridge. New Haven: Yale University Press, 1923.

Ashton, Rosemary. *George Eliot: A Life*. London: Hamish Hamilton, 1996.

Avalon, Jean. "Restif de la Bretonne fétichiste." *Aesculape* (April 1912): 89–93.

Barras, Louis. *Le Fétichisme: Restif de la Bretonne, fut-il fétichiste?* Paris: Maloine, 1913.

Baudrillard, Jean. *For a Critique of the Political Economy of the Sign*. Translated by Levin Charles. St. Louis, MO: Telos, 1981.

Beer, Gillian. *George Eliot*. Bloomington: Indiana University Press, 1986.

Bell, Bill. "Beyond the Death of the Author: Matthew Arnold's Two Audiences, 1888–1930." *Book History* 3 (2000): 155–65.

Benedict, Ruth. *Patterns of Culture*. 1934. Boston: Houghton Mifflin, 1959.

Bennett, William J. "'To Reclaim a Legacy': Text of Report on Humanities in Education." *Chronicle of Higher Education* 28 (November 1984): A16–21.

Bernheimer, Charles. "Fetishism and Decadence: Salome's Severed Heads." In Apter and Pietz, *Fetishism*, 62–83.

Berrios, German E. "Obsessional Disorders during the Nineteenth Century: Terminological and Classificatory Issues." In *The Anatomy of Madness: Essays in the History of Psychiatry*, edited by W. F. Bynum, Roy Porter, and Michael Shepherd, 1:166–87. London: Tavistock, 1985.

Bidney, David. *Theoretical Anthropology*. New York: Schocken, 1967.

Binet, Alfred. "Le fétichisme dans l'amour." *Revue Philosophique* 12, no. 2 (1887): 143–67.

Birkett, Dea. *Mary Kingsley: Imperial Adventuress*. Basingstoke: Macmillan, 1992.

Boas, Franz. *A Franz Boas Reader: The Shaping of American Anthropology, 1883–1911*. Edited by George W. Stocking. Chicago: University of Chicago Press, 1982.

———. "The Limitations of the Comparative Method of Anthropology." *Science* 4 (1896): 901–8.

Boas, George. *Essays on Primitivism and Related Ideas in the Middle Ages*. Contributions to the History of Primitivism. New York: Octagon, 1966.

Bodenheimer, Rosemarie. *The Real Life of Mary Ann Evans: George Eliot, Her Letters and Fiction*. Ithaca: Cornell University Press, 1994.

Bonnell, Victoria E., and Lynn Hunt. Introduction to *Beyond the Cultural Turn: New Directions in the Study of Society and Culture*, 1–32. Berkeley: University of California Press, 1999.

Bourdieu, Pierre. *Distinction: A Social Critique of the Judgement of Taste*. Translated by Richard Nice. Cambridge: Harvard University Press, 1984.

[Brewster, David]. Review of *Cours de philosophie positive*, by Auguste Comte. *Edinburgh Review* 67 (1838): 271–308.

British Periodicals. In *C19: The Nineteenth Century Index*. ProQuest Information and Learning. http://collections.chadwyck.com (search: keywords fetish* fetich*; accessed 29 April 2007).

Bromwich, David. "The Genealogy of Disinterestedness." *Raritan* 1 (1982): 62–92.

Bronfen, Elisabeth. *The Knotted Subject: Hysteria and its Discontents*. Princeton: Princeton University Press, 1998.

Burnham, John C. "The 'New Freud Studies': A Historiographical Shift." *Journal of the Historical Society* 6, no. 2 (June 2006): 213–33.

Buzard, James. *Disorienting Fiction: The Autoethnographic Work of Nineteenth-Century British Novels*. Princeton, NJ: Princeton University Press, 2005.

Carabelli, Giancarlo. *In the Image of Priapus*. London: Duckworth, 1996.

Carlyle, Thomas. *On Heroes, Hero-Worship, and the Heroic in History*. New York: D. Appleton, 1841.

———. *Sartor Resartus*. London: Dent, 1908. Reprint, New York: Chelsea House, 1983.

Cashdollar, Charles D. *The Transformation of Theology, 1830–1890: Positivism and Protestant Thought in Britain and America*. Princeton, NJ: Princeton University Press, 1989.

Charcot, Jean-Martin, and Valentin Magnan. "Inversion du sens génital." *Archives de neurologie* 3–4 (January-February, November 1882): 53–60, 296–322.

Charpentier, Louis. *Restif de la Bretonne, son fétichisme*. Bordeaux: Destout, 1912.

Chaucer, Geoffrey. *The Works of Geoffrey Chaucer*. Edited by F. N. Robinson. 2nd ed. Boston: Houghton Mifflin, 1957.

Christ, Carol T. *Victorian and Modern Poetics*. Chicago: University of Chicago Press, 1984.

Claessen, Henri J. M. "Evolution and Evolutionism." In *Encyclopedia of Social and Cultural Anthropology*, edited by Alan Barnard and Jonathan Spencer, 213–17. New York: Routledge, 1996.

Clarke-Evans, Christine. "Charles de Brosses and Diderot: Eighteenth-Century Arguments concerning Primitive Language, Particular Natural Languages, and a National Language." *History of European Ideas* 16 (1993): 183–88.

Clifford, James. "Introduction: Partial Truths." In Clifford and Marcus, *Writing Culture*, 1–26.

———. *The Predicament of Culture: Twentieth-Century Ethnography, Literature, and Art*. Cambridge: Harvard University Press, 1988.

Clifford, James, and George E. Marcus, eds. *Writing Culture: The Poetics and Politics of Ethnography*. Berkeley: University of California Press, 1986.

Cohen, William A. *Sex Scandal: The Private Parts of Victorian Fiction*. Durham, NC: Duke University Press, 1996.

Coleridge, Samuel Taylor. *The Friend*. Edited by Barbara E. Rooke. 16 vols. Vol. 4 (2 vols.). Bollingen series 75. London: Routledge, 1969.

Collini, Stefan. *Arnold*. Oxford: Oxford University Press, 1988.

Comte, Auguste. *Auguste Comte: Correspondance générale et confessions*. Edited by de Berrêdo Carneiro, Pierre Arnaud, Paul Arbousse-Bastide, and Angèle Kremer-Marietti. 8 vols. Paris: Ecole des Hautes Etudes en Sciences Sociales, 1973–90.

———. *Cours de philosophie positive*. Edited by Michel Serres, François Dagognet, Allal Sinaceur, and Jean-Paul Enthoven. 2 vols. Paris: Hermann, 1975.

———. *The Positive Philosophy of Auguste Comte*. Translated by Harriet Martineau. New York: Calvin Blanchard, 1855. Reprint, New York: AMS Press, 1974.

———. *System of Positive Polity*. Translated by John Henry Bridges, Frederic Harrison, Edward Spencer Beesly, Richard Congreve, and H. D. Hutton. 4 vols. 1851–1854. London: Longman, 1875.

Comte, Auguste, and Pierre Laffitte. *Lettres d'Auguste Comte á M. Valat, 1815–1844*. Paris: Dunod, 1870.

Darwin, Charles. *Journal of Researches into the Natural History and Geology of the Countries Visited During the Voyage of H.M.S. Beagle Round the World, under the Command of Capt. Fitz Roy, R.N.* 2 vols. New York: Harper, 1846.

Davis, Norman, Douglas Gray, Patricia Ingham, and Anne Wallace-Hadrill. *A Chaucer Glossary*. Oxford: Clarendon, 1979.

Dawson, Carl, and John Pfordresher, eds. *Matthew Arnold: Prose Writings*. Critical Heritage. London: Routledge, 1979.

DeLaura, David J. *Hebrew and Hellene in Victorian England*. Austin: University of Texas Press, 1969.

———. "What, Then, Does Matthew Arnold Mean?" *Modern Philology* 66 (1969): 345–55.

De Lauretis, Teresa. *The Practice of Love: Lesbian Sexuality and Perverse Desire*. Bloomington: Indiana University Press, 1994.

Demarest, Marc. "Arnold and Tylor: The Codification and Appropriation of Culture." *Bucknell Review* 34, no. 2 (1990): 26–42.

De Quincey, Thomas. "Letters to a Young Man Whose Education Has Been Neglected." In *The Collected Writings of Thomas De Quincey*, edited by David Masson, 10:46–52. Edinburgh: Adam and Charles Black, 1889–90.

Dulaure, Jacques Antoine. *The Gods of Generation: A History of Phallic Cults among Ancients and Moderns*. 1805. New York: Panurge, 1933.

Dupuis, Charles François. *The Origin of All Religious Worship*. 1794. New Orleans, 1872.

Eagleton, Terry. *The Idea of Culture*. Chapman's Quarterly Series. Oxford: Blackwell, 2000.

———. *Ideology: An Introduction*. London: Verso, 1991.

———. *Literary Theory: An Introduction*. 2nd ed. 1983. Minneapolis, MN: University of Minnesota Press, 1996.

Edgeworth, Maria. "The Grateful Negro." In *Tales and Novels*, 5:231–61. London: Baldwin and Cradock, 1832.

Eisen, Sydney. "Frederic Harrison: The Life and Thought of an English Positivist." Ph.D. diss., Johns Hopkins University, 1957.

Eliot, George. *Essays of George Eliot*. Edited by Thomas Pinney. New York: Columbia University Press, 1963.

———. *The George Eliot Letters*. Edited by Gordon S. Haight. 9 vols. New Haven: Yale University Press, 1954–78.

———. *The Journals of George Eliot*. Edited by Margaret Harris and Judith Johnston. Cambridge: Cambridge University Press, 1998.

———. *The Mill on the Floss*. Edited by Gordon S. Haight. Oxford: Clarendon, 1980.

———. "The Natural History of German Life." *Westminster Review* 66 (July 1856): 51–79.

———. *Selected Critical Writings*. Edited by Rosemary Ashton. Oxford: Oxford University Press, 1992.

———. *Selected Essays, Poems, and Other Writings*. Edited by A. S. Byatt and Nicholas Warren. New York: Penguin, 1990.

———. *A Writer's Notebook, 1854–1879, and Uncollected Writings*. Edited by Joseph Wiesenfarth. Charlottesville: University Press of Virginia, 1981.

Eliot, T. S. "The Perfect Critic." In *The Sacred Wood: Essays on Poetry and Criticism*. London: Methuen, 1948.

Ellen, Roy. "Fetishism." *Man* N.S. 23, no. 2 (1988): 213–235.

Ellenberger, Henri F. *The Discovery of the Unconscious: The History and Evolution of Dynamic Psychiatry*. New York: Basic, 1970.

Ellis, Alfred Burdon. *The Land of Fetish*. London: Chapman, 1883.

Ellis, John M. *Literature Lost: Social Agendas and the Corruption of the Humanities*. New Haven: Yale University Press, 1997.

Emerson, Ralph Waldo. "The American Scholar: An Oration Delivered before the Phi Beta Kappa Society at Cambridge, August 31, 1837." In *Nature, Addresses, and Lectures*. Chadwyck-Healey, 1999. Reprinted from London: Routledge, 1849.

English Poetry. 2nd ed. In *Chadwyck-Healey Literature Collections*. ProQuest Information and Learning. http://collections.chadwyck.com (search: keywords fetish* fetich* fetisch*; accessed 28 April 2007).

Epicurus. *The Essential Epicurus: Letters, Principal Doctrines, Vatican Sayings, and Fragments.* Translated by Eugene O'Connor. Great Books in Philosophy. Amherst, NY: Prometheus, 1993.

Errington, Shelly. *The Death of Authentic Primitive Art and Other Tales of Progress.* Berkeley: University of California Press, 1998.

Esquirol, Jean Étienne. *Mental Maladies: A Treatise on Insanity.* Translated by E. K. Hunt. Philadelphia: Lea and Blanchard, 1845.

Evans, Brad. *Before Cultures: The Ethnographic Imagination in American Literature, 1865–1920.* Chicago: University of Chicago Press, 2005.

Feuerbach, Ludwig. *The Essence of Christianity.* Translated by George Eliot. Great Books in Philosophy. New York: Prometheus, 1989.

ffrench, Yvonne. *The Great Exhibition: 1851.* London: Harvill, 1950.

Foucault, Michel. *The History of Sexuality: An Introduction.* Translated by Robert Hurley. Vol. 1. New York: Vintage, 1990.

———. *The Order of Things: An Archaeology of the Human Sciences.* London: Routledge, 2001.

Freud, Sigmund. *Group Psychology and the Analysis of the Ego.* Translated by James Strachey. New York: Norton, 1959.

———. *The Standard Edition of the Complete Psychological Works of Sigmund Freud.* Translated by James Strachey. 24 vols. London: Hogarth, 1953–.

Froude, James Anthony. *The Nemesis of Faith.* London: Chapman, 1849.

Frow, John. *Cultural Studies and Cultural Value.* Oxford: Clarendon, 1995.

Gallagher, Catherine. *The Body Economic: Life, Death, and Sensation in Political Economy and the Victorian Novel.* Princeton, NJ: Princeton University Press, 2005.

———. "Raymond Williams and Cultural Studies." *Social Text 30* 10, no. 1 (1992): 79–89.

Gallagher, Catherine, and Stephen Greenblatt. *Practicing New Historicism.* Chicago: University of Chicago Press, 2000.

Goh, Robbie B. H. "Unwritten Fetishes and Rhetorical Strategies in Matthew Arnold's Criticism." In *The Silent Word: Textual Meaning and the Unwritten,* edited by Robert Young, Robbie B. H. Goh, and Kan Choon Ban, 135–44. Singapore: Singapore University Press, National University of Singapore, World Scientific, 1998.

Goldstein, Jan. *Console and Classify: The French Psychiatric Profession in the Nineteenth Century.* Cambridge: Cambridge University Press, 1987.

Goodnough, Abby. "Survivors of Tsunami Live on Close Terms with Sea." *New York Times,* 23 January 2005, 6.

Graff, Gerald. "Arnold, Reason, and Common Culture." In *Culture and Anarchy,* by Matthew Arnold, edited by Samuel Lipman, 186–201. Rethinking the Western Tradition. New Haven: Yale University Press, 1994.

———. *Professing Literature: An Institutional History*. Chicago: University of Chicago Press, 1987.

Grafton, Anthony. Introduction to *New Science: Principles of the New Science Concerning the Common Nature of Nations*, by Giambattista Vico, translated by David Marsh, 3rd ed., xi–xxxiii. New York: Penguin, 1999.

Greenslade, William. *Culture, Degeneration, and the Novel*. Cambridge: Cambridge University Press, 1994.

Grosz, Elizabeth. "Lesbian Fetishism?" In Apter and Pietz, *Fetishism*, 101–15.

Haggard, H. Rider. *She: A History of Adventure*. London: Longman, 1887.

Haight, Gordon S. *George Eliot: A Biography*. New York: Oxford University Press, 1968.

Hall, Stuart. "Cultural Studies: Two Paradigms." In *Culture / Power / History: A Reader in Contemporary Social Theory*, edited by Nicholas B. Dirks, Geoff Eley, and Sherry B. Ortner, 520–38. Princeton: Princeton University Press, 1994.

Hardy, Barbara. *The Appropriate Form: An Essay on the Novel*. London: Athlone, 1964.

Hare, E. H. "Masturbatory Insanity: The History of an Idea." *Journal of Mental Science* 108 (1962): 2–25.

Harrison, Frederic. "The Life of George Eliot." Review of *George Eliot's Life, as Related in Her Letters and Journals*, by John Cross. *Fortnightly Review* 37 n.s. (1 March 1885): 309–22.

———. *Tennyson, Ruskin, Mill, and Other Literary Estimates*. London: Macmillan, 1900.

Hartman, Geoffrey H. *The Fateful Question of Culture*. The Wellek Library Lecture Series at the University of California, Irvine. New York: Columbia University Press, 1997.

Harvey, William John. *Character and the Novel*. London: Chatto, 1965.

Hauser, Renate. "Krafft-Ebing's Psychological Understanding of Sexual Behaviour." In *Sexual Knowledge, Sexual Science: The History of Attitudes to Sexuality*, edited by Roy Porter and Mikulás Teich, 210–27. Cambridge: Cambridge University Press, 1994.

Hegeman, Susan. "Franz Boas and Professional Anthropology: On Mapping the Borders of the 'Modern.'" *Victorian Studies* 41, no. 3 (Spring 1998): 455–83.

———. *Patterns for America: Modernism and the Concept of Culture*. Princeton: Princeton University Press, 1999.

Heilbroner, Robert L. *The Worldly Philosophers: The Lives, Times, and Ideas of the Great Economic Thinkers*. New York: Simon and Schuster, 1986.

Herbert, Christopher. *Culture and Anomie: Ethnographic Imagination in the Nineteenth Century*. Chicago: University of Chicago Press, 1991.

Herrnstein Smith, Barbara. *Contingencies of Value: Alternative Perspectives for Critical Theory*. Cambridge, MA: Harvard University Press, 1988.

Hirsch, E. D., Jr. *Cultural Literacy: What Every American Needs to Know*. New York: Vintage, 1988.

Hirst, Francis Wrigley. *Early Life and Letters of John Morley*. 2 vols. London: Macmillan, 1927.

Hoctor, Thomas Marion. Introduction to *Matthew Arnold's Essays in Criticism: First Series*, vii–xliii. Chicago: University of Chicago Press, 1968.

Hodgen, Margaret T. *Early Anthropology in the Sixteenth and Seventeenth Centuries*. Philadelphia: University of Pennsylvania Press, 1964.

Honan, Park. *Matthew Arnold: A Life*. Cambridge, MA: Harvard University Press, 1983.

Howe, Anthony. *Free Trade and Liberal England, 1846–1946*. Oxford: Clarendon, 1997.

Hume, David. *The Natural History of Religion*. Edited by H. E. Root. A Library of Modern Religious Thought. 1777. Stanford, CA: Stanford University Press, 1956.

Hunter, Richard, and Ida Macalpine. *Three Hundred Years of Psychiatry, 1535–1860: A History Presented in Selected English Texts*. London: Oxford University Press, 1963.

Ian, Marcia. *Remembering the Phallic Mother: Psychoanalysis, Modernism, and the Fetish*. Ithaca: Cornell University Press, 1993.

Inwood, Brad, and Lloyd P. Gerson, eds. *Hellenistic Philosophy: Introductory Readings*. 2nd ed. Indianapolis, IN: Hackett, 1997.

James, Henry. *The Art of Criticism: Henry James on the Theory and the Practice of Fiction*. Edited by William Veeder and Susan M. Griffin. Chicago: University of Chicago Press, 1986.

Jameson, Fredric. "The Cultural Logic of Late Capitalism." In *Postmodernism, or The Cultural Logic of Late Capitalism*, 1–54. Durham, NC: Duke University Press, 1991.

———. *The Political Unconscious: Narrative as a Socially Symbolic Act*. Ithaca: Cornell University Press, 1981.

Jones, Howard. *The Epicurean Tradition*. London: Routledge, 1989.

Kant, Immanuel. *Religion within the Limits of Reason Alone*. Translated by Theodore M. Greene and Hoyt H. Hudson. Chicago: Open Court, 1934.

Kettle, Arnold. *An Introduction to the English Novel*. 2nd ed. 2 vols. London: Hutchinson, 1967.

Kingsley, Mary H. *Travels in West Africa: Congo Français, Corisco, and Cameroons*. 1897. London: Cass, 1965.

Kitchel, Anna Theresa. *George Lewes and George Eliot: A Review of Records*. New York: John Day, 1933.

Knoepflmacher, U. C. *George Eliot's Early Novels: The Limits of Realism*. Berkeley: University of California Press, 1968.

Konstan, David. "Epicureanism." In *The Blackwell Guide to Ancient Philosophy*, edited by Christopher Shields, 237–52. Blackwell Philosophical Guides. Madden, MA: Blackwell, 2003.

Krafft-Ebing, Richard von. *Psychopathia Sexualis, with Especial Reference to the Antipathetic Sexual Instinct: A Medico-Forensic Study*. Translated by F. J. Rebman. 12th ed. New York: Physicians and Surgeons, 1922. Reprint, 1935.

Kroeber, A. L., and Clyde Kluckhohn. *Culture: A Critical Review of Concepts and Definitions*. Papers of the Peabody Museum of American Archaeology and Ethnology 47, no. 1. Cambridge, MA: Peabody Museum, 1952.

Kuklick, Henrika. "The British Tradition." In *A New History of Anthropology*, edited by Henrika Kuklick. Oxford: Blackwell, 2007.

———. *The Savage Within: The Social History of British Anthropology, 1885–1945*. Cambridge: Cambridge University Press, 1991.

Lang, Andrew. "Edward Burnett Tylor." In Tylor, *Collected Works* 8:1–15.

Laqueur, Thomas W. *Solitary Sex: A Cultural History of Masturbation*. New York: Zone Books, 2003.

Lauden, Larry. "Towards a Reassessment of Comte's 'Méthode Positive.'" *Philosophy of Science* 38, no. 1 (1971): 35–53.

Leopold, Joan. *Culture in Comparative and Evolutionary Perspective: E. B. Tylor and the Making of Primitive Culture*. Beitrage Zur Kuulturanthropologie. Berlin: Reimer, 1980.

Levine, George. *The Realistic Imagination: English Fiction from Frankenstein to Lady Chatterley*. Chicago: University of Chicago Press, 1981.

Lewes, G. H. "Auguste Comte." *Fortnightly Review* 3 (1866): 390, 400, 402–10.

———. *Comte's Philosophy of the Sciences: Being an Exposition of the Principles of the "Cours de Philosophie Positive" of Auguste Comte*. London: Bohn, 1853.

Logan, Peter Melville. "Conceiving the Body: Realism and Medicine in *Middlemarch*." *History of the Human Sciences* 4 (1991): 197–222.

———. *Nerves and Narratives: A Cultural History of Hysteria in Nineteenth-Century British Prose*. Berkeley: University of California Press, 1997.

Louis, Dr. "Un Romancier fétichiste: Restif de la Bretonne." *La Chronique médicale* 1 (June 1904): 353–57.

Louis, Margot K. "Gods and Mysteries: The Revival of Paganism and the Remaking of Mythography through the Nineteenth Century." *Victorian Studies* 47, no. 3 (2005): 331–61.

Lovejoy, Arthur O., and George Boas. *Primitivism and Related Ideas in Antiquity*. Contributions to the History of Primitivism. 1935. New York: Octagon, 1965.

Lowie, Robert H. "Edward B. Tylor." *American Anthropologist* 19 (1917): 262–68.

———. "Edward B. Tylor." In *The History of Ethnological Theory*, 68–85. New York: Holt, Rinehart, and Winston, 1937.

Lucretius. *The Way Things Are: The "De Rerum Natura" of Titus Lucretius Carus.* Translated by Rolfe Humphries. Bloomington: Indiana University Press, 1968.

Mace, Ruth, and Mark Pagel. "The Comparative Method in Anthropology." *Current Anthropology* 35, no. 5 (1994): 549–64.

Machann, Clinton. Preface to *The Essential Matthew Arnold: An Annotated Bibliography of Major Modern Studies*, vii–x. New York: G. K. Hall, 1993.

Malinowski, Bronislaw. *Argonauts of the Western Pacific: An Account of Native Enterprise and Adventure in the Archipelagoes of Melanesian New Guinea.* London: Routledge, 1922.

Mannoni, Octave. *Freud: The Theory of the Unconscious.* Translated by Renaud Bruce. London: Verso, 1983.

Manuel, Frank E. *The Eighteenth Century Confronts the Gods.* Cambridge, MA: Harvard University Press, 1959.

Marett, R. R. *Tylor.* New York: J. Wiley, 1936.

Martineau, Harriet. Preface to *The Positive Philosophy of Auguste Comte*, by Auguste Comte, 3–11. New York: Calvin Blanchard, 1855. Reprint, New York: AMS Press, 1974.

Marx, Karl. *Capital: A Critique of Political Economy.* Translated by Ben Fowkes. Vol. 1. New York: Vintage, 1977.

Matlock, Jann. "Masquerading Women, Pathologized Men: Cross-Dressing, Fetishism, and the Theory of Perversion, 1882–1935." In Apter and Pietz, *Fetishism*, 31–61.

McClintock, Anne. *Imperial Leather: Race, Gender, and Sexuality in the Colonial Contest.* New York: Routledge, 1995.

McGann, Jerome J. *A Critique of Modern Textual Criticism.* Charlottesville: University Press of Virginia, 1992.

McGee, John Edwin. *A Crusade for Humanity: The History of Organized Positivism in England.* London: Watts, 1931.

McKeon, Michael. *The Origins of the English Novel, 1600–1740.* Baltimore: Johns Hopkins University Press, 1987.

McLaverty, James. "Comtean Fetishism in *Silas Marner*." *Nineteenth-Century Fiction* 36, no. 3 (Dec. 1981): 318–36.

Meiners, Christoph. *Allgemeine kritische Geschichte der Religionen.* 2 vols. Hannover: Im Verlage der Helwingischen Hof-Buchhandlung, 1806.

Mill, John Stuart. *Autobiography of John Stuart Mill.* Edited by John Jacob Coss. 1924. New York: Columbia University Press, 1960.

———. *On Liberty*. Edited by Gertrude Himmelfarb. 1859. New York: Penguin, 1974.

Nassau, Robert Hamill. *Fetichism in West Africa: Forty Years' Observation of Native Customs and Superstitions*. New York: Young People's Missionary Movement, 1904.

Nelson, Cary, Paula Treichler, and Lawrence Grossberg. "Cultural Studies: An Introduction." In *Cultural Studies*, edited by Lawrence Grossberg, Cary Nelson, and Paula Treichler, 1–22. New York: Routledge, 1992.

Nichols, James H., Jr. *Epicurean Political Philosophy: The "De Rerum Natura" of Lucretius*. Ithaca: Cornell University Press, 1976.

Nietzsche, Friedrich. "On Truth and Lying in a Non-Moral Sense." In *The Birth of Tragedy and Other Writings*, edited by Raymond Geuss and Ronald Speirs, translated by Ronald Speirs, 141–53. Cambridge Texts in the History of Philosophy. Cambridge: Cambridge University Press, 1999.

The Nineteenth-Century Fiction Database. Edited by Danny Karlin and Tom Keymer. In *Chadwyck-Healey Literature Collections*. ProQuest Information and Learning. http://collections.chadwyck.com (search: keywords fetish* fetich*; accessed 28 April 2007).

Nye, Robert A. "The Medical Origins of Sexual Fetishism." In Apter and Pietz, *Fetishism*, 13–30.

O'Connor, Eugene. *Introduction to The Essential Epicurus: Letters, Principal Doctrines, Vatican Sayings, and Fragments*, 9–15. Amherst, NY: Prometheus, 1993.

Okely, Judith, and Helen Callaway, eds. *Anthropology and Autobiography*. New York: Routledge, 1992.

Oosterhuis, Harry. *Stepchildren of Nature: Krafft-Ebing, Psychiatry, and the Making of Sexual Identity*. Chicago Series on Sexuality, History, and Society. Chicago: University of Chicago Press, 2000.

Ouida. *Under Two Flags: A Story of the Household and the Desert*. 3 vols. London: Chapman and Hall, 1867. Literature Online, 2000. http://gateway.proquest.com/.

Paley, William. *Natural Theology: Or, Evidences of the Existence and Attributes of the Deity, Collected from the Appearances of Nature*. 6th ed. London: R. Faulder, 1803.

Parrinder, Geoffrey. *West African Religion: A Study of the Beliefs and Practices of Akan, Ewe, Yoruba, Ibo, and Kindred Peoples*. New York: Barnes and Noble, 1969.

Pater, Walter. *The Renaissance*. New York: Oxford University Press.

Patmore, Coventry. "The Ethics of Art." *British Quarterly Review* 10 (1849): 441–462.

Paxton, Nancy L. "Feminism and Positivism in George Eliot's *Romola*." In *Nineteenth-Century Women Writers of the English-Speaking World*, edited by Rhoda B. Nathan, 143–150. Contributions in Women's Studies. New York: Greenwood, 1986.

———. *George Eliot and Herbert Spencer: Feminism, Evolutionism, and the Reconstruction of Gender.* Princeton, NJ: Princeton University Press, 1991.

Peckham, Morse. *Victorian Revolutionaries: Speculations on Some Heroes of a Culture Crisis.* New York: George Braziller, 1970.

Periodicals Index Online. In *C19: The Nineteenth Century Index.* ProQuest Information and Learning. http://collections.chadwyck.com (search: keywords fetish* fetich*; accessed 28 April 2007).

Pickering, Mary. *Auguste Comte: An Intellectual Biography.* Vol. 1. New York: Cambridge University Press, 1993.

Pietz, William. "Fetishism and Materialism: The Limits of Theory in Marx." In Apter and Pietz, *Fetishism*, 119–51.

———. "The Problem of the Fetish, I." *Res* 9 (1985): 5–17.

———. "The Problem of the Fetish, II: The Origin of the Fetish." *Res* 13 (1987): 23–106.

———. "The Problem of the Fetish, IIIa: Bosman's Guinea and the Enlightenment Theory of Fetishism." *Res* 16 (1988): 105–23.

Pocock, J. G. A. *The Machiavellian Moment: Florentine Political Thought and the Atlantic Republican Tradition.* Princeton, NJ: Princeton University Press, 1975.

Poignant, Roslyn. *Professional Savages: Captive Lives and Western Spectacle.* New Haven: Yale University Press, 2004.

Poole's Index to Periodical Literature, 1802–1907. In *C19: The Nineteenth Century Index.* ProQuest Information and Learning. http://collections.chadwyck.com (search: keywords fetish* fetich*; accessed 28 April 2007).

Porter, Roy. *Mind-Forg'd Manacles: A History of Madness in England from the Restoration to the Regency.* Cambridge, MA: Harvard University Press, 1987.

Pratt, Mary Louise. *Imperial Eyes: Travel Writing and Transculturation.* New York: Routledge, 1992.

Rabinow, Paul. *Reflections on Fieldwork in Morocco.* Berkeley: University of California Press, 1977.

Radcliffe-Brown, A. R. "The Comparative Method in Social Anthropology." *Journal of the Royal Anthropological Institute of Great Britain and Ireland* 51, no. 1/2 (1951): 15–22.

———. "On Social Structure." *Journal of the Royal Anthropological Institute* 70 (1940): 1–12.

Radin, Paul. Introduction to *Religion in Primitive Culture*, by Edward B. Tylor, ix–xvii. New York: Harper, 1958.

Reinhard, Philipp Christian. *Abriss einer Geschichte der Entstehung und Ausbildung der religiösen Ideen.* Jena, 1794.

Ricks, Christopher. "Poetry and Repression." *New York Times Book Review*, 14 March 1976, 2.

Robert, Marthe. "Origins of the Novel." In *Theory of the Novel: A Historical Approach*, edited by Michael McKeon, 57–69. Baltimore: Johns Hopkins University Press, 2000.

Ross, Andrew. "Giving Culture Hell: A Response to Catherine Gallagher." *Social Text 30* 10, no. 1 (1992): 98–101.

Ruskin, John. *Modern Painters: Of Many Things.* Vol. 3. Boston: Estes, 1873.

———. *Sesame and Lilies.* Edited by Harold Bloom. Prophets of Sensibility: Precursors of Modern Cultural Thought. New York: Chelsea House, 1983.

Saussure, Ferdinand de. *Course in General Linguistics.* New York: McGraw-Hill, 1966.

Schapera, I., and Milton Singer. "Wenner-Gren Foundation Supper Conference: Comparative Method in Social Anthropology." *American Anthropologist* N.S. 55, no. 3 (1953): 353–366.

Schor, Naomi. *Reading in Detail: Aesthetics and the Feminine.* New York: Methuen, 1987.

Semmel, Bernard. *George Eliot and the Politics of National Inheritance.* New York: Oxford University Press, 1994.

Sewell, William H., Jr. "The Concept(s) of Culture." In *Beyond the Cultural Turn*, edited by Victoria E. Bonnell and Lynn Hunt, 35–61. New Directions in the Study of Society and Culture. Berkeley: University of California, 1999.

Shuttleworth, Sally. Introduction to *The Mill on the Floss*, by George Eliot, ix–xxix. London: Routledge, 1991.

Simon, Walter M. *European Positivism in the Nineteenth Century: An Essay in Intellectual History.* Ithaca: Cornell University Press, 1963.

Simpson, David. *Fetishism and Imagination: Dickens, Melville, and Conrad.* Baltimore: Johns Hopkins University Press, 1982.

Smith, Adam. *An Inquiry into the Nature and Causes of the Wealth of Nations.* Edited by Edwin Cannan. New York: Modern Library, 1937.

Stacer, Jud. "Horrific Hat Fad Takes Over Athens." *Redandblack.com*, 27 October 2003.

Stang, Richard. *The Theory of the Novel in England: 1850–70.* London: Routledge, 1959.

Stocking, George W. *After Tylor: British Social Anthropology, 1888–1951.* Madison: University of Wisconsin Press, 1995.

———. "Edward Burnett Tylor and the Mission of Primitive Man." In Tylor, *Collected Works*, 1:ix–xxvi.

———. "The Ethnographer's Magic: Fieldwork in British Anthropology from Tylor to Malinowski." In *History of Anthropology*, edited by George W. Stocking, 1:70–119. Madison: University of Wisconsin Press, 1983.

———. "Franz Boas and the Culture Concept in Historical Perspective." In *Race, Culture, and Evolution: Essays in the History of Anthropology*, 195–232 New York: Free Press, 1968.

———. Introduction to *Researches into the Physical History of Man*, by James Cowles Prichard, ix–cx. Chicago: University of Chicago Press, 1973.

———. "Matthew Arnold, E. B. Tylor, and the Uses of Invention." *American Anthropologist* 65 (1963): 783–99.

———. *Victorian Anthropology*. New York: Free Press, 1987.

Taine, Hippolyte. *History of English Literature*. Translated by Henri Van Laun. 4 vols. 1883. New York: Ungar, 1965.

Taylor, Jenny Bourne, and Sally Shuttleworth, eds. *Embodied Selves: An Anthology of Psychological Texts: 1830–1890*. Oxford: Clarendon, 1998.

Teggart, Frederick J. *Theory and Processes of History*. Berkeley: University of California Press, 1977.

Thompson, E. P. "The Long Revolution (Part 1)." *New Left Review* 1, no. 9 (May–June 1961): 24–33.

Trilling, Lionel. *Matthew Arnold*. New York: Harcourt, 1977.

Tylor, Edward B. *Anthropology: An Introduction to the Study of Man and Civilization*. New York: D. Appleton, 1898.

———. *The Collected Works of Edward Burnett Tylor*. Edited by George W. Stocking. 8 vols. London: Routledge/Thoemmes, 1994.

———. "On a Method of Investigating the Development of Institutions; Applied to Laws of Marriage and Descent." *Journal of the Anthropological Institute of Great Britain and Ireland* 18 (1889): 245–72.

———. *Primitive Culture: Researches into the Development of Mythology, Philosophy, Religion, Language, Art, and Custom*. 2nd ed. 2 vols. London: John Murray, 1873.

———. *Researches into the Early History of Mankind and the Development of Civilization*. Edited by Paul Bohannan. Chicago: University of Chicago Press, 1964.

Venuti, Lawrence. *The Translator's Invisibility: A History of Translation*. New York: Routledge, 1995.

Vico, Giambattista. *New Science: Principles of the New Science Concerning the Common Nature of Nations*. Translated by David Marsh. 3rd ed. New York: Penguin, 1999.

Vogeler, Martha Salmon. "George Eliot and the Positivists." In "George Eliot: 1880–1980." Special issue, *Nineteenth-Century Fiction* 35, no. 3 (1980): 406–31.

———. "Matthew Arnold and Frederic Harrison: The Prophet of Culture and the Prophet of Positivism." *SEL: Studies in English Literature, 1500–1900* 2 (1962): 441–62.

Von Hendy, Andrew. *The Modern Construction of Myth*. Bloomington: Indiana University Press, 2002.

Waddington, Ivan. *The Medical Profession in the Industrial Revolution*. Dublin, Ire.: Gill, 1984.

Watt, Ian. *The Rise of the Novel: Studies in Defoe, Richardson, and Fielding*. Berkeley: University of California Press, 1957.

Wellesley Index to Victorian Periodicals, 1824–1900. In *C19: The Nineteenth Century Index*. ProQuest Information and Learning. http://collections.chadwyck.com (search: keywords fetish* fetich*; accessed 28 April 2007).

Wernick, Andrew. *Auguste Comte and the Religion of Humanity: The Post-Theistic Program of French Social Theory*. Cambridge: Cambridge University Press, 2001.

Wilde, Oscar. *The Major Works*. Edited by Isobel Murray. Oxford: Oxford University Press, 1989.

Williams, Raymond. *Culture and Society: 1780–1950*. New York: Columbia University Press, 1958.

———. *Keywords: A Vocabulary of Culture and Society*. New York: Oxford University Press, 1983.

Wimsatt, William K., and Cleanth Brooks. *Literary Criticism: A Short History*. New York: Knopf, 1957.

Winterbottom, Thomas Masterman. *An Account of the Native Africans in the Neighbourhood of Sierra Leone: To Which is Added, An Account of the Present State of Medicine among Them*. 2 vols. London: John Hatchard and J. Mawman, 1803.

Wyngaard, Amy S. "The Fetish in/as Text: Rétif de la Bretonne and the Development of Modern Sexual Science and French Literary Studies, 1887–1934." *PMLA* 121 (2006): 662–86.

———. "New Perspectives on Rétif de la Bretonne: Introduction." *Symposium (Washington, D.C.)* 60, no. 3 (Fall 2006): 131–33.

Žižek, Slavoj. *The Plague of Fantasies*. London: Verso, 1997.

———. *The Sublime Object of Ideology*. London: Verso, 1989.